THE MEDIEVAL
MILITARY
REVOLUTION

THE MEDIEVAL MILITARY REVOLUTION

STATE, SOCIETY, AND MILITARY CHANGE IN
MEDIEVAL AND EARLY MODERN EUROPE

Edited by

ANDREW AYTON
and
J. L. PRICE

I.B.Tauris Publishers
LONDON • NEW YORK

First published in paperback in 1998 by
I.B.Tauris & Co. Ltd
Victoria House, Bloomsbury Square
WC1B 4DZ

175 Fifth Avenue
New York, NY 10010

In the United States of America
and in Canada distributed by
St Martin's Press
175 Fifth Avenue
New York, NY 10010

A full CIP record for this book is available from the British Library

A full CIP record for this book is available from the Library of Congress

ISBN 1 86064 353 1

Library of Congress catalog card number available

Printed and bound in the United States of America

Contents

Abbreviations

APC	*Acts of the Privy Council of England, 1542–1631*, new series, 46 vols (London, 1890–1964)
BL	British Library
CCR	*Calendar of Close Rolls, 1272–1509*, 47 vols (1900–63)
CIPM	*Calendar of Inquisitions Post Mortem, Henry III–Richard II*, 16 vols (1904–74)
CPR	*Calendar of Patent Rolls, 1216–1578*, 73 vols (1901–81)
CSPD	*Calendar of State Papers, Domestic, Edward VI–James I*, 12 vols (1856–72)
CSPF	*Calendar of State Papers, Foreign, 1547–89*, 25 vols (1861–1950)
CSPI	*Calendar of State Papers Relating to Ireland, Henry VIII–Elizabeth*, 11 vols (1860–1912)
EcHR	*Economic History Review*
EHR	*English History Review*
GEC	G.E. Cokayne, ed, *The Complete Peerage*, revised edn, 12 vols in 13 (London, 1910–57)
HMC	Historical Manuscripts Commission
PRO	Public Record Office, London
RCHM	Royal Commission on Historical Monuments
TRHS	*Transactions of the Royal Historical* Society
VCH	*Victoria History of the Counties of England*

Introduction: The Military Revolution from a Medieval Perspective

Andrew Ayton and J.L. Price

Although there is continuing disagreement concerning the essential nature of the military revolution, and also with regard to its timing, there is nevertheless general agreement that it occurred in the early modern period of European history. Both the general history of warfare in European society during these centuries,[1] and more specifically the military revolution itself,[2] have been well covered by recent publications. Only a brief historiographical sketch of the early modern period needs to be given here, therefore, and the greater part of this introduction will consider to what extent viewing the military revolution from a medieval perspective suggests a reinterpretation of both its nature and, consequently, its timing.

The idea of a military revolution was introduced by Michael Roberts, who argued that the tactical reforms pioneered by the Dutch army at the end of the sixteenth century and perfected by the Swedish army under Gustavus Adolphus, together with the accompanying rise in the size and cost of these new armies, constituted a radical break with the immediate past.[3] Subsequently, the concept of such a revolution has been very generally accepted by historians of the period, but only with considerable disagreement over both its content and its timing. Geoffrey Parker criticized Roberts for overlooking the developments, especially in the Spanish armed forces, of the earlier years of the sixteenth century,[4] and it has since become conventional to stretch out the military revolution to cover the period from the beginning of the sixteenth century to the middle of the seventeenth,[5] although Jeremy Black has recently suggested that more importance should be given to the century after 1660.[6] Similarly, with regard to the nature of the revolution, the emphasis has moved from the rather specific changes in tactics and organization highlighted by Roberts to a range of broader, perhaps less well-defined, but certainly more far-

1

reaching developments which took place in the course of the early modern period.

Three elements have been regarded as constituting the essence of the military revolution, but there is as yet no consensus as to their relative importance. Firstly, there is the supplanting of heavily armoured cavalry by infantry as the most effective component of armies in battle, first in the form of English longbowmen and dismounted men-at-arms and of Swiss pikemen, then by varying combinations of pike and shot throughout western and central Europe.[7] Associated with this development was the introduction of gunpowder weapons, which in the form of artillery rapidly – though perhaps only briefly – transformed siege warfare,[8] and as hand-held weapons rather less swiftly changed the character of infantry fighting. The third aspect of the revolution, closely involved with the other two, but in the end perhaps even more far reaching in its consequences, was the rise in the size of armies. All these developments were intertwined: for example, the switch from heavily armoured knight to footsoldier not only changed the social basis of battlefield strength but – as infantry could be trained more quickly and could be hired simply for wages – made possible the expansion in the size of armies from the late fifteenth century onwards. Similarly, the new siege warfare of the sixteenth century required large armies to surround towns and fortresses, and the development and diffusion in this period of new types of fortification designed to combat artillery meant that these besieging forces had to be held together for increasing lengths of time. Thus there is also a fourth element, rarely given the importance it deserves, of the new warfare: time. Campaigns were slower to achieve definite results, and wars tended to become a series of long sieges and to last years, often with indecisive results. The decision as to what should be considered most important among these developments depends in part on the historian's perspective: from a purely military point of view, infantry, firearms and siege-techniques (both offensive and defensive) must loom large but, when the impact of the revolution on European society in general is considered, the continuous growth of the size, and thus the cost, of armies can be seen as the most important. Perhaps the best example of this line of argument has been the attempt to link the military revolution to the growth of the state in this period.

Recent theories concerning the relationship between the development of the early modern state and war have approached the problem from a number of directions – political, fiscal and bureaucratic – but all centre very largely on the effects of the increase in the costs of war. Briefly, the argument is that the military revolution encouraged something akin to an arms race among the competing states of Europe, which stretched their resources to the utmost. The leading powers spent up to, and beyond, the level of bankruptcy to keep up with their rivals; the chief problem facing most governments was how to squeeze the maximum of resources out of what were still essentially low-productivity economies. The answers were found in the strengthening of royal power, and of central government in general, at the expense of local autonomy, and in the growth of bureaucracies.[9] The other side of the coin is that these apparently stronger governments were permanently hag-ridden by the problem of satisfying the insatiable financial demands of military expenditure.

In what became a contemporary cliché, attributed to a number of prominent generals, it was said that there were three necessities for making war successfully – money, money, and more money. The main reason for the escalation in the cost of warfare in the early modern period was the rise in the size of armies, together with the greater length of time such armies had to be kept together. In this period, all other things being equal, the biggest armies won, and thus governments were under heavy pessure to produce the largest forces they could possibly muster and support. In consequence, it often seems that few states could wage a major war for long in the sixteenth and seventeenth centuries without coming close to ruining their finances. The general increase in real costs was exacerbated by the inflation of the sixteenth century, which racked up the apparent costs of warfare at a time when governments were finding it politically difficult to ensure that revenues rose enough to compensate for the fall in the value of the money.

Of all the costs of warfare, the payment of troops was by far the most important. From the late fifteenth century onwards the size of armies increased enormously. Field armies grew, but there was at least a practical limit to the number of men who could be organized and supplied on the battlefield; there was no such limit to the total number of troops in the pay of a state, and this is where the most spectacular rises can be seen, notably the estimated 200,000 men supported by Spain in the 1590s and the 400,000 soldiers employed by France a hundred years later. (This latter figure needs to be treated with some scepticism, but so do all the figures of troop strength in this period.) The real weight of these large numbers of troops was greatly increased by the length of time they needed to be kept under arms. After a brief period in the later fifteenth century when the use of the new artillery rendered most fortifications in Europe obsolete, there were few decisive battles and warfare became a series of sieges and manoeuvres around sieges. Campaigns were lengthened by the introduction of effective anti-artillery fortifications, and towns and fortresses had to be reduced by starvation or by technically elaborate and time-consuming sieges. The consequence was that wars could, and did, drag on indecisively for years and, although some troops could be paid off in the autumn, they had to be re-engaged in the spring, and the saving was meagre in comparison with the cost of ever longer wars.

The changes in naval warfare consequent on the introduction of firearms and especially shipboard artillery were perhaps slower to take universal effect, but in the end they were similarly burdensome to state finances. The particular nature of galley warfare in the Mediterranean limited the effects of big guns, and even the consequences of the introduction of handguns was perhaps less than might have been expected at first,[10] but the need for large numbers of troops on board meant that costs rose just the same. Elsewhere, until well into the seventeenth century governments were able to limit the cost of naval defence by hiring merchant vessels for particular campaigns, thus avoiding as far as possible the expense of a permanent navy. They also tried to shift the military costs of colonial competition to the private sector through privateering and, especially, monopoly trading companies, but by the middle of the seventeenth century the slow shift from boarding and hand-to-hand fighting to artillery duels at a distance, together with the related growth in the size of ships, brought about the need for permanent navies using specialist warships and thus another standing drain on state resources.[11]

When the costs of building the new anti-artillery fortifications to protect strategic towns and fortresses and of supplying the ever-growing armies with firearms are added to those already considered, then it is hardly surprising that states seemed almost permanently to be on the verge of collapsing under the financial strain.[12]

Indeed, if the functions of the early modern state are assessed by what they spent their money on, then they were primarily organizations for the preparation or prosecution of war. The expenditure of governments in this period is notoriously difficult to estimate and even more difficult to analyse, but it seems tolerably clear that in all states it was devoted largely to supplying the cost of war in one way or another.[13] It is difficult to express the cost of war as a percentage of total expenditure, because such a high proportion of the spending of all states was in the form of repayment of loans; although many if not most of such debts were incurred to finance war, it is rarely possible to give anything like an accurate estimate. The figures that can be presented – however cautiously they must be treated – are impressive enough: France in the last years of Louis XIV's reign was spending 75 per cent of its income on war, and in England in the 1650s about 90 per cent of government expenditure went to the upkeep of the army and navy.[14] Under Philip II the proportion in Spain rose to over 75 per cent in the 1570s and if anything the situation was even more starkly unambiguous during the dominance of Olivares.[15]

Those that live by the sword shall die by the sword, and this can be applied in a sense to governments and even states as well. States went bankrupt, at least technically, through the cost of war, and the fiscal strain of long-term involvement in warfare was perhaps the single most important threat to political stability even in this most turbulent of periods. From the middle of the sixteenth century, Spain had to suspend payment of its debts and employ other expedients which were damaging to its credit at frequent, almost regular intervals (1575, 1596, 1607, 1627, 1647, 1653),[16] and increasing fiscal pressure led directly to the Catalan revolt and the collapse of the *monarchía* as a major power in Europe after 1640. This is only an extreme case of a general phenomenon: heavy involvement in war over a prolonged period overstrained the financial capacities of states and caused severe internal political problems. Even England's small-scale war with Scotland at the end of the 1630s exceeded the financial capacity of royal government and proved to be the trigger for the collapse of the state.[17]

Admittedly, most states survived through one expedient or another, but in the process their very nature was affected: the demands of war finance encouraged political centralization, with its accompanying bureaucratization and the strengthening of governments at the expense of local rights and privileges.[18] The basic argument is relatively straightforward: the cost of warfare overstretched the fiscal resources of the early modern state but was unavoidable, so some way of increasing revenue from reluctant taxpayers, in economies which produced little surplus wealth, had to be found. In order to achieve this end, central governments had to take control over taxation away from representative institutions, and also find ways of enforcing its demands for increased taxes. In other words, absolutism was the standard answer to the problem of how to pay for war in this period. This solution also brought its own problems, with the growth in the number of officials needed to collect taxes and administer the increased revenues as well as to organize and supply the new armies, navies and fortifications. In practice, absolutism may well not have been very efficient, but it did enable states to survive in the dangerous world of early modern Europe. France survived severe internal problems to become the ideal type of the militarily successful absolutist state by the late seventeenth century; Poland-Lithuania retained its ancient aristocratic freedoms and ceased to be able to compete as a major power, suffering the ultimate fate of the militarily incompetent in the eighteenth century by disappearing altogether. In contrast, while Spain may have faded as a power on a European scale, the monarchy survived, and even managed to retain most of its territories. England is a special case to the extent that its island position largely freed it from the necessity of developing a modern military system, until increased prosperity enabled it from the end of the seventeenth century to pay for large modern armies and navies and yet retain a constitutional system of government. Even here the scare of 1588 and the invasion of 1688 remind us how vulnerable the English state remained before it modernized its military system. As J.L. Price discusses in chapter 9, only the Dutch Republic (together with the English state after the 1690s) proved capable of supporting the enormous costs of the new forms of warfare while maintaining traditional political freedoms.

If such considerable consequences are to be attributed to the military revolution, it becomes all the more necessary to be clear about what it was and when it happened. Was it really an early modern phenomenon? Although there are few recent general studies of war and society in the later Middle Ages to compare with those available for the early modern centuries, enough is emerging from more specialist works to cast at least some doubt on the picture of the military revolution developed by historians of the early modern period.

Some aspects of the early modern military revolution were firmly rooted in the experience of the later medieval period: this is certainly the case with the emergence of gunpowder weapons and innovations in fortification design, together with the effects that these developments had on the character of warfare. If some of the weapons most characteristic of the Middle Ages – crossbow, longbow, trébuchet and *arme blanche* – do indeed mark it out as a quite separate era of warfare, then it must also be conceded that gunpowder weapons were known and used in western Europe before the mid-fourteenth century; and it would not be an exaggeration to suggest that the fifteenth century actually witnessed an 'artillery revolution'.[19] It is true that slow rate of fire, modest range and immobility severely limited the effectiveness of gunpowder artillery on most battlefields, and continued to do so until the early seventeenth century.[20] But cannon had proved their worth in siege warfare, for both attack and defence,[21] by the early decades of the fifteenth century, and by the middle of that century, an artillery train had become a potentially decisive weapon. Indeed, the mere threat of bombardment might be enough to induce surrender, as we find, for example, in Charles VII's rapid reconquest of Normandy in 1449–50.

Admittedly, the supremacy of tactical offence in siege warfare, so evident at the end of the fifteenth century, was not to last for very long, for as Philippe Contamine has noted, 'by a dialectical process which may be found in all periods, progress in the art of siege was answered by progress in the art of fortification, and vice versa'.[22] Charles VIII's invasion of Italy in 1494 demonstrated the potency of siege artillery; but in this region by the early years of the sixteenth century there were beginning to emerge fortifications which had been designed specifically to resist artillery bombardment.[23] If the full impact the fifteenth-century 'artillery revolution' was comparatively quickly blunted by the development of the bastion and the *trace italienne*, the military supremacy which the possession of a powerful siege train conferred contributed in no small degree to that strengthening of royal authority which we find in some European states in the later fifteenth century.[24]

With the exploitation of gunpowder weapons, then, we find that the origins of one major thread of the early modern military revolution stretched back to, and indeed flourished in, the last century of the Middle Ages; and continuity from the medieval centuries had further dimensions. The emphasis on fortifications and siege warfare during the early modern period represented in effect a return to the conditions of the fourteenth century and earlier.[25] This is one matter upon which most medievalists who have written on war have agreed: medieval warfare revolved essentially around the control of castles and fortified towns, strongpoints with which western Europe was thickly studded. In these cautious wars of attrition, battle was avoided because the outcome was too often unpredictable; far more energy was expended on the pillaging of the countryside – the aim being to destroy an enemy's economic resources and undermine his political credibility – and on the control of fortresses.[26]

This characterization of war in the Middle Ages (which bears more than a slight resemblance to early modern warfare) does not, of course, fit the circumstances of each and every medieval conflict. Not every experienced medieval commander had fought as few real battles as Richard I (or indeed his father) after 25 years of campaigning.[27] Yet it must be seen as significant that the period during which fortifications were temporarily at the mercy of siege artillery – from about 1450 to about 1530 – was also a period marked by 'an exceptional number of pitched battles in European warfare'.[28] As for systematic ravaging, this too was a feature of much campaigning activity throughout medieval Europe, from Scotland to the

Balkans; there are exceptions, but they serve only prove the rule.[29] Unfortunately it is rarely possible to trace the economic impact of ravaging with any precision.

This is where Domesday Book has been thought to be of considerable value, since it contains voluminous data on manorial wealth for the periods before and after the Norman Conquest, and it has often been argued that its folios preserve a clear imprint of 'the Conqueror's footprints' in various parts of England. Re-examining the Domesday evidence, J.J.N. Palmer (chapter 1) questions 'the assumption that war damage inflicts characteristic patterns which can almost always be detected in the record of Domesday valuations', and suggests, in particular, that the course of Duke William's campaigning in south-eastern England between October and December 1066 is largely undetectable in Domesday Book.

Altogether more enduring as landmarks of the Conquest were the castles which the Conqueror and his followers built in England. But, as Barbara English argues in chapter 2, the earliest urban castles were likely to have been improvized affairs, 'ring-works, perhaps of small size, built as quickly as possible in difficult military circumstances ... usually within the angle of former town defences'. The mottes – and the great stone keeps, epitomized by the White Tower – which are so closely associated with the arrival of the Normans, came later. Despite the spate of castle-building in the post-Conquest period, England, comparatively secure behind its 'moat defensive', was not to be one of the more intensively fortified kingdoms of Europe. Recent studies of castle-building in later medieval England have stressed the importance of structural symbolism and status affirmation, rather than military considerations;[30] and, similarly, D.M. Palliser, surveying the 'patchy picture of urban fortification' in England (chapter 5), concludes that 'enhancing the communal image' was one of the chief motives lying behind the construction of town walls. This is certainly a far cry from continental Europe, where towns were more uniformly protected by mural defences. In Saintonge in south-western France, a sensitive 'frontier of war' during the Hundred Years War, there were 70 castles and fortified towns and about 90 fortified churches.[31] On the south-eastern fringe of Christendom, the survival of the kingdom of Hungary in the fifteenth century depended very largely upon two lines of fortifications along its southern border.[32] Whilst most of Europe adopted the *trace italienne* during the sixteenth century, England remained a lightly fortified kingdom. As R.W. Ambler shows in chapter 8, 'repair rather than fundamental refurbishment' was the order of the day; and when an Englishman became what passed for an expert in siege-craft and fortification design, as we find with Sir William Pelham, this expertise was learned, and largely given expression, overseas.

Turning from military engineering to the manpower employed in war, here surely we will find that the developments of the early modern period – the massive increase in the size of armies, swelled by unprecedented numbers of infantry – do indeed mark a significant break with the later Middle Ages. It is not that infantry played an insignificant part in medieval warfare; far from it. The defeat of heavy cavalry by armies fighting on foot is one of the most striking features of warfare in the first half of the fourteenth century: witness the triumphs of the urban militias of Flanders at Courtrai (1302), of the Scots at Bannockburn (1314), the Swiss at Mortgarten (1315) and Laupen (1339), and of the English at Crécy (1346).[33] Admittedly some of the most effective 'foot soldiers' were in fact 'mounted infantry', troops who shared the day-to-day mobility of mounted men-at-arms and who dismounted merely to fight, rather in the fashion of the dragoons of later centuries.[34] But even if the real 'transformation of the infantry' did not occur until the mid-fifteenth century,[35] it is nevertheless undeniable that a more prominent role for foot soldiers – for men of sub-genteel status – from the early to mid-fourteenth century did have practical consequences. Foot soldiers were cheaper and much more plentiful than aristocratic men-at-arms. They also had an effect on the nature of warfare. Lacking the chivalric mentality of the knightly class and armed with weapons designed for indiscriminate slaughter, the infantryman's rise 'made the European battlefield a much more sanguinary place'.[36]

Yet it would surely be wrong to argue that mastery in battle had passed from the heavily armoured, mounted man-at-arms to the 'common infantryman' by the middle of the fourteenth century. The aristocratic warrior was not so easily to be ousted from the battlefield; the fabric of medieval warfare has a more complex pattern woven into it. Solutions to the challenges posed by pike and arrow were actively sought. The English developed a tactical system based upon the dismounting of men-at-arms, to allow them to fight in a coordinated fashion with archers; they would remount their warhorses only to pursue a beaten enemy or to retreat from the field. These tactics proved spectacularly successful for the English; but experiments with dismounted men-at-arms by other European states often led to disaster – as at Poitiers (1356), Nicopolis (1396) and Agincourt (1415)[37] – and, by and large, the enduring importance of the aristocratic warrior in continental Europe was not to rest upon the abandonment of his warhorse. The full development, in the fifteenth century, of plate armour for both man and horse, combined with the use of the *arrêt* (lance rest) which could support a heavier lance, ensured that the heavy cavalryman remained a formidable warrior, providing the 'core and the most prestigious arm of every major fifteenth-century army, including the new standing armies of France, Burgundy, Brittany, Venice and Milan'.[38] Charles VIII's army for the invasion of Italy in 1494 is notable not only for its powerful siege-train, but also for the number of its heavy cavalrymen.[39] It would not be an exaggeration to say that 'without cavalry, a fifteenth-century army was unlikely to achieve a decisive victory on the field of battle'; that 'the issue of a battle might be decided by archers or pikemen, [but] a retreat could only be cut off effectively or followed-up by cavalry'.[40]

It was only in the sixteenth century that the heavily armoured warrior was overwhelmed by massed infantry armies, hand-held firearms and field artillery. It was only then that aristocratic warriors no longer comprised a proportionately substantial elite contingent in field armies. Yet even in the early modern period they remained a 'military class' in so much as they provided the bulk of the professional officer corps of armies composed very largely of their social inferiors.[41] Although lacking a standing army, Elizabethan England was not without such men. As R.W. Ambler shows in chapter 8, Sir William Pelham was both landowner and 'wise and experimented in martial affairs'; and like many medieval younger sons of gentry stock, he had actually made his way in the world, and had established his landed estate, through his career in arms.

Admittedly, much in the character of war had changed since the later fourteenth century, when Pelham's counterparts gave evidence before the Court of Chivalry. Indeed, the central matter of the disputes discussed by Andrew Ayton in chapter 4 – rightful possession of certain armorial bearings, which were essential for battlefield recognition, as well as for aristocratic self-esteem and family honour – would have hardly seemed relevant to the warfare of the later sixteenth and seventeenth centuries, conducted as it was by armies in which uniforms and rank insignia, tight discipline, drill and training had become commonplace.[42] But there *is* a continuous thread of mentality connecting such exploits as Sir Richard de Baskerville's feat of arms outside Paris in 1360, as recalled by the veteran Sir Thomas Gray in his military memoirs,[43] and those of the teenaged Captain John Evans in the Crimea and the Indian Mutiny, commemorated by a tablet in Chagford parish church, Devon.[44] The medieval idea of a warrior class, in which the pursuit of honour bulked large, lasted long after the early modern military revolution converted the aristocratic soldier from a numerically significant battlefield player to an army officer.

Soldiering, hitherto the spiritual *raison d'être* of the secular landholding class, had become a profession for gentlemen.

The watershed in warfare which we see with the early modern military revolution rests not on the emergence of a prominent battlefield role for infantry, but on the sheer numbers of fighting men that were involved. The heavy cavalryman was overwhelmed by numbers; the major change was in the size of armies. The largest armies raised in the fourteenth and fifteenth centuries were no more than a few tens of thousand men strong. The largest English royal army of the Middle Ages was probably the host raised by Edward I for the Falkirk campaign of 1298 – perhaps 3,000 heavy cavalry and over 25,700 infantry;[45] but once the unwieldy and poorly disciplined infantry armies of the Anglo-Scottish wars had been abandoned, very few English field armies exceeded 10,000 men. Most of the classic *chevauchées* of the fourteenth century were conducted by armies of half this size.[46] J.R. Strayer has doubted whether Philip IV of France 'ever had more than 30,000 men concentrated in one theater of war',[47] whilst surviving pay accounts suggest that, in September 1340 in northern and south-western France combined, Philip VI fielded 28,000 men-at-arms and 16,700 foot soldiers. The very differently composed permanent French army of the late fifteenth century numbered 20,000 to 25,000 fighting men.[48] The permanent peacetime armies of Milan and Venice in the fifteenth century fluctuated in size from about 10,000 men to over 20,000, though it was not impossible to mobilize larger numbers.[49] In 1486 King Mátyás Corvinus of Hungary's standing army, mustered at Vienna, numbered 28,000 men, over two-thirds of whom were cavalry.[50] These were the largest armies that late medieval European states could manage to raise; most were on an altogether smaller scale, consisting of a few thousand men.[51] Only the huge Ottoman hosts of the later Middle Ages (for example, 100,000 men at the siege of Belgrade in 1456) rival, in terms of size, the standing armies of the major states of early modern Europe. By comparison with the military might of the sultan, crusading expeditionary forces were often very small: for example, Count Amadeus of Savoy took the fortress of Gallipoli in August 1366 with an army numbering no more than 3,000 to 4,000 men.[52]

If the early modern period witnessed a massive increase in the size of armies, then it should surely follow that the cost of war at this time also reached unprecedented levels. Whilst this cannot be denied, it must also be recognized that the later Middle Ages did experience wars that were both prolonged and extremely expensive. For most states of Europe the later medieval period witnessed profound changes in military institutions: the disappearance of unpaid service based upon various forms of obligation, and the emergence of wholly paid armies. As Bernard Guenée has neatly put it: 'between the age of the feudal army and that of the standing army, the fourteenth and fifteenth centuries were the era of the contract army'.[53] It has become customary to see the late thirteenth century as marking the start of a 'new age' of war,[54] as paid armies were mobilized for ambitious, large-scale wars and the costs of war soared to levels not previously experienced, prompting novel fiscal and institutional developments.

Just how far the later thirteenth century marked a watershed in European warfare is open to debate. Paid military service was certainly not a new phenomenon. In England, mercenaries were routinely employed during the eleventh and twelfth centuries,[55] and it is consequently no surprise to find that the wars waged during the reigns of Richard I and John were indeed very costly. Perhaps, therefore, we should view the 'new age' of expensive warfare ushered in during the last decades of the thirteenth century as 'a reversion to earlier levels of expenditure'.[56] The monumental scale of warfare in the 1290s was certainly thrown into sharper relief for contemporaries by the relative peace of Henry III's reign; but, for the modern historian, what makes this decade seem so significant as the start of a new age of war is that, thereafter, there was to be scarcely any abatement for a century and a half. Edward I's multi-faceted military operations in 1294–98 cost £750,000, while his grandson, Edward III, spent so heavily in the early years of the Hundred Years War (£400,000 in 1337–40) that his government slipped into financial chaos, helping to bring about the ruin of the Florentine merchant-bankers Bardi and Peruzzi, who had provided war loans.[57] The particularly intensive phase of warfare from 1369 to 1380, which witnessed no decisive battles and the loss to the French of many of the earlier territorial gains, cost the English government over £1 million.[58] Since the 'ordinary' revenues of the English crown amounted, in the later thirteenth century, to less than £30,000 per annum, such ambitious and costly campaigning could be paid for only by recourse to 'extraordinary' fiscal measures: direct taxation of the laity and clergy, and indirect taxation, principally customs duties and subsidies levied on wool and cloth exports. By these means, the English crown raised more than £9.5 million during the course of the Hundred Years War.[59]

Opinion has been divided over the institutional effects of so massive an exploitation of the financial resources of the kingdom to support the war: whether state-building was advanced more by war or peace; whether war strengthened or weakened royal authority.[60] What is clear is that later medieval England did acquire distinctive *military* institutions. This period did not witness the establishment of a proper standing army, but this was not because England was backward in the military sphere: she had experienced her 'military revolution' during the middle decades of the fourteenth century.[61] This involved, amongst other things, the development of contract armies composed of privately recruited aristocratic retinues serving for the king's pay for prescribed periods. Such a degree of 'privatization' of the war effort brought with it potential problems of control; but rigorous 'muster and review' sought to ensure that manpower numbers and standards of equipment were maintained, and the crown issued ordinances to regulate the conduct of armies in the field (the first surviving version dates from 1385). Moreover, the martial courts – the Court of Chivalry and the courts with temporary jurisdiction in individual hosts – would deal with disputes and disciplinary matters that arose during the course of campaigns. Perhaps most notably, these courts ensured the orderly settlement of armorial disputes, such as those, discussed by Andrew Ayton in chapter 4, which erupted during Richard II's campaign in Scotland in 1385. Such disputes became more frequent as contract armies drew their personnel from all corners of the realm and as heraldic arms were increasingly adopted by men of sub-knightly status, while the cult of chivalric knighthood made all members of the armigerous community jealous of their armorial sense of identity and sensitive to encroachments by others.

The English contract armies of the fourteenth century, at their best composed of mounted retinues of men-at-arms and archers, fast-moving and tactically proficient if brought to battle, were wholly appropriate to a war strategy based upon the *chevauchée*. They were, however, less well suited to strategic commitments requiring long-term occupation. The 'indenture system' had to be adapted to meet the military demands of conquest and occupation in Lancastrian Normandy.[62] This can be seen, for example, in the parliamentary legislation of 1439, which made desertion the breach, not merely of a private contract with a captain, but of a more solemn *public* undertaking. But neither the demands of garrisoning Normandy and the *pays de conquête* – nor indeed those which required permanent garrisons at Calais and in the northern marches with Scotland – were such as to bring about the establishment of a standing army in England. The force which Edward IV led to France in 1475 was recruited and organized along lines very similar to those employed for the contract armies of the fourteenth century, and English armies continued to be based upon aristocratic retinues until the 1540s.[63]

Turning to the experience of the kingdom of France, here too the end of the thirteenth century witnessed an escalation in the scale and cost of war, as a state 'whose capacity for fighting had mounted significantly in the general administrative development' of the relatively peaceful thirteenth century flexed its muscles.[64] J.R. Strayer has shown that Philip IV spent as heavily as Edward I on the Anglo-French war of 1294–1303.[65] Yet, by comparison with England, the war finance of the French crown 'shows a distinctly more ramshackle, *ad hoc* character': it was only during the decade after Poitiers (1356) that the taxes of early modern France emerged and began to be levied frequently – *aides*, *gabelles* and *fouages* (later, *tailles*).[66] Moreover, the Hundred Years War plunged the Valois kings of France into a maelstrom in which the kingdom, weakened by provincial particularism, was torn asunder by the *chevauchées*, battlefield triumphs and territorial gains of the English, by periods of civil war and by the depredations of *routiers*.[67] From these desperate conditions emerged, in several stages, a reformed royal army, which in the guise fashioned under Charles VII achieved the decisive victory against the English in 1449–53, and which by the last decades of the century had become established as a standing army.[68] Given the circumstances, it is hardly surprising that France's late medieval 'military revolution' went a good deal further than England's. Nor is it surprising that it set France on the road to absolutism, for the Hundred Years War had left Frenchmen with a 'sentimental attachment' not to assemblies but to a strong ruler. In England, parliament was strengthened by the king's wars of the later Middle Ages, the crown's financial needs ensuring that the Commons, whose members – representatives of shire and borough communities with full power to consent to royal requests for taxation – became an active and essential element (over 80 per cent of parliaments held during the period of the Hundred Years War involved grants of taxation). 'Parliamentary assent was no real barrier to continuous taxation in time of war [consent was 'procedural' in cases of military necessity], but it did force the crown into a dialogue with its subjects over their respective political obligations'.[69] By contrast, in France no such national assembly had ever become established, and the multiplicity of general and regional Estates were never able to check the development of *royal* fiscal authority.[70] Small wonder that, in order to finance the standing army, the *taille* was increased threefold between 1470 and 1484, while in England, parliament played a significant part in the process whereby yields from both direct and indirect taxation declined in the later fourteenth and the fifteenth centuries, the fall denoting 'an inability on the part of the state to adapt to new economic conditions' and 'a reduction in the willingness ... of the political community to pay'.[71]

How far should the development of standing armies be regarded as a distinctive characteristic of the last century of the Middle Ages? Some states, like England, resisted the transition from contract armies to a standing army; some, indeed, continued to rely upon the unpaid service of able-bodied men, mobilized at times of crisis (for example, Scotland, and Moldavia and Wallachia).[72] Then again, there had been 'permanent' forces before the fifteenth century. Long-service garrisons and the military households of kings and magnates were commonplace, while the free companies, which both Charles V and Charles VII drew upon to man their reformed armies, have been rightly described as 'autonomous martial societies, already mustered as miniature standing armies, and internally well organised, with their own governing councils, treasuries and secretariats'.[73]

Another institutional model of sorts was provided by the military orders. At their best, as *La Règle du Temple* sought to ensure, these were strictly regulated and rigorously trained permanent forces;[74] and, as John Walker considers in chapter 3, they were (in theory at least) properly resourced permanent forces, fuelled by aristocratic manpower and revenue-generating preceptories in western Europe.[75] But as 'standing armies', the military orders were pitifully small (the garrison of Rhodes at the time of the 1480 siege included no more than a few hundred Hospitallers; the Teutonic Order had only about 1,200 brethren in Livonia and Prussia in the early fifteenth century),[76] and for the emergence of true standing armies it is necessary to focus on developments in several fifteenth-century European states.[77] The *ordonnance* companies of France provided a model, in the 1470s, for Duke Charles the Bold of Burgundy's own army reforms; and regular forces can also be seen in Castile at the very end of the fifteenth century. The major Italian states established 'permanent, well-trained and loyal armies' during the fifteenth century (indeed, Philippe de Commynes suggested that Charles VII's army reforms were strongly influenced by Italian military structures). These forces – the companies of *condottieri*, together with individual soldiers paid directly by the state – consumed about half of the disposable revenue of Italian states.[78]

Nor was the standing army a uniquely western European phenomenon. If we turn to the kingdom of Hungary, Christendom's bulwark against the Ottoman advance in the fifteenth century, we find that the cultural renaissance under Mátyás Corvinus was accompanied by the establishment of a permanent army. Mátyás recruited mercenaries from a variety of central and eastern European peoples and his army's effectiveness was based upon the synergy brought about by the mixing of complementary military skills. The army was financed, somewhat precariously, by a combination of existing taxes, more rigorously administered, and extraordinary taxation (*subsidia*), the latter levied almost annually once the Diet had been won over by the confirmation of their privileges.[79] As in France, Mátyás's army was a response to a formidable military challenge; but unlike France, the military pressures of a border defence war were near-continuous and the financial burden was crippling, particularly since the mercenary army was employed mostly in wars in Moravia, Bohemia, Silesia and Austria – wars of conquest aimed at expanding the kingdom's tax base, in order, ultimately, to mount a decisive campaign against the Ottomans (a grand strategy which collapsed, along with the standing army, following Mátyás's untimely death in 1490).

The militant pacifism of Erasmus, considered in chapter 7 by Howell A. Lloyd, can be regarded as a reaction to the changing nature of warfare at the beginning of the early modern period, with the increasing scale and evident brutality of these wars calling into question the conventional arguments in favour of the 'just war'. However, it may be that there is another line of continuity between the conditions of late-medieval and early-modern Europe to be perceived here, as Peter Heath's chapter on Gower and Erasmus suggests that even in court circles the changing nature of the English experience of warfare in the later fourteenth century may have inspired a similar revulsion to that shown by Erasmus in reaction to the shock of the 'military revolution'. So, even when viewed from the perspective of changing perceptions of the reality of war, developments which have been seen as peculiar to the early modern period, and as a specific response to the changing nature of warfare of the time, would now seem to have a history which stretches back into the fourteenth century, if not earlier.

In so far as a conclusion can be drawn from such reconsiderations, it would seem to be that the main innovations which have been seen as the core of the 'military revolution' of the early modern period of European history do not appear so new when viewed from a medieval perspective. The rise of infantry to dominance on the battlefield was a steady rather than a revolutionary process and can be traced back to the fourteenth century at least, while even the introduction of firearms was less of a novelty and changed military practice less than was once thought. Even in the case of siege warfare, the transformation brought about by artillery was relatively short-lived as a consequence of the development of new types of fortification effective against gunfire. Long sieges became common again, and it was the success or failure of such sieges rather than pitched battles which determined the outcome of campaigns – much as in the late Middle Ages. Even in the case of the significant growth in the size of armies in the early-modern period, the supposed consequences – as a result of fiscal pressure – for the nature of the state in the form of increased centralisation and a drift towards absolutism were not as ineluctable as is often argued. The main point of J.L. Price's chapter is that the Dutch Republic was able to fight modern wars with 'medieval' political institutions.

The military revolution of the early-modern period, as identified by some scholars, needs, therefore, to be placed in the context of the almost equally radical changes which took place in the later Middle Ages, not to mention the very varied military experiences of the Middle Ages as a whole. The period covered by the military revolution must in consequence be extended backwards well into the later medieval centuries, but this change would bring the question whether a transformation which took place over such a long period – perhaps from the early fourteenth to the end of the eighteenth century – can be usefully called a revolution at all.

Notes

1. J.R. Hale, *War and Society in Renaissance Europe, 1450–1620* (London, 1985); M.S. Anderson, *War and Society in Europe of the Old Regime, 1618–1789* (London, 1988); F. Tallett, *War and Society in Early-Modern Europe, 1495–1715* (London, 1992); A. Corvisier, *Armies and Societies in Europe in Europe, 1494–1789* (Bloomington, 1979).
2. G. Parker, *The Military Revolution. Military Innovation and the Rise of the West, 1500–1800* (Cambridge, 1988); J. Black, *A Military Revolution? Military Change and European Society, 1550–1800* (Basingstoke, 1991).
3. M. Roberts, *The Military Revolution, 1560–1660* (Belfast, 1956).
4. G. Parker, 'The "military revolution", 1550–1660 – a myth?', *Journal of Modern History* 48 (1976), pp 195–214, reprinted in his *Spain and the Netherlands, 1559–1659* (London, 1979).
5. E.g. B.M. Downing, *The Military Revolution and Political Change. Origins of Democracy and Autocracy in Early Modern Europe* (Princeton, 1992), pp 64–74.
6. Black, *A Military Revolution?*, pp 20–34.
7. The conditions in much of eastern Europe allowed cavalry to play a dominant role almost until the eighteenth century.
8. See C. Duffy, *Siege Warfare. The Fortress in the Early Modern World, 1494–1660* (London, 1979).
9. For this general argument, see M. Mann, *The Sources of Social Power,* 2 vols (Cambridge, 1986; 1993), I, pp 453–8, 475–83.
10. Cf. J.F. Guilmartin, *Gunpowder and Galleys. Changing Technology and Mediterranean Warfare at Sea in the Sixteenth Century* (Cambridge, 1974).

11 . For these changes in naval warfare in one particularly significant case, see J.R. Bruijn, *The Dutch Navy in the Seventeenth and Eighteenth Centuries* (Columbia, SC, 1993).

12 . See also W. Brulez, 'Het gewicht van de oorlog in nieuwe tijden. Enkele aspecten', *Tijdschrift voor Geschiedenis* 91 (1978), pp 386–406.

13 . See Mann, *The Sources of Social Power*, I, chapter 14.

14 . Parker, *The Military Revolution*, p 62.

15 . See also Tallett, *War and Society in Early-Modern Europe*, pp 176–8.

16 . Parker, *The Military Revolution*, p 63.

17 . Cf. C. Russell, *The Fall of the British Monarchies, 1637–1642* (Oxford, 1991), pp 72ff; C. Russell, *The Causes of the English Civil War* (Oxford, 1990), chapter 7; A. Hughes, *The Causes of the English Civil War* (Basingstoke, 1991), pp 13–15.

18 . R. Bean, 'War and the birth of the nation state', *Journal of Economic History* 33 (1973); Downing, *The Military Revolution and Political Change, passim*.

19 . On the development of gunpowder weapons, see P. Contamine, *War in the Middle Ages*, trans. M. Jones (Oxford, 1984), pp 137–50, 193–207; see also R. Smith, 'Artillery and the Hundred Years War: myth and interpretation', in A. Curry and M. Hughes, *Arms, Armies and Fortifications in the Hundred Years War* (Woodbridge, 1994), pp 151–60. For the concept of an 'artillery revolution', see C.J. Rogers, 'The military revolutions of the Hundred Years War', *The Journal of Military History* 57 (1993), pp 258–75.

20 . Contamine, *War in the Middle Ages*, pp 198–200. Such battles as Castillon (1453) were exceptions, as were the *Wagenburg* tactics, involving guns mounted on carts, employed by the Hussites in the 1420s and later by János Hunyadi's Hungarian armies against the Ottomans: J.W. Sedlar, *East Central Europe in the Middle Ages, 1000–1500* (Seattle and London, 1994), pp 234, 247.

21 . On the use of handguns and artillery for defence, see M. Vale, *War and Chivalry* (London, 1981), pp 133ff.

22 . Contamine, *War in the Middle Ages*, p 101.

23 . J. Hale, 'The early development of the bastion: an Italian chronology, c. 1450–c.1534', in J. Hale, J.R.L. Highfield and B. Smalley, eds, *Europe in the Late Middle Ages* (London, 1965), pp 466–94; Contamine, *War in the Middle Ages*, pp 202–5. Cf. Vale, *War and Chivalry*, p 133, for the earthwork *boulevards* constructed to protect Gascon towns in the 1430s and '40s.

24 . Rogers, 'The military revolutions of the Hundred Years War', pp 272–5.

25 . It is true that, from the sixteenth century, effective fortifications tended to be larger than before, with consequential increases in building and garrisoning costs, and encouraging the deployment of larger siege armies.

26 . For eloquent expression of this view, see J. Gillingham, 'Richard I and the science of war in the Middle Ages', in J. Gillingham and J.C. Holt, eds, *War and Government in the Middle Ages* (Woodbridge, 1984), pp 78–91; on the strategy of devastation, see H.J. Hewitt, *The Organisation of War under Edward III* (Manchester, 1966), chapter 5.

27 . Gillingham, 'Richard I and the science of war', p. 80–81. Cf. János Hunyadi's military career and the Turco-Hungarian wars in general: J. Held, *Hunyadi: Legend and Reality* (New York, 1985), chapters 5–9; yet much

also hinged on the control of fortresses (F. Szakály, 'Phases of Turco-Hungarian warfare before the battle of Mohács (1365–1526)', *Acta Orientalia Academiae Scientiarum Hungaricae* 33 (1979), pp 65–111). Civil wars in England, by the fifteenth century a lightly fortified realm by continental standards, were unusually battle-oriented: J. Gillingham, *The Wars of the Roses* (London, 1981), chapter 2; A. Goodman, *The Wars of the Roses* (London, 1981), chapter 8.

28 . Vale, *War and Chivalry*, p 171.

29 . See, for example, A. Tuck, 'War and society in the medieval north', *Northern History* 21 (1985), pp 33–52; L. Carolus-Barré, 'Benoît XII et la mission charitable de Bertrand Carit dans les pays dévastés du nord de la France', *Mélanges d'archéologie et d'histoire* 62 (1950), pp 165–232, on which cf. H.J. Hewitt, *The Organisation of War under Edward III*, pp 123–31, and R.W. Kaeuper, *War, Justice and Public Order: England and France in the Later Middle Ages* (Oxford, 1988), pp 80–88. See also, on the impact of war on the French countryside, R. Boutruche, 'The devastation of rural areas during the Hundred Years War and the agricultural recovery of France', in P.S. Lewis, ed, *The Recovery of France in the Fifteenth Century* (London and Basingstoke, 1971), pp 23–59; M. Jones, 'War and fourteenth-century France', in Curry and Hughes, *Arms, Armies and Fortifications in the Hundred Years War*, pp 103–20. Cf., for other parts of Europe, M. Burleigh, *Prussian Society and the German Order* (Cambridge, 1984), pp. 73–6, 87–8; R.C. Hoffmann, *Land, Liberties and Lordship in Late Medieval Countryside. Agrarian Structures and Change in the Duchy of Wroclaw* (Philadelphia, 1989), chapter 10.

30 . For example, C. Coulson, 'Some analysis of the castle of Bodiam, east Sussex', in C. Harper-Bill and R. Harvey, eds, *Medieval Knighthood IV* (Woodbridge, 1992), pp 51–107; cf. M.W. Thompson, *The Decline of the Castle* (Cambridge, 1987).

31 . Jones, 'War and fourteenth-century France, pp 110–11.

32 . E. Fügedi, 'Medieval Hungarian castles in existence at the start of the Ottoman advance' and F. Szakály, 'The Hungarian-Croatian border defense system and its collapse', both in J. Bak and B. Király, eds, *From Hunyadi to Rakoczi* (Brooklyn, 1982), pp 59–62; 141–58. See also E. Fügedi, *Castle and Society in Medieval Hungary, 1000–1437* (Budapest, 1986).

33 . J.F. Verbruggen, *The Art of Warfare in Western Europe During the Middle Ages* (Amsterdam, 1977), chapter 3: 'The foot soldiers'. Cf. C.C. Giurescu, 'Les armées Roumaines dans la lutte pour la défense et l'indépendance du pays du XIVe au XVIe siècle', *Revue internationale d'histoire militaire* 34 (1975), pp 6–7, for the defeat of King Charles I's Hungarian army in a defile at Posada (9–11 November 1330), which the author compares with the better-known battle of Mortgarten (1315). Clifford Rogers has recently argued strongly for an 'infantry revolution' in this period: 'The military revolutions of the Hundred Years War', pp 247–57.

34 . On the 'mounted archers' recruited by various states of Europe, see Contamine, *War in the Middle Ages*, pp 129–30; and A. Borosy, 'The *militia portalis* in Hungary before 1526', in Bak and Király, eds, *From Hunyadi to Rakoczi*, pp 63–80. The English mounted archer was described by J.E. Morris as the

'finest fighting man of the Middle Ages': 'Mounted infantry in medieval warfare', *TRHS*, 3rd series, 8 (1914), p 78.

35 . Contamine, *War in the Middle Ages*, pp 132–7; and Vale, *War and Chivalry*, pp 154–61.

36 . Rogers, 'The military revolutions of the Hundred Years War', p 256.

37 . T.F. Tout, 'Some neglected fights between Crécy and Poitiers', *EHR* 20 (1905), pp 726–30; M. Bennett, *Agincourt, 1415: Triumph Against the Odds* (London, 1991), pp 61–85. At Nicopolis, the western European contingents 'leaped off their horses, as is their custom, intending to fight as foot-soldiers': János Thuróczy, *Chronicle of the Hungarians*, ed F. Mantello and P. Engel (Bloomington, Indiana, 1991), pp 57–8.

38 . M. Vale, *War and Chivalry* (London, 1981), pp 100–28, at 101; M. Mallett, *Mercenaries and their Masters* (London, 1974), pp 146–51.

39 . F. Lot, *Recherches sur les effectifs des armées françaises des Guerres d'Italie aux Guerres de Réligion, 1494–1562* (Paris, 1962), chapter 1.

40 . Vale, *War and Chivalry*, p. 127.

41 . On one aspect of this development, see J.R. Hale, 'The military education of the officer class in early modern Europe', in J.R. Hale, *Renaissance War Studies* (London, 1983), pp 225–46. On duelling, 'a compensatory interest' for the nobility: Vale, *War and Chivalry*, pp 165–6.

42 . Vale, *War and Chivalry*, pp 147–54.

43 . H. Maxwell, ed, *Scalacronica. The Reigns of Edward I, Edward II and Edward III as Recorded by Sir Thomas Gray* (Glasgow, 1907), p 157.

44 . Evans, of the 88th Connaught Rangers, fought at the siege of Sebastapol in 1855, where he took part in the attack on 'the quarries' (7 June) and the Redan (18 June), and where he was badly wounded in the trenches on 8 August. In India, he was severely wounded at Cawnpore on 27 November 1857, 'from the effect of which he died at Babbicombe on 5 October 1861, at the early age of 23 years'.

45 . M. Prestwich, *War, Politics and Finance under Edward I* (London, 1972), p 113; M. Prestwich, *Edward I* (London, 1988), p 479. Edward III's army for the siege of Calais in 1346–7 is unlikely to have been as large as this: on the difficulties of interpreting the well-known but misleading 'Calais roll', see A. Ayton, 'The English army and the Normandy campaign of 1346', in D. Bates and A. Curry, eds, *England and Normandy in the Middle Ages* (London, 1994), pp 260–68.

46 . A. Ayton, 'English armies in the fourteenth century', in Curry and Hughes, eds, *Arms, Armies and Fortifications in the Hundred Years War*, pp. 21–38.

47 . J.R. Strayer, *The Reign of Philip the Fair* (Princeton, 1980), p 379.

48 . P. Contamine, *Guerre, état et société à la fin du Moyen Age* (Paris, 1972), pp 68–70, 313–19; Contamine, *War in the Middle Ages*, pp 169–71; P. Contamine, ed, *Histoire militaire de la France: I – Des origines à 1715* (Paris, 1992), pp 135–9, 230–32. From 16,000 to 20,000 French combatants served in Charles VIII's *grande armée* in Italy in 1494–95: Lot, *Recherches sur les effectifs des armées françaises*, p. 21.

49 . Mallett, *Mercenaries and their Masters*, pp 116–19.

50 . G. Rázsó, 'The mercenary army of King Matthias Corvinus', in Bak and Király, eds, *From Hunyadi to Rakoczi*, pp 125–40.

51 . See, for example, M.C. Bartusis, *The Late Byzantine Army: Arms and Society, 1204–1453* (Philadelphia, 1992), pp 258–69. Duke Charles the Bold of Burgundy's 'model army' of the 1470s numbered no more than 10,000 combatants: Contamine, *War in the Middle Ages*, p. 171; R. Vaughan, *Valois Burgundy* (London, 1975), chapter 7, especially pp 123–4.

52 . E. Cox, *The Green Count of Savoy. Amadeus VI and Transalpine Savoy in the Fourteenth Century* (Princeton, 1967), p. 220, note 41; N. Housley, *The Avignon Papacy and the Crusades, 1305–1378* (Oxford, 1986), pp 44–5.

53 . B. Guenée, *States and Rulers in Later Medieval Europe* (Oxford, 1985), p 142.

54 . See Kaeuper, *War, Justice and Public Order*, pp 88–9 and citations there.

55 . See, for example, C.W. Hollister, *Anglo-Saxon Military Institutions on the Eve of the Norman Conquest* (Oxford, 1962), chapter 1; J.O. Prestwich, 'War and finance in the Anglo-Norman state', *TRHS*, 5th series, 4 (1954), pp 19–43; and S.D.B. Brown, 'Military service and monetary reward in the eleventh and twelfth centuries', *History* 74 (1989), pp 20–38.

56 . M. Prestwich, 'War and taxation in England in the thirteenth and fourteenth centuries', in J-P. Genet and M. Le Mené, eds, *Genèse de l'état moderne* (Paris, 1987), pp 181–92, especially p 183.

57 . On the cost of the war effort under Edward I, see M. Prestwich, *War, Politics and Finance under Edward I* (London, 1972), pp 169–76; and Prestwich, 'War and taxation in England in the thirteenth and fourteenth centuries'. On Edward III, see Kaeuper, *War, Justice and Public Order*, pp 52–4; but cf. E.S. Hunt, 'A new look at the dealings of the Bardi and Peruzzi with Edward III, *Journal of Economic History* 50 (1990), pp 149–62.

58 . J. Sherborne, 'The cost of English warfare in the later fourteenth century', *Bulletin of the Institute of Historical Research* 50 (1977), pp 135–50.

59 . W.M. Ormrod, 'The domestic response', in Curry and Hughes, *Arms, Armies and Fortifications in the Hundred Years War*, pp 87–94, which revises K.B. McFarlane's calculations in *England in the Fifteenth Century* (London, 1981), pp 142–3.

60 . G. Harriss, 'Political society and the growth of government in late medieval England', *Past and Present* 138 (February 1993), pp 28–57; recent writing on this subject is surveyed on pp 28–32.

61 . See Ayton, 'English armies in the fourteenth century'.

62 . For an excellent discussion, see A. Curry, 'English armies in the fifteenth century', in Curry and Hughes, *Arms, Armies and Fortifications in the Hundred Years War*, pp 39–68. Apart from 'brief experimentation in 1430–1', garrison troops continued to be paid through their captain, not individually: cf. government pressure to shift to a system of individual payments in the 1560s and 1580s (C.G. Cruickshank, *Elizabeth's Army*, 2nd edn (Oxford, 1966), pp 152–3; and R.W. Ambler's chapter in this volume).

63 . J.R. Lander, 'The Hundred Years War and Edward IV's 1475 campaign in France', in Lander, *Crown and Nobility, 1450–1509* (London, 1976), pp 220–41 and appendix E; H. Miller, *Henry VIII and the English Nobility* (Oxford, 1986), pp 159–60.

64 . Kaeuper, *War, Justice and Public Order*, p 23.

65 . J.R. Strayer, 'The costs and profits of war: the Anglo-French conflict of 1294–1303', in H.A. Miskimin, D. Herlihy and A.L. Udovitch, eds, *The Medieval City* (New Haven and London, 1977), pp 269–91.

66 . Kaeuper, *War, Justice and Public Order*, p 63ff; E. Fryde, 'Royal fiscal systems and state formation in France from the thirteenth to the sixteenth centuries, with some English comparisons', *Journal of Historical Sociology* 4 (1991), pp 236–87.

67 . On the control of the free companies by recruiting them into standing companies in the service of the French crown, see M. Keen, 'War, peace and chivalry', in B. McGuire, ed, *War and Peace in the Middle Ages* (Copenhagen, 1987), pp 106–12. An alternative approach was to re-direct the routiers' energies into a crusade: N. Housley, 'The mercenary companies, the papacy and the crusades, 1356–1378', *Traditio* 38 (1982), pp 253–80.

68 . Contamine, *War in the Middle Ages*, pp 168–71: a convenient summary of his own work.

69 . G. Harriss, 'War and the emergence of the English Parliament, 1297–1360', *Journal of Medieval History* 2 (1976), pp 35–56.

70 . P.S. Lewis, 'The failure of the French medieval Estates', in P.S. Lewis, ed, *The Recovery of France in the Fifteenth Century* (London and Basingstoke, 1971), pp 294–311; Guenée, *States and Rulers in Later Medieval Europe*, pp 180–81, 185–7.

71 . Ormrod, 'The domestic response', pp 93–4.

72 . A. Grant, *Independence and Nationhood: Scotland, 1306–1469* (London, 1984), pp 34–5; Sedlar, *East Central Europe in the Middle Ages, 1000–1500*, p 255.

73 . Keen, 'War, peace and chivalry', in McGuire, ed, *War and Peace in the Middle Ages*, p 103.

74 . M. Bennett, '*La Règle du Temple* as a military manual, or how to deliver a cavalry charge', in C. Harper-Bill, C.J. Holdsworth and J.L. Nelson, eds, *Studies in Medieval History Presented to R. Allen Brown* (Woodbridge, 1989), pp 7–19; A. Forey, *The Military Orders from the Twelfth to the Early Fourteenth Centuries* (Basingstoke, 1992), chapter 5.

75 . See also Forey, *The Military Orders*, chapter 4.

76 . N. Housley, *The Later Crusades, 1274–1580* (Oxford, 1992), pp 228, 340.

77 . Contamine, *War in the Middle Ages*, pp 165–72.

78 . Mallett, *Mercenaries and their Masters*, chapter 5, at p 109; M. Mallett and J.R. Hale, *Military Organisation of a Renaissance State: Venice, c. 1400 to 1617* (Cambridge, 1984), chapter 4.

79 . Rázsó, 'The mercenary army of King Matthias Corvinus'; J. Bak, 'The price of war and peace in late medieval Hungary', in McGuire, ed, *War and Peace in the Middle Ages*, pp 161–78, especially pp 172–4; J. Bak, 'The late medieval period, 1382–1526', in P. Sugar, *A History of Hungary* (London and New York, 1990), pp 70–76. Cf. Muscovy, where the 'crown had neither the technical means nor the economic resources to create a military establishment of the type coming into being in Western Europe ... pay, as always, came largely in the form of booty': G. Alef, 'Muscovite military reforms in the second-half of the fifteenth century', in G. Alef, *Rulers and Nobles in Fifteenth–Century Muscovy* (London, 1983), chapter 7, at p 81.

1. The Conqueror's Footprints in Domesday Book

J.J.N. Palmer

Agrarian history becomes more catastrophic as we trace it backwards.

F.W. Maitland, *Domesday Book and Beyond*

The principal strategy of early medieval armies was to lay waste the countryside,[1] with potentially devastating social and economic consequences which can all too rarely be assessed. If we are to believe the chroniclers, the land was ravaged from 'sea to sea', reduced to a desert, 'stripped of all means of sustenance', or totally depopulated, on all too many occasions in the early medieval centuries before Europe had acquired a dense network of fortifications which offered a measure of protection to the open countryside.[2] But historians, of course, are now rarely so naive as to believe the chroniclers where large numbers are concerned or where hyperbole may be suspected.[3] For the most part, this leaves a void in the evidence; but there is one source in which the effects of early medieval warfare appear to be abundantly, indeed overwhelmingly, documented, and that is in Domesday Book.

As a test case for the impact of early medieval warfare, Domesday England could scarcely be bettered. It was a land where 'the plough was King'[4] and where the countryside was largely unprotected by fortifications. Due to the circumstances of the Norman Conquest, it was also a land extensively ravaged by warfare – warfare which contemporary chroniclers tell us left swathes of devastated land across most counties.[5] For once the statements of the chroniclers can apparently be verified, and in the minutest of detail. It has been claimed that in Domesday Book 'the Conqueror's footprints' of 1066 can be traced for mile after mile across 450 miles of English countryside by the evidence of the damage they left in their wake, meticulously accounted for in Domesday's record of wasted and devalued manors.

This claim has a lengthy pedigree. It was some two centuries ago that a certain Mr Hayley, a Sussex antiquarian, first suggested that the 'ravages of the two armies of the Conqueror and King Harold' had left their imprint in Domesday Book, and that we could trace 'the footsteps of King Harold's army' on its way to defeat at Hastings by the trail of devastated manors recorded there. The giants of Victorian Domesday studies – Sir Henry Ellis, E.A. Freeman, J.H. Round, and F.W. Maitland – agreed that the waste recorded in Domesday signified war damage. Ellis, who had independently arrived at the same conclusion as Hayley, gave him full credit for the observation and, like Maitland, applied the method to Yorkshire, the county with more waste than all others combined. Freeman, while accepting the basic premise, predictably objected to the role allocated to King Harold. It was 'the height of absurdity' to suggest that Harold would have been guilty of ravaging the lands of his own subjects in a county where the landed interests of his family were dominant. There was 'no doubt that all these [waste] entries record ravages done by the army of William', in an attempt to provoke Harold to battle. The waste was certainly war damage, but it was Norman war damage, all of it. Inevitably, Freeman's pronouncements evoked a characteristic response from Round. In *Feudal England*, Freeman's 'hasty', 'contemptuous', and 'careless' attack upon Hayley was rebutted, and his errors remorselessly catalogued. He had misrepresented Hayley; he had 'not read his Domesday "with common care"'; and he had demonstrably reached the wrong conclusion: the disputed footsteps were indeed Harold's, not William's.[6]

Round had the better of the argument – though Freeman probably reached the correct conclusion[7] – but he had little time to savour his triumph before the next contributor to the debate altered its entire complexion, enlarging its scope to the point where Round's controversy with Freeman was too trivial to merit even a footnote. In a seminal paper on 'The Conqueror's footprints in Domesday' published in 1898, Francis Baring argued that the full range of Domesday valuations – not merely the waste or zero values – could be used to document the damage caused by the armies of the period in those counties for which the two earliest valuations – those for 1066 and shortly afterwards – were recorded.[8] At a stroke, this extension of Hayley's methodology vastly enlarged the potential for documenting military activity, particularly in southern England, where waste was infrequently noted but where the two earliest manorial valuations were regularly recorded throughout ten counties.[9] In these counties there were a hundred devalued manors after the Conquest for every one said to be waste.[10] Against this background, the relative claims of King Harold and King William to have left their imprint on a handful of Sussex manors sank into an obscurity from which they have never since emerged. Even Round turned his energies to exploiting the new methodology rather than pursuing old quarrels, though with a somewhat ill grace.[11]

Baring's methodology was simple. Of the three valuations often supplied by Domesday, the earlier two – just before and just after the Conquest – could be used to calculate the immediate economic impact of the Conquest. If this were serious, Baring argued, it might indicate military activity; and if the *pattern* of damage were marked, it certainly did so. Plotted on a map, the more heavily devalued manors would therefore reveal the paths traced out by the armies of the period by the damage they had inflicted, which could thus be assessed with some precision.

Baring's technique had its weaknesses. It has been fairly described as 'a naked-eye comparison' of the valuations, with all the lack of sophistication that this phrase implies.[12] He was somewhat arbitrary in his selection of the data. He excluded manors because they were too small, or because their values were unchanged and therefore suspect. All his figures related to manors rather than vills; he ignored the problems posed by complex manors; and he used absolute numbers when percentages would have facilitated comparisons.[13] Later writers have improved upon his technique in these respects.[14] But these rough edges did not affect the essentials of his thesis, or invalidate his findings. No one else has analysed the campaign in such detail, and no other military episode is anything like as well served by the valuations as the Conqueror's campaign of 1066. For all its pioneering faults, therefore, Baring's original paper remains the classic exposition of his thesis, and his data the best test of its validity.

Prior to Baring's paper, the campaign of 1066 had been reconstructed only in the broadest of outlines, from the few clues afforded by the chroniclers.[15] After the battle of Hastings the Norman army passed through Romney, Dover and Canterbury, and approached London before turning west to march through Hampshire, then northwards to cross the Thames at Wallingford. After that, only an insecurely identified 'Berkhamsted' was named in the sources. On this basis, it was believed that the Conqueror went from Canterbury to Rochester by Watling Street, then struck west through Surrey and Hampshire – the North Downs ridgeway was the obvious route – before marching north through Berkshire to cross the Thames at Wallingford. 'Berkhamsted' was identified as Great

Berkhamsted, which implied that the army followed the Icknield Way north-east from Wallingford before turning south-east through the Chilterns to reach London via Great Berkhamsted, St Albans and Watling Street (Map 1).[16]

In outline, Baring's reconstruction bore some resemblance to this route, if for no other reason than that the crossing of the Thames at Wallingford imposed severe constraints upon plausible alternatives. But Baring did far more than simply confirm the chroniclers' story. He extended the scale of the campaign, adding two counties[17] and almost 150 miles to the march; and in every county through which the Conqueror passed, he proposed significant changes of route. Above all, he claimed to be able to plot the movement of the army with such precision that he could name more than 200 villages along the 450-mile route. He specified not only the path followed by the main force but also the routes taken by columns and sometimes even by individual patrols. More than that, he identified reinforcements arriving from Normandy, their place of disembarkation, and the trails they followed to join the main force, all without the help of a single reference in the chronicles. He was so confident of the methodology that he felt able on occasions to determine the location of camps, the length of daily marches and the number of days spent at resting places, even correcting the chroniclers on these matters. He also believed that it was possible to calculate the size of the army, and one of his more enthusiastic disciples has even claimed to be able to distinguish the infantry from the cavalry and to deduce the precise size of individual patrols.[18]

Although Baring's thesis has encountered some scepticism,[19] it has never been seriously challenged.[20] An analysis of the first stage of the campaign of 1066 should make it possible to appreciate why. The Norman army spent three weeks near Hastings and a week encamped at Dover[21] and these two areas suffered the worst devastation recorded anywhere in the south of England. Within a few years of the Conquest, many manors around Hastings were without any value at all, and the values of almost all others had plunged dramatically. In the three coastal hundreds of the rape of Hastings, values fell by over 80 per cent; and in Netherfield hundred, in which the battle of Hastings took place, the decline was almost 90 per cent. Overall, the rape lost about three-quarters of its value in the years immediately after 1066.[22] This was twice the level of loss in the remainder of the county.

Although the damage near Dover was not as extreme, the pattern was even more sharply defined. The town itself was burnt by the Norman

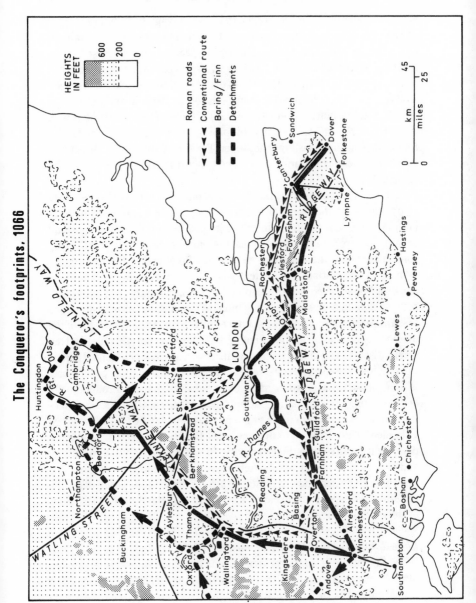

The Conqueror's footprints, 1066

army,[23] and the surrounding areas extensively ravaged. Within five miles of Dover, vills lost on average over 70 per cent of their value; within 10 miles, 54 per cent; and within 15 miles, 34 per cent. To put these figures into perspective, even the lowest of them (34 per cent) was more than seven times greater than losses elsewhere in the county, where decline averaged a mere 5 per cent.[24] Military activity is the only plausible explanation for such distinctive patterns, and the military activity of October 1066 is well documented. Baring claimed that this proved his method – as, indeed, it did for the areas around Hastings and Dover. Taking this as proof of the general validity of the thesis, Baring proceeded to apply it to the remainder of the campaign.

His confidence here may have been misplaced, for the next stage of the campaign took a different course, presenting different and more intractable problems. Up to this point, damage had been concentrated around encamped armies, in fixed locations, for known periods of time, allowing some estimate of the areas that were under threat and of the scale of the damage to be anticipated. After Dover, however, damage would be dispersed along the lines of march of an unknown number of columns, moving at unknown speeds, along unknown routes, towards destinations that are specifically identified in only two cases in the entire length of the march between Dover and its eventual destination, some 400 miles and ten weeks distant. Attributing damage to their virtually undocumented activities inevitably involves a considerable element of speculation, particularly in view of the widespread distribution of devalued manors throughout the entire region.[25] Occasionally, Baring's method may still produce convincing results: the choice of route might be unavoidable; the trail of devalued vills clearly marked; and adjacent areas largely unaffected, producing patterns indicative of military activity. In western Kent, western Surrey, and along the flank of the Chilterns, such conditions are met in some measure. But such ideal conditions are the exception. Elsewhere, the pattern of damage is not so easily reconciled with the Baring thesis. Four problems can be identified.

Little damage along the line of march
In the first place, Domesday often records little damage where we should most expect to find it. Wallingford provides the clearest example. After Canterbury, it is the only place through which the army is known with certainty to have passed. It concentrated there in order to cross the Thames; and since the Conqueror remained long enough to lay out a camp (*castra*) and to receive the submission of Archbishop Stigand, a stay of some days

at least is indicated.[26] We might, therefore, expect that the area around Wallingford would produce something of the pattern observed near Dover. But this is far from being the case.

On the Oxfordshire side of the Thames, astonishingly little damage is recorded.[27] Neither Crowmarsh – the probable location of the Conqueror's camp – nor any of the other manors in that hundred for which we have comparable figures declined in value after 1066. The aggregate value of the eight hundreds of southern Oxfordshire actually increased slightly (1.4 per cent), and the vills which lay within a ten-mile radius of Crowmarsh jumped in value by almost 10 per cent. The Oxfordshire valuations are eccentric, with few losses between 1066 and 1070 but substantial increases thereafter. Baring suggested that the pre-Conquest values had been depressed by the depredations of the northern rebels of 1065. But even if this were the case – which has been disputed by one of his own disciples[28] – it would have affected only northern and central Oxfordshire and would in any case not explain why there was no further fall in values after 1066. The Oxfordshire valuations are undoubtedly puzzling. But the one certain conclusion which they do permit is that the county sustained no serious losses after the Conquest. They provide no evidence whatsoever that the Norman army passed this way, and strongly imply that it did not. Yet we know that it did.

On the Berkshire side, the decline in values, though significantly higher, was still modest by comparison with any substantial part of the route, let alone with the area around Dover. Vills within a five-mile radius of Wallingford suffered an average decline of under 9 per cent; within 10 miles, 11 per cent; and within 15 miles, 12 per cent.[29] All these figures are below the average for the county (-18 per cent). The greatest losses were suffered at its extremities, at the furthest remove from Wallingford. Beyond 15 miles, the average loss was 26 per cent. In short, the greater the distance from Wallingford, the higher the losses. This is a mirror image of the situation around Dover and Hastings. If the evidence of the valuations were all we had to go on, we would not place the crossing of the Thames at Wallingford, nor would we imagine that the Conqueror had entered Oxfordshire at all.[30]

Serious damage away from the line of march

Apart from the lack of major damage where it should be found, the thesis fails to account for serious damage where we have little reason to expect it on military grounds. In Surrey, the worst-affected area lies along a north–south axis on the eastern edge of the county: the loss of value in the three eastern hundreds amounts to almost 45 per cent, twice the average for the remainder of the county. Yet this area lies at right angles to any plausible line of march for the main army. The oddity of this distribution is emphasized by the fact that it is flanked by two sections of the route in western Kent and central Surrey where damage is modest. Between Maidstone and Guildford – perhaps a week's march – the loss of value averages about 20 per cent,[31] below that for the county generally and less than half that for eastern Surrey.

This pattern has embarrassed all the commentators. Several have sought to explain it by the activities of detachments; but this presupposes that detachments could cause substantially more damage than the main army, which, if true, would seriously weaken the whole thesis. Baring actually changed his mind about this section of the route, first sending the army in a sweep along the south bank of the Thames from Dartford to East Molesey, then revising this to a zigzag across the downs in an effort to encompass more of the damage. Later commentators have found his second thoughts implausible. J. Beeler combined elements from both proposals, with a twist of his own. D. Butler agreed with Baring's original interpretation, which at least solved the problem of the modest damage between Maidstone and Guildford, though at the expense of ignoring the heavy damage in eastern Surrey. R.W. Finn acknowledged that there was no coherent military pattern in the data for eastern Surrey and abandoned any attempt to map it, sending the army along the ridgeway across central Surrey in despite of the healthy state of the valuations along this stretch, in effect abandoning the Baring thesis for this part of the route.[32]

An even more striking example of devastation where we have no plausible military reason to locate it is in western Middlesex and the adjacent part of south-eastern Buckinghamshire. Here, in an area encompassing 49 vills, every one had declined in value, a situation without parallel even around Dover and Hastings. The loss of value averaged almost 50 per cent, more than four times the level around Wallingford, and comparable to that around Dover.[33] Yet the army could not have come this way.

This is another section of the route about which Baring had second thoughts,[34] a sure sign that the data could not easily be accommodated to his thesis. He eventually attributed the damage to a detachment sent across the Thames to protect the Conqueror's flank. But there is no warrant in the sources for this manoeuvre, which appears both unnecessary and danger-ous: unnecessary because the Thames and the Chilterns themselves provided flanking cover; and dangerous because neither force could support the other if required to do so. Even if these implausibilities are swallowed, it does not explain the pattern to the data. The losses are widespread; they lead in no direction; they are isolated from other areas of military activity; and they are far more substantial than those caused by the main army, wherever it is located. The drastic losses in this area are as mysterious as the modest decline around Wallingford.

There are several other areas where damage is heavier than military factors would warrant, but two more examples must suffice. In Hampshire, the extensive decline in values around Winchester, and to the south and east of the city, appears to be quite unrelated and has been explained only by the twin suppositions that reinforcements landed in south Hampshire and that the Conqueror directed his main army south-west – well away from the natural line of march along the ridgeway between Farnham and Basingstoke – towards Winchester, in order to obtain its submission before turning north to the Thames. The first supposition has no warrant in the sources, and the second disregards the one source to mention Winchester, which records that the Conqueror accepted tribute and left the city in peace, as a courtesy to Queen Edith, the Confessor's widow.[35]

Finally, Sussex. Of all the counties traversed by William's armies, none suffered more than Sussex. In part, this was the result of the prolonged stay around Hastings and the devastation inflicted there. But even excluding the rape of Hastings, the losses in Sussex (-37.5 per cent) were greater than those in any other county except Middlesex (-40 per cent). Throughout the whole of the county south of the Weald between Pevensey and Bosham (some 60 miles east to west), the majority of the vills lost value, and no area was entirely unscathed. Since this area extends inland for about 15 miles for much of its length, and up to 25 miles in the west of the county, it would require an army of two or three columns marching parallel to the coast to account for a significant proportion of this damage; but this, of course, would make no military sense.

Several alternative military explanations of the losses in Sussex have been proposed. Reinforcements landing at Fareham and elsewhere on the coast have, for instance, been held partly responsible, as have the activities of the Norman fleet. But neither of these events is documented; and neither naval landings on the coast nor reinforcements marching away from the coast will explain such dispersed damage, affecting east and west, inland and coastal areas alike. Other explanations – the ravages of Tostig in May 1066, or the defensive measures taken by Harold between May and September 1066 – have little more to commend them.[36] The very variety of explanations offered for the damage in Sussex testifies to the difficulty of accounting for it. One thing is certain. Whatever the explanation of the losses in Sussex west of Hastings, the passage of armies is not the answer, since no intelligible military pattern can be discerned.

Widespread damage where there are no clearly defined lines of march

The example of Sussex points to a third weakness of the Baring thesis. In some areas devalued manors are so widespread that they can no longer be taken as *prima facie* evidence of military activity since the very basis of that thesis is that the *pattern* of damage is itself the proof of military activity: no pattern, no proof. Baring repeatedly emphasized the significance of patterns which defined areas of military activity by their contrast with the undamaged territory which surrounded them. In Kent, Surrey and northern Hampshire there were no 'considerable losses' other than those along the line of march, thereby defining it; in Buckinghamshire and Oxfordshire, no damage outside a defined area in which the army operated; and in Hertfordshire and Middlesex none beyond their eastern boundaries. In most of these areas, he claimed, the line of march was narrow, or at least clearly defined, separating it from the adjacent territory spared by the Conqueror's army. 'Outside the line of march,' he concluded, 'the immediate effect of the Conquest on the value of land seems to have been very slight.'[37]

But in many areas where values had declined significantly, lines of march are not clearly distinguishable. This is the case in Sussex, and arguably in Hampshire and Buckinghamshire too. It is certainly the case in Middlesex, Hertfordshire and Bedfordshire. In these counties, damage is so dispersed that the identification of lines of march depends more upon the strategic vision of the analyst than upon the logic of the data.

In Bedfordshire, for instance, over two-thirds of the vills had lost 25 per cent or more of their value, every second vill had declined by over a third, and almost one-third by 50 per cent or more. Only two small areas escaped serious damage.[38] For the remainder – four-fifths of the county – modest and heavy damage were interspersed in a fairly even manner. Every hundred contained undamaged or lightly damaged vills, and every hundred contained vills which had lost 50 per cent or more of their value (except the hundred in which Bedford itself lay). No vill lay more than two or three miles from a seriously damaged neighbour. In such circumstances, identifying 'routes' is only too easy; the trick would be to find a path through the county which did not encompass serious damage.

In the absence of clear patterns, commentators have been tempted to account for this damage by constructing a multiplicity of routes across the

county. Finn has no fewer than ten columns entering or leaving Bedfordshire, and he does not incorporate all the routes plotted across the county
by other commentators. Even so, this multiplicity of columns does not
explain the extent of the damage or its distribution. Damage in the vicinity
of Bedford itself, which should have been the heaviest in the county in view
of the convergence of all routes upon the borough, was actually below the
average for the county as a whole (-33.7 per cent). In Bucklow, the hundred
in which Bedford lay, manors lost 27 per cent of their value, and a circle
of ten miles' diameter with Bedford as its centre enclosed damage
averaging just 30 per cent.

Both Finn and Baring acknowledged that the Bedfordshire data was
difficult to explain. At one point, Baring exclaimed, almost in despair, that
'William ... must have crossed Bedfordshire somewhere', and Finn
acknowledged that his map 'shows few clear signs of the possible
movements of a campaigning force', a situation he ascribed to a general-
ized 'requisitioning from as much of the countryside as possible'.[39] This
may have been the case; but, if so, it deprived the valuations of a clear
pattern and hence of their status as *prima facie* evidence of military
activity.

This has serious consequences for Baring's reconstruction of the final
stages of the Conqueror's campaign of 1066, because there is no other
evidence that his army marched through Bedfordshire, Cambridgeshire
and eastern Hertfordshire. All other indications are that it made for London
through Great Berkhamsted.

This was the traditional view. Until Baring outlined his thesis, the
surrender of the English leaders at 'Berkhamsted', and the effective
termination of the campaign there, was taken to refer to Great Berkhamsted
in western Hertfordshire, not Little Berkhamsted in the east, in which case
the Conqueror's army would have gone nowhere near Bedfordshire or
Cambridgeshire and would only have touched the western edge of Hertfordshire. Many factors appeared to support the identification of
'Berkhamsted' as Great Berkhamsted. On the basis of the name alone, it
is the obvious choice. Great Berkhamsted was a borough, and a manorial
centre belonging to one of the richest laymen in Anglo-Saxon England,[40]
important enough to become the seat of the honour of the Conqueror's
half-brother, Robert of Mortain, the site of his castle, and probably his
personal residence.[41] Little Berkhamsted, by contrast, was a insignificant
manor belonging to insignificant men.

Strategically, too, the route through Great Berkhamsted is the more
plausible choice. After a march of some 300 miles through enemy territory,

the direct route to London along major Roman roads, through the first considerable gap in the Chilterns, had everything to commend it. A wide sweep to the north away from London, adding almost 150 miles to the itinerary just as winter set in, can have had little appeal to either leaders or rank and file.

One last factor lends additional weight to the traditional view. Archbishop Stigand had surrendered at Wallingford. The submission of the main English leaders at Great Berkhamsted a few *days* later seems rather more likely than their submission at Little Berkhamsted some *weeks* later. All these factors indicate that the 'Berkhamsted' of the English surrender is most likely to have been Great Berkhamsted in western Hertfordshire and not its minor namesake in the east. If they chose otherwise, the leaders on both sides certainly showed a remarkable lack of ceremony or sense of history.

Against this, Baring argued that the devastation around Great Berkhamsted was insufficient to account for the presence of the Norman army, and that the extensive devaluations around Little Berkhamsted indicated the Conqueror must have come this way, via Bedfordshire and Cambridgeshire, even though the route he had taken was not clearly defined. The damage around Little Berkhamsted was, indeed, the greater, but it was far from insignificant around Great Berkhamsted. Within a ten-mile radius of each, vills had lost on average 37 per cent and 25 per cent of their value. But although it is the lower of the two, the figure for Great Berkhamsted is, of course, more than double that for the area around Wallingford, which we know supported the Conqueror's army for some days. In view of this, and in the absence of clearly defined trails of damage in Bedfordshire and eastern Hertfordshire, the case for Little Berkhamsted must be regarded as unproven, and implausible.[42]

Disagreements over lines of march

The fourth weakness of the Baring thesis is a particularly revealing one: that is, the inability of its advocates[43] to agree upon the lines of march. If the essential proof of an hypothesis is that it should always produce the same results from the same data, the Baring thesis manifestly fails this test. All too frequently different commentators have reached different conclusions, proposing divergent paths for significant stretches of the route. This is the case in every county through which the army passed.

Even in Kent and Surrey, where the line of the downs circumscribes plausible routes, none of the commentators agree exactly with each other. Baring was categoric that the main force took the road south of the downs, from Canterbury to Maidstone, and did not use the Roman road north of the downs via Rochester; yet this last was precisely the route favoured by Finn. Beyond Maidstone, Butler had the main army march directly on Southwark, a choice considered and rejected by Baring. The trails proposed for detachments are as various as those for the main army, rarely coinciding at all except for short stretches.

Even more divergent paths have been suggested in Surrey (Map 2),[44] though the route through this county would seem almost to choose itself for an army heading for Hampshire from Kent.[45] The ridgeway was the major east–west line of communication and had everything to commend it from a military point of view.[46] It kept to the high ground, commanding the Thames to the north and the passages of the downs and communications with the coast to the south; it was at a safe distance from London; it was the strategic choice, as evidenced by battles fought along its course during earlier centuries. But only one of the commentators – Finn – selected this route, and he did so in the teeth of the evidence supplied by the valuations which, as already noted, showed moderate levels of damage between Maidstone and Guildford. Baring – although he had the army entering and leaving the county at the same points as Finn – sent it on a north-west march across the downs from Godstone to Cuddington, before turning south-west towards Guildford. Butler thought the main army must have entered the county from Eltham in Kent and followed the Thames round to East Molesey before heading south-west to Guildford, Baring's original suggestion. In short, one analyst had the army traversing the north of the county, another the centre, and a third zigzagging from centre to north and back again.

Although divergences in other counties are not as marked as in Surrey, in no county is there anything like a consensus among the commentators about the lines of march. In no county, for instance, do they agree upon the route taken by the main force, and in Surrey, Hampshire, Buckinghamshire and Bedfordshire they all differ about this crucial identification. In most counties they disagree on the number of columns, the discrepancies in some amounting to more than half an army. In no county do the commentators concur on the paths taken by these columns, and in several they all disagree. Their record on the routes followed by detachments is little more harmonious, with particularly sharp divergencies in Hampshire and significant variations in Kent, Buckinghamshire and Middlesex. Every commentator marches his columns across territory untouched by the others, or spares areas which they ravage. Examples can be found in most counties. In some – Buckinghamshire and Bedfordshire, for instance

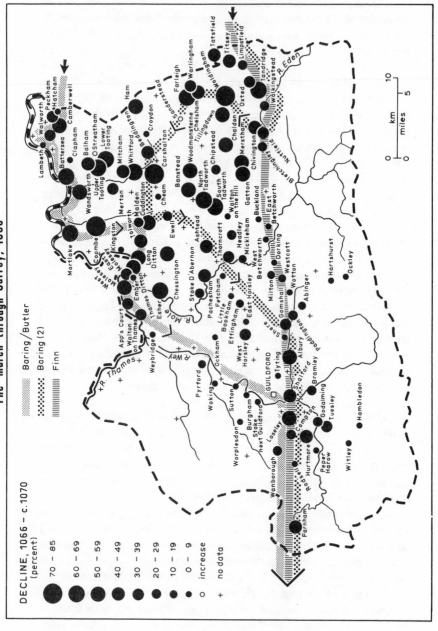

The march through Surrey, 1066

– the lines of march even go in different directions, one commentator proposing a north–south orientation, another an west–east one. In short, nothing is more damaging to the Baring thesis than the enthusiasm of its advocates in applying it.

It would be ungracious to conclude this essay without mentioning that Baring subsequently showed some unease about aspects of his thesis. When his article was reprinted with corrections in *Domesday Tables* in 1909, one of the corrections he made was to abandon his title, substituting the bland 'On the Domesday valuations, with special reference to William's march from Hastings to London' for the more provocative 'The Conqueror's footprints'.[47] He revealed further doubts by changing his mind about two significant stretches of the route, and acknowledging that there must be 'an element of conjecture' in his reconstruction. The most scholarly of his disciples, R.W. Finn, has indicated the problems to which the application of the thesis gives rise in many counties, and has admitted that it does not yield intelligible results in some instances.

Neither scholar was led to question the basis of the methodology, yet that is precisely what should be questioned. Its underlying assumption that war damage inflicts characteristic patterns which can almost always be detected in the record of Domesday valuations is flawed. There are a few areas where the pattern of devastation is so distinctive that it is evidently the result of military activity, as around Hastings and Dover. But even encamped armies – the easiest test of the thesis – did not always leave distinctive traces, as the case of Wallingford reveals. As for armies on the march, there are few cases where the trails they left are so sharply distinguished from the undamaged countryside around them as to be unambiguously recognizable. Military activity of a messier nature – widespread requisitioning – will by its very nature not leave distinctively 'military' patterns. In short, the Baring thesis has more limited application than has been claimed for it. It is not a precision tool, and on occasions not even useful as a blunt instrument.

And this is surely what we should expect. Some of the commentators treat the valuations as though they had been collected by commissioners following immediately in the wake of the Norman army. In reality, the interval between the pre-1066 and the intermediate values was a matter of years, more years in some cases than others. During that interval, manors would have recovered at different rates or suffered additional damage from civil unrest, manorial reorganization, later military activity, bad weather, poor harvests, famine, murrain, mortality and plague. Every change which occurred after 1066 scuffed the footprints left by the Conqueror between October and December or buried them under the debris of later events.

Appendix

Although Baring's thesis greatly extended the range of Domesday valuations that could be used to document military activity, it still left outside its scope those areas which lacked either waste or intermediate values. Some ingenuity has been employed to fill this void, first by Baring himself, then by a succession of scholars, including J.H. Round, F.M. Stenton, G.H. Fowler, Finn and H.C. Darby.[48] Their attention has been focused mainly upon the midland counties of circuit four – Leicestershire, Northampton-shire, Oxfordshire, Staffordshire and Warwickshire – and upon some parts of circuit five. These counties saw considerable military activity both before and after the Conquest, and their failure to record an intermediate, or third, valuation, has therefore been particularly frustrating. Of the two valuations normally given, one is for 1086 and the other for an earlier date, often stated to be 1066. Where this is not the case, it is usually assumed to have been so, though there are known hazards in this assumption.[49]

The technique used to exploit this unpromising data has been described by Fowler – its principal exponent – as an 'inductive method' whereby it is possible to 'infer the original depreciation from the extent of the recovery or appreciation', by calculating the 1086 value as a percentage of the 1066 one. A significant *increase* in value between these dates would, in Fowler's words, 'imply a catastrophe to the village about the time of the Conquest',[50] that is, before 1065, or at least at some time before the date of the 1066 valuations. This technique, therefore, could be used to analyse the impact of pre-Conquest warfare, and notably the 1065 campaign of the northerners which ravaged Northamptonshire and the surrounding coun-ties 'so that the shire and other neighbouring shires were the worst for it for many years'.[51]

Like the Baring thesis itself, this extension has never been submitted to critical scrutiny, though the data for testing it are readily to hand in Domesday Book. Fowler's method assumes – a rather large assumption – that increases in value between 1066 and 1086 imply corresponding decreases before the Conquest: that the depressed valuations of 1066 are a deviation from the norm, represented by the valuations for 1086. This cannot, of course, be tested directly, since we have no pre-1065 valuations. But we can apply Fowler's assumption to those counties for which three valuations are recorded. In these counties, the 1086 valuations can be calculated as a percentage of the depressed (i.e, intermediate) valuations to 'infer the original depreciation'. This inferred depreciation can then be compared to the *actual* depreciation between 1066 and about 1070.

The results are sobering. In few instances do the estimated depreciations come at all close to the true ones, even for data aggregated at a high level. If the discrepancies between the actual and inferred depreciations for each county are calculated, for instance, they differ from each other by as much as 15 per cent in circuit three, by 28 per cent in circuit one and by almost 40 per cent in the two circuits combined. Aggregation at the circuit and county level has, of course, smoothed out most variations. In circuit three, for instance, the discrepancies between estimated and actual depreciations from one hundred to another was 70 per cent, and those from one vill to another exceeded 1200 per cent. In Bedfordshire, Buckinghamshire and Cambridgeshire the variations from hundred to hundred within each county were approximately 50 per cent, and in Hertfordshire over 25 per cent; only in Middlesex did they fall below 20 per cent, and then only by one point. These are very substantial margins of error: in a fifth of the hundreds, the margin of error actually exceeded the amount of the depreciation. Only the most extreme forms of ravaging would have left scars which were still clearly visible through this statistical smog after the lapse of more than 20 years.

Notes

1. N. Hooper, 'The Anglo-Saxons at war', in S.C. Hawkes, ed, *Weapons and Warfare in Anglo-Saxon England* (Oxford, 1989), pp 191–201; J. France, 'La guerre dans la France féodale à la fin du IXe et au Xe siècle', *Revue belge d'histoire militaire* 23 (1979), pp 177–98; M. Strickland, ed, *Anglo-Norman Warfare* (Woodbridge, 1992), pp 150–55, 199–201, 214–17, 232–4; J. France, *Victory in the East: A Military History of the First Crusade* (Cambridge, 1994), pp 42–51.

2. M. Bloch, *Feudal Society*, trans. L.A. Manyon (London, 1961), pp 1–56; M. Strickland, 'The conduct and perception of war under the Anglo-Norman and Angevin kings', unpublished PhD thesis, University of Cambridge, 1989, pp 237–79, 325, 350.

3. See, among many others, the comments of P.H. Sawyer, *The Age of the Vikings*, 2nd edn (London, 1971), chapter 6; J. Gillingham, '"The most precious jewel in the English crown": levels of danegeld and heregeld in the early eleventh century', *EHR* 104 (1989), pp 379, 384. S. Keynes, 'The historical context of the battle of Maldon', in D. Scragg, ed, *The Battle of Maldon* (Oxford, 1991), p 100, puts the case succinctly: 'medieval chroniclers were nothing if not prone to the wilful misrepresentation of facts and the gross exaggeration of numbers'.

4. J.H. Round, 'The Domesday survey', *VCH: Surrey*, i (London, 1904), p 291.

5 . D. Whitelock, D.C. Douglas, and S.I. Tucker, eds, *Anglo-Saxon Chronicle* (London, 1961), p 144; Florence of Worcester, *Chronicon ex chronicis*, ed B. Thorpe, English Historical Society, 2 vols (London, 1848–9), I, pp 228–9.

6 . Sir Henry Ellis, *A General Introduction to Domesday Book*, 2 vols (London, 1833), I, pp 314–20, quoting extensively from Hayley on pp 315–18; E.A. Freeman, *The History of the Norman Conquest*, 6 vols (Oxford, 1867–79), III, pp 413–14, 741–5; J.H. Round, *Feudal England* (London, 1895), pp 149–52; F.W. Maitland, *Domesday Book and Beyond* (Cambridge, 1897), pp 363–5.

7 . But see note 36 below.

8 . F.H. Baring, 'The Conqueror's footprints in Domesday', *EHR* 13 (1898), pp 17–25, reprinted with corrections in *Domesday Tables for the Counties of Surrey, Berkshire, Middlesex, Hertford, Buckingham and Bedford, and for the New Forest* (London, 1909), pp 207–16; F.H. Baring, 'William the Conqueror's march through Hampshire in 1066', *Proceedings of the Hampshire Field Club and Archaeological Society* 7 (1915), pp 33–9. Domesday records manorial valuations for three dates: 1066, 1086 and an intermediate date, of indeterminate year, traditionally assigned to *c.* 1070, but probably a year or two earlier for many of the manors in southern England, particularly those south of the Thames. Which of the three were normally recorded varied from circuit to circuit. Four broad patterns are discernible, though subject to individual variations and some ambiguity: (1) all three valuations (circuits one and three); (2) three valuations, but irregularly (circuits five and seven); (3) 1066 and 1086 (circuits four and six); and (4) *c.* 1070 and 1086 (circuit two). There is a useful distribution map in H.C. Darby, *Domesday England* (Cambridge, 1977), p 212.

9 . See Appendix to this chapter for later efforts to extend Baring's method to the data of circuit four. I hope to deal with circuit six elsewhere.

10 . 1777 manors in these ten counties recorded a loss in value immediately after the Conquest, compared to 17 which were recorded as waste.

11 . He made some grudging remarks about the Baring thesis in his contribution to the 'Domesday survey' chapter in the *Victoria County History* (*VCH*) for Surrey but ignored it in those for Buckinghamshire, Hampshire, Hertfordshire and Bedfordshire, except by implication. When he turned to territory which Baring had not exploited before him, however, he devoted several pages to applying a variation of Baring's technique to the Northamptonshire data: *VCH: Surrey,* i (London, 1902), pp 278–9; *VCH: Hampshire,* i (London, 1900), pp 399–447; *VCH: Bedfordshire*, i (London, 1904), p 213; *VCH: Hertfordshire*, i (London, 1902), pp 280–81, 292–3; *VCH: Buckinghamshire,* i (London, 1905), pp 207–28; *VCH: Northamptonshire,* i (London, 1902), pp 260–63. He also assisted L.F. Salzmann with the Sussex volume (*VCH: Sussex,* i [London, 1905], pp 362–3), which accepted the Baring thesis with reservations.

12 . G.H. Fowler, 'The devastation of Bedfordshire and the neighbouring counties in 1065 and 1066', *Archaeologia* 72 (1922), p 41.

13 . Both absolute numbers and percentages have their disadvantages: percentages give undue weight to small manors or vills, absolute numbers to large

ones. For this reason, this essay uses data aggregated for larger areas than single vills wherever this is appropriate since the disadvantages of percentages are thereby significantly reduced. It has the further advantage of diminishing the arbitrary factor involved in plotting 'by eye'. Since armies normally marched in columns, throwing out lines of foragers, the damage they did should be conveyed more accurately by average losses astride lines of march than by pockets of damage to individual vills.

14 . Fowler, 'Devastation of Bedfordshire', pp 41–50; C.H. Lemmon, 'The campaign of 1066', in Dorothy Whitelock *et al*, eds, *The Norman Conquest: Its Setting and Impact* (London, 1966), pp 77–122; R.W. Finn, *The Norman Conquest and its Effects upon the Economy, 1066–1086* (London, 1971); Darby, *Domesday England*, pp 233–59.

15 . Freeman, *Norman Conquest*, III, pp 532–55, 794–5. The principal chronicle sources are: *Anglo-Saxon Chronicle*, pp 143–4; Florence of Worcester, *Chronicon*, pp 228–9; William of Jumièges, *Gesta Normannorum ducum*, ed J. Marx, Société de l'histoire de Normandie (Rouen, 1914), p 136; and William of Poitiers, *Histoire de Guillaume le Conquérant*, ed R. Foreville (Paris, 1952), pp 210–22. The *Carmen de Hastingae Proelio of Guy, bishop of Amiens*, ed C. Morton and H. Muntz (Oxford, 1972), is now regarded with suspicion: R.H.C. Davis, 'The *Carmen de Hastingae Proelio*', *EHR* 93 (1978), pp 241–61; R.H.C. Davis, L.J. Engels *et al*, 'The *Carmen de Hastingae Proelio*: a discussion', *Proceedings of the Battle Conference on Anglo-Norman Studies* 2 (1979), pp 1–20.

16 . The map shows only the major lines of march. Note the wide sweep north of the Thames, taking in Oxford, Buckingham, Bedford, Northampton, Cambridge, and Hertford.

17 . Bedfordshire and Cambridgeshire, with a foray into Wiltshire.

18 . Lemmon, 'Campaign of 1066', pp 117–18.

19 . Round led the way (see note 11 above). Later sceptics include G.J. Turner, 'William the Conqueror's march to London in 1066', *EHR* 17 (1912), pp 209–25; J. Blair, 'An introduction to the Surrey Domesday', *The Surrey Domesday*, Alecto edn (London, 1989), p 5; J. Blair, *Early Medieval Surrey: Landholding, Church and Settlement Before 1300* (Stroud, 1991), p 9; R. Eales, 'An introduction to the Kent Domesday', *The Kent Domesday*, Alecto edn (London, 1992), pp 10, 43. Others, including Stenton and Darby, have been ambivalent or have changed their minds. H.C. Darby and E.M.J. Campbell, eds, *The Domesday Geography of South-East England* (Cambridge, 1971), pp 26–7, 72–3, 164, 209, 260, 316, 383, 441, 569–75, reflects varying shades of opinion.

20 . In addition to the works by Fowler, Finn, Lemmon and Darby cited in note 14 above, see: F.M. Stenton, *William the Conqueror and the Rule of the Normans* (London, 1908), pp 215–25; J. Beeler, *Warfare in England, 1066–1169* (New York, 1966), pp 25–31, 326–9; D. Butler, *1066: The Story of a Year* (London, 1966), pp 258–92; R.A. Brown, *The Normans and the Norman Conquest* (London, 1969), pp 176–81; F.M. Stenton, *Anglo-Saxon England*, 3rd edn (Oxford, 1971), pp 596–8; Morton and Muntz, eds, *Carmen*, pp xlvii–liii; H.R. Loyn, *The Norman Conquest*, 3rd edn (London, 1982), p 99; D.N. Hall, 'An introduction to the Northamptonshire Domes-

day', *The Northamptonshire Domesday*, Alecto edn (London, 1987), pp 13–14; D. Bates, *William the Conqueror* (London, 1989), pp 70–71; K.P. Witney, 'Development of the Kentish marshes in the aftermath of the Norman Conquest', *Archaeologia Cantiana* 107 (1989), pp 30–33; R.P. Abels, 'An introduction to the Bedfordshire Domesday', *The Bedfordshire Domesday*, Alecto edn (London, 1991), pp 22–23; R.P. Abels, 'An introduction to the Hertfordshire Domesday', *The Hertfordshire Domesday,* Alecto edn (London, 1991), pp 18–19.

21 . Brown, *Norman Conquest*, pp 154, 176–7; Beeler, *Warfare*, pp 25–6, 326: 29 September to 21 October.

22 . The precise figures were 81.8 per cent, 88.4 per cent, and 74.2 per cent.

23 . *Domesday Book: Kent*, ed P. Morgan (Chichester, 1983), D7: 'In ipso [sc. Willelmo] primo adventu in Angliam fuit ipsa villa combusta'.

24 . The exact figures within each five-mile band were 70.4 per cent, 50.1 per cent and 14.9 per cent, giving cumulative losses of 70.4 per cent, 53.85 per cent and 34.15 per cent.

25 . Approximately two-thirds of all manors in the ten counties of circuits one and three declined in value to some extent after 1066 (1777 of 2774 manors). Only 4 per cent rose in value. Many of the remainder whose values are recorded as unchanged have rightly been suspected of revealing only ignorance, more likely to conceal a decline than anything else.

26 . William of Jumièges, *Gesta*, p 136; William of Poitiers, *Histoire*, p 216. Jumièges, the better source, is explicit about the camp and its situation: 'ad Warengeforth divertit urbem, transmeatoque vado fluvii, legiones ibi castra metari jussit'.

27 . Only about one holding in eight has intermediate values in Oxfordshire; nevertheless, they are widely distributed and include many substantial manors. There is no reason to believe that they are unrepresentative.

28 . F.H. Baring, 'Oxfordshire traces of the northern insurgents of 1065', *EHR* 13 (1898), pp 295–7; Finn, *Norman Conquest*, pp 116–22. See also Fowler, 'Devastation of Bedfordshire', pp 48–9.

29 . It is worth recalling that the corresponding figures around Dover were -70 per cent, -54 per cent, and -35 per cent.

30 . The Wallingford crossing is mentioned by the Norman chroniclers – William of Jumièges and William of Poitiers – but not by the English ones. However, the English chroniclers do lend general plausibility to the Norman tradition by their statements that (1) the Conqueror's army marched through Hampshire and (2) the Conqueror received the English submission at 'Berkhamsted'. Both statements can be reconciled with Wallingford as the crossing, and the latter virtually guarantees it if 'Berkhamsted' is taken to mean Great Berkhamsted.

31 . The precise figure depends upon how wide the net is cast to the west of Maidstone and in the Guildford area, and how wide the width of the line of march is taken to be. The figure in the text has included all the damaged vills picked out by Baring in the Maidstone and Guildford areas but otherwise included only vills on or very close to the North Downs ridgeway. If the line of march is defined as a swathe some ten miles wide, the loss of value rises

– mainly due to the vills in eastern Surrey – but is still below 25 per cent, barely more than half the damage between Godstone and Southwark.

32 . See pp 34–37 for further discussion of this point.

33 . The southern 'peninsula' of Buckinghamshire: that is, the southern half of Burnham and Stoke hundreds and the most southerly vill in Desborough. The losses were 48.5 per cent overall: 49.8 per cent in western Middlesex and 44.1 per cent in south-east Buckinghamshire.

34 . Baring, *Domesday Tables*, p 211; cf 'Footprints', pp 20–21.

35 . Baring, 'March through Hampshire', pp 33–9; Morton and Muntz, eds, *Carmen*, pp 40–41. There is no suggestion in the text that the Conqueror or his army approached Winchester. See note 15 above for the reliability of the *Carmen* as a source.

36 . Tostig's attack was a coastal raid, and it is improbable that Harold would have tolerated widespread devastation in the county in which his family estates were so dominant. Significantly, the average decline in value on the estates of the Godwinson family – almost a third of the county – was virtually identical to that of the county in general – 39.4 per cent as compared to 38.8 per cent. These figures tend to confirm that any devastation was Norman work and hence the tradition recorded by Wace that, in the interests of his subjects, Harold rejected out of hand the scorched-earth policy recommended by his brother Gyrth: *Le roman de Rou de Wace*, ed A.J. Holden, 3 vols (Paris, 1970–73), II, pp 140–42 (lines 6901–50).

37 . Baring, *Domesday Tables*, pp 216, 208, 209–10, 212, 214–15.

38 . The northern part of Stodden hundred and the eastern part of Biggleswade. The observations made about widespread damage in Bedfordshire in the following paragraphs apply in almost equal measure to eastern Hertfordshire. Eight points of entry to the county have been identified by commentators.

39 . Baring, 'Footprints', p 22; Finn, *Norman Conquest*, p 94. For Bedfordshire and Hertfordshire, see in addition to Baring and Finn, Fowler, 'Devastation of Bedfordshire', pp 41–50; Abels, 'Introduction to Bedfordshire Domesday, pp 23–4; Abels, 'Introduction to Hertfordshire Domesday', pp 18–19.

40 . Edmer Atre, for whom see P.A. Clarke, *The English Nobility Under Edward the Confessor* (Oxford, 1994), pp 280–81.

41 . Round, *VCH: Hertfordshire*, i, pp 280–81.

42 . Whatever caused the damage in these counties, its consequences were more long-term there than south of the Thames. In Kent, Surrey, Hampshire and Berkshire the recovery was complete by 1086, values even increasing beyond their 1066 level, spectacularly so in Kent. Only Sussex still had some considerable distance to go towards complete recovery (-11 per cent). But all the counties north of the Thames failed to recover fully, and in Bedfordshire (-23.5 per cent), Hertfordshire (-20 per cent) and Middlesex (-18 per cent) the level of loss was actually higher than that suffered by Kent and Berkshire in the immediate aftermath of the Conquest. This is another indication that the Baring thesis affords an inadequate explanation of the patterns in these counties.

43 . Baring, *Domesday Tables*, pp 207–16; Fowler, 'Devastation of Bedfordshire', pp 41–50; Butler, *1066*, pp 258–92; Lemmon, 'Campaign of 1066',

pp 115–22; Beeler, *Warfare*, pp 25–31, 326–9; and Finn, *Norman Conquest*, pp 3–115, for what follows.

44 . Only the major detachments are shown on the map.

45 . Unless a direct attack upon London was to be attempted, but this was not a viable proposition from south of the Thames and William can scarcely have been ignorant of this. For what it is worth – his geography is confused – William of Poitiers has a story about a force of 500 cavalry sent forward to attack skirmishers from the city (*Histoire*, p 216) but none of the sources suggests an assault on London from south of the river.

46 . I.D. Margary, 'The north downs main trackway and the pilgrims' way', *Archaeological Journal* 75 (1918), pp 39–53.

47 . He did not, however, remove all references to footprints from the text.

48 . Baring, 'Oxfordshire traces', pp 295–7; Round, 'The Domesday survey', *VCH: Northamptonshire*, i (London, 1902), pp 260–63; F.M. Stenton, 'The Domesday survey', *VCH: Leicestershire*, i (1907), pp 282–5; Fowler, 'Devastation of Bedfordshire', pp 41–50; Finn, *Norman Conquest*, pp 115–39; Darby, *Domesday England*, pp 236–8.

49 . Particularly for Leicestershire. This is a compressed account of a complex subject. For present purposes, the complexities, which are additional weaknesses in the Fowler thesis, are not essential. For a fuller exposition, see Maitland, *Domesday Book*, p 469; Stenton, *VCH: Leicestershire*, i, pp 282–5; Finn, *Norman Conquest*, pp 227–33; Darby, *Domesday England*, pp 233, 242.

50 . This is an ambiguous formulation which points to some ambiguity in Fowler's thinking, notably with regard to Oxfordshire: 'Devastation of Bedfordshire', pp 42, 47–8.

51 . *Anglo-Saxon Chronicle*, p 138.

2. Towns, Mottes and Ring-works of the Conquest

Barbara English

William the Conqueror built some 36 castles in England during his reign; two-thirds of these, 24, were attached to major urban centres, and about half lay within the city or town limits.[1] Precision in the numbers is hindered by ambivalence in the evidence, and the lack of a clear definition of urban status. This essay is an examination of the sites and construction of some of the urban castles, and in particular the form they took when they were first created.

The importance of towns to the Anglo-Norman government is demonstrated by their treatment in Domesday Book. The arrangement of material within the county sections is hierarchical: the lists of tenants in chief, and the sequence of their holdings, begin with the greatest lords headed by the king, and end with entries of lesser men and women, such as the king's thanes. In such ordered listings, it must be significant that almost all the county sections begin with the shire towns. Where very great towns were omitted from Domesday Book (for instance, London and Winchester), spaces were left at the head of the county entries suggesting that here, too, the inclusion of the towns had been intended.[2]

The towns were politically important for several reasons. They produced a considerable revenue; they contained the largest clusters of population; they were often located at significant road junctions or river crossings. They contained the Anglo-Saxon administrative structures for the shire and the sheriff, with fiscal and military connections, which implies the existence of some official buildings, or at least sites. Towns had mints, law courts and markets, and often Roman or Anglo-Saxon defences. Many (and the Conqueror was to increase these) were also episcopal sees. They could be centres of revolt; early rebellions against the Conqueror centred on towns such as Hereford, Exeter, York, Durham and Chester.

The planting of castles was an essential, and successful, part of the Conqueror's strategy for holding England, recognized by his contemporaries; 'the fortifications called castles by the Normans were scarcely known in the English provinces, and so the English – in spite of their courage and warlike spirit – could put up only a weak resistance'.[3] It was logical, therefore, that when William I built strongholds in England most were in towns.

The siting of the urban castles seems to have been governed by two principles: they were normally set at the edge of the town, and they also normally used existing Roman or Anglo-Saxon fortifications, or, in the case of Old Sarum, even older circuits, to provide part of their defences. A rare exception to the peripheral location is Colchester, where the central site of the temple of Claudius was reused; at Norwich, Oxford and Stamford, where the castle sites now appear central in relation to the present urban area, the castles may have been on the edge of the Anglo-Saxon *burhs*.[4] Many urban castles were placed in an angle of existing defences, and there seems to have been some preference for a southern location.

Domesday Book recorded that of a total of 112 boroughs, 30 had some 3500 waste or destroyed houses.[5] Urban property became waste for many reasons, sometimes stated in Domesday Book but often not: misfortune, poverty and fire at Lincoln, for the king's fishpool at York, for the archbishop's new lodging in Kent. Some destruction was specifically related to castle-building,[6] and some may with much less certainty be assigned to the same cause.[7] A castle built within a town almost invariably destroyed property and displaced existing houses, churches and streets.[8] The property may have been taken by compulsory eviction (Dover), or by agreement (Rochester and Exeter), but in most cases there is no evidence to show how or when it was obtained. Information about both towns and castles in Domesday Book is unevenly recorded: some town entries are much fuller than others, and while 50 castles, urban or rural, were included, a further 21 castles built before 1086 and known from other sources were omitted.[9] Domesday provides a partial record only: in many towns the amount of property destroyed for castle-building is unknown.

Urban castles with destruction of property recorded in Domesday Book

Town	Date built	Properties destroyed	Type of property (Latin word)
Cambridge	1068	27 (a ward)	*domus*
Canterbury	1066	21? + 11	not named
Gloucester	*ante* 1086	14	*domus*
Huntingdon	1068	21? (a quarter)	*mansio*
Lincoln	1068	166	*mansio*
Norwich	?1068	98	*mansura*
Shrewsbury	*ante* 1069	51	*ma(n)sura*
Stamford	?1068	4 (a ward)	*mansio*
Wallingford	*ante* 1071	8	*haga*
Warwick	1068	4	*ma(n)sura*
York 1 & 2	1068 or 1069	a shire	not named

Source: Domesday Book

It can be seen that there is considerable variation in the amount and type of property destroyed for different castles, from the four *masure* at Warwick to the 166 *mansiones* at Lincoln. The shire at York, laid waste for the castles, was one of seven shires of the city. The words used for the types of property included in the table apparently change their meaning from one part of Domesday Book to another, even within the entry for one place.[10]

No correlation seems possible between the acreage of the castle site and the number of properties lost in castle construction.[11] The acreage of the castle sites at their first building, or in 1086 when the destruction was recorded, is unknown, and the initial building is likely to have been enlarged as the hurried fortifications of the 1060s were developed as permanent administrative centres for the shires. Castles were rebuilt, extended, or even moved to different sites (as at Canterbury and Gloucester). Little is known about eleventh-century properties, but enough to suggest there was a range of sizes (archaeologists have found evidence of destroyed Anglo-Saxon huts at or beside the castle sites at Northampton, Norwich, Oxford and Winchester).[12] Nothing is known of the housing density in the areas requisitioned. At some time, or at several times, between the first phase of the castle and 1086, property was lost: when this was recorded in Domesday, the loss may relate to any castle works undertaken within a 20-year span. In spite of uncertainty about what was destroyed and when, the first construction of an urban castle made a considerable impact upon the town, and it is this, the primary fortification, which is now investigated further.

Early castles were generally built of earth and timber, and the earthworks survive in two principal forms, mottes and baileys (earth mounds with associated defensive areas), and ring-works (ditches and banks creating an enclosure).[13] In the late twentieth century, castle earthworks in England and Wales show a ratio of mottes to ring-works of approximately four to one (c. 750 mottes and c. 190 ring-works).[14] This ratio, however, may not represent the pattern of castles when first built.[15] Brian Davison, in a remarkable paper published in 1969, was the first to challenge the assumption that the motte-and-bailey castle was the characteristic type of early Anglo-Norman fortification, and suggested that in both England and Normandy simple enclosures formed a large proportion of the earthwork castles in existence in the 1060s.[16] Davison made out an excellent case for the earliest castles in England being ring-works created by rampart and ditch. He included those constructed in 1066, and two subsequent castles, Winchester (1067) and Exeter (1068). After this, Davison believed, the pattern changed, and the castles of the northern campaign of 1068–70 were built with motte and bailey from the beginning.[17] This essay, while reiterating and supporting Davison's thesis, suggests that he might have carried it further, to include the midland and northern castles of 1068–70 and perhaps beyond. These castles are as likely as those of 1066 and 1067 to have been in origin enclosure or ring-work castles. They conform to the previous pattern, demonstrated by Davison, of defences which were necessarily constructed at great speed in a situation of extreme danger, built in the angles of existing walls wherever possible, and demolishing town properties in the process. Most of these castles were subsequently rebuilt as motte-and-bailey castles, with more elaborate defences, often in stone.

The first requirement of an occupying force, after the initial victory, was to create a defensive enclave. For the commander it was essential that he himself, his senior staff and, if possible, his troops should be protected from the enemy and the elements. In 1066 Duke William built his first defences at Pevensey as soon as his army disembarked. Pevensey, the first royal castle in England, is the prototype of the Conqueror's castles, and two main themes of this essay can be explored in the context of Pevensey: the nature of the early defences and the location of the fortification in relation to existing structures.

On landing at Pevensey on 28 September 1066 William 'at once built a fortification [*castrum*] with a very strong rampart'.[18] The word translated as rampart is *vallum*, which can mean either a wall or a ditch; the word reappears in the description of York castle. The fortification, a ring-work of ditch and bank, was formed by cutting off the south-east corner of the much larger area of an Anglo-Saxon *burh*, which itself was located within the former Roman fort of Anderida, using the stone walls built by the Romans to form two sides of the enclosure.[19] The first castle the duke built, therefore, reused existing walls and (because it did so) was on the periphery of the settlement, but within it. Two further deductions might be made: that the duke himself planned the fortification at Pevensey, as we are told he did later at Exeter, and that the defences were made very quickly indeed, for within a few days William had moved his force to the better site at Hastings.

The building of Hastings castle at the end of September or the beginning of October 1066 is a major difficulty in one of the themes of this essay. According to the *Anglo-Saxon Chronicle*, as soon as William's men had recovered from their journey they built a castle at Hastings.[20] The Bayeux Tapestry provides a graphic picture of the building of this castle, with the legend 'this man ordered that a castle be dug at Hastings' camp ('iste iussit ut foderetur castellum at Hestenga ceastra').[21] On two other occasions the Tapestry refers to Hastings by its name alone, but here the suffix *ceastra* is added. The wording suggests an earlier fortification was being adapted by the duke, for Hastings was an Anglo-Saxon *burh* within, or related to, an Iron Age hill-top fortress. The historical value of the *Carmen de Hastingae Proelio* is debated by historians, but, for what it is worth, Guy of Amiens refers to Duke William restoring the destroyed forts ('*diruta ... castella*'), which had formerly stood at both Pevensey and Hastings.[22] In addition, in a story told by William of Poitiers, when it was suggested to the duke at Hastings that he should stay within his fortifications, he replied he would not take shelter behind a rampart (*vallum*) or walls.[23] Nevertheless, the Bayeux Tapestry clearly shows a motte being built at Hastings, topped by a wooden tower.

There is a curious feature about the fortification at Hastings shown in the tapestry. While it is generally assumed that the castles of the first months of the Conquest were built primarily to protect and to shelter the military commander and his staff, the Bayeux Tapestry shows the duke's feast and his war council on the eve of battle being held, within buildings, before the construction of the motte began. It is accepted that on two occasions the tapestry reverses the normal order of events (the messengers sent to Guy de Ponthieu, and the death and burial of Edward the Confessor); is this a third such reversal? Or is the tapestry recording that the building of the motte was a development of the duke's first camp, perhaps by the castellan?[24]

A historian proposing that every castle built in the first years after the Conquest was initially a ring-work has to try to explain the depiction of Hastings in the tapestry. It is extremely unlikely that the Hastings motte (*c.* 6 metres high) of the tapestry could have been constructed in 16 days between 28 September and 14 October 1066. It is conceivable, however, that an original primary defence of a ring-work type within the Iron Age fort was subsequently turned into a motte-and-bailey castle. Is it possible that the tapestry designer represented the most familiar form of castle at the time he was working (probably in the 1070s) rather than some less graphic rampart of 1066? Excavation at Hastings of the castle has proved inconclusive, and much of the castle site has been eroded by the sea.[25]

Hastings remains an anomaly. The depiction of mottes in the Bayeux Tapestry, however, not only at Hastings but in France before 1066, remains the dominant image of early Norman castles, producing resistance to the suggestion that castles could come in any other form.

After Hastings William moved to Dover and there, according to William of Poitiers, he 'spent eight days adding fortifications [*firmamenta*] to it'.[26] Again, as at Pevensey, his fortifications were a ditch and bank which cut off a section of the Anglo-Saxon *burh* which was defended by surviving Iron Age earthworks.[27] The bank and ditch ran close to the Anglo-Saxon church of St Mary in Castro and cut through the cemetery beside it; the requisition of such sanctified areas, even of churches themselves, was to happen elsewhere.[28] At Dover, also, it is first recorded that the duke 'ordered the English to evacuate their houses'.[29]

William next moved his force to Canterbury, where the town surrendered to him. A fortification was built, in the southern part of the city, just inside the Roman city walls which in 1066 protected an Anglo-Saxon *burh*.[30] The first castle at Canterbury was on the site now called Dane John; to make the castle, Domesday recorded that 32 houses were waste, that is, 11 for the ditch (*fossa*) of the city or castle, and 21 by exchange with the archbishop and the abbot.[31] At the end of the Conqueror's reign the castle was rebuilt further to the west. The form of the first Canterbury castle is not known. It is possible that the first urgently created fortifications were, as at Pevensey and Dover, a ditch, bank or both that cut off a corner of the existing defences. For some days William stayed near Canterbury, in an unidentified place called by William of Poitiers the 'Broken Tower' (*fracta turris*), possibly Richborough;[32] again, there is an implication that he was using an earlier Roman or Anglo-Saxon defence to protect his headquarters. As November 1066 ended, William was master of south-eastern England, with a number of fortifications to protect his line of retreat, but before he could consolidate his conquest, in Douglas's evocative phrase, 'London lay enigmatic and formidable across his path'.[33]

He made an approach to London from the south, but perhaps being unwilling to cross London Bridge against opposition he moved west, crossing the Thames at Wallingford.[34] There, either at this time or subsequently (for Wallingford castle is not mentioned until 1071), he constructed a fortification: on the now familiar pattern, within the walls of the Anglo-Saxon *burh*, cutting off the north-eastern corner and destroying eight house sites.[35]

While William was at 'Berkhamsted' he sent men into London to make a fortress (*munitio*) in the city, and after his coronation William withdrew to Barking while fortifications (*firmamenta*) were completed 'against the inconstancy of the huge and savage population'.[36] There were to be four early castles in London and, although it is not clear which was the first built, the one that was to become the most important was the Tower of London.[37] Excavations at the Tower in 1962–3 showed that the first earthwork was a bank and ditch running north from the river and then turning east, designed to cut off the south-east angle of the Roman city wall (which protected part of the Saxon city) to make an enclosure.[38] At the Tower there is no sign that there was ever a motte; the White Tower, standing four-square on the level ground, was perhaps begun in 1078. Baynard's castle may have been built at the same time; it also incorporated the city wall where it joined the river, on the south-west to balance the Tower on the south-east.[39]

After William's coronation in 1066, two further castles were built which Davison added to his tally of early ring-work castles. At Winchester, the castle of 1067 was made by enclosing an area in the south-west corner of the old Roman and later Anglo-Saxon defences of the town, digging a ditch and bank through the occupied area, destroying streets and houses which have been found in twentieth-century excavations. The motte was built later, *c.* 1071–2.[40] The castle at Exeter, built in 1068, was set into the north-east angle of the Roman town walls, cut off by a rampart and ditch; a site chosen by the king himself after his entry into the city.[41] Exeter was never rebuilt as a motte.

It has been shown that most and perhaps all of these first castles were not mottes, but ring-works built within earlier fortifications. Could mottes have ever been the primary buildings in these early castles? There seems to be an insuperable problem of time. Even when there was a motte on the site subsequently, surely the first act of the castle-builder in hostile territory was to create a ditch, using the earth to make a rampart, and improving the rampart with a palisade. Then the motte could be built while the precinct was defended; perhaps the motte is always a later feature, even if only by a matter of months.

Various calculations have been made of the number of hours of labour required to create mottes. E.W. Holden and T. McNeill have independently estimated that a small motte approximately 5.6 metres high and 39.5 metres at the base would have taken 50 men, working a ten-hour day, 42 days to build in reasonable weather. A large motte ten metres high would take a little over three times as long to build, 120 days; the motte at Castle Neroche, added to an earlier ring-work, may have taken between four and six months to construct and Bramber about nine months. The higher the motte, the slower the progress, because of the difficulty of lifting material, and indeed of finding material as the diggers used up the topsoil in ditch and bailey, and had to bring suitable material from further away. Increasing the number of labourers would not solve the problem, because of space restrictions in the access to the top of an inherently unstable structure. If, in addition to the motte itself, the associated bailey defences and timber buildings were taken into account (for an earthen motte alone could not provide any shelter), McNeill calculated that a large earthwork castle would take one to two years to build. N.J.G. Pounds used a late-nineteenth-century War Office manual to show that a soldier equipped with simple entrenching tools could shift about 80 cubic feet a day, in reasonable conditions; he could throw soil a maximum of 12 feet horizontally and four feet vertically. The need to move earth further than the 'throw', either horizontally or vertically, greatly slowed down the building operations. Pounds calculated the man-days required to build the known mottes in East Anglia and the East Midlands, and showed the building time for one man building one motte varying from 1000 days to a staggering 24,000 days.[42] Yet the Conqueror's castles are twice recorded as having been built in around eight days, at Dover and at York.[43] These 'eight-day castles' must surely have been of the simplest kind and, it is suggested, ring-works rather than mottes.

In 1068 William was forced to go north after Whitsun (11 May) because of difficulties in Northumbria, and on his journey he established castles at Warwick, Nottingham and York. He returned south by a different route, building castles at Lincoln, Huntingdon and Cambridge.[44] A further castle was made at York in 1069. These seven northern castles are believed by Davison to have been motte-and-bailey in type from the outset. It is suggested here, however, that five of the seven may have originally been of the same type as the early southern castles, such as Pevensey and Dover; that is, that they were set within the angles of pre-existing walls, defended by ditch and rampart, with the mottes and baileys being later developments. These five were Cambridge, Lincoln, Huntingdon, Warwick and possibly York (Old Baile), placed within corner angles of Roman, Anglo-Saxon or Danish urban defences.[45] The castle at Nottingham was outside the Danish walls and was an oval enclosure or enclosures formed by ditches and ramparts placed on and around a rocky outcrop.[46] York (Clifford's Tower) may have used river defences. All these castles, except Nottingham, destroyed urban property: in the case of York a whole district and at Lincoln 166 properties, substantial areas of the towns. Although the pattern seems to be the same as in the south, there has been no extensive excavation of the castles of the northern campaign. The argument must depend, therefore, upon the model of the southern castles of the Conquest, where there is some excavation evidence, being extended to suggest the probability that the same practices of castle-building applied in the midlands and the north, as they were being constructed in similar circumstances.

At Lincoln the castle reused the south-western corner of the Roman city wall. The present area of Lincoln castle contains two mottes (the bases of the Observatory Tower and the Lucy Tower). Historians have consistently assumed that the Observatory Tower motte was part of the castle of 1068 and that the Lucy Tower motte was later.[47] Excavation in the 1970s, however, showed that the rubble core of the Observatory motte contains fragments of twelfth-century pottery, so that the motte cannot date from 1068.[48] Lincoln castle has a peripheral urban site, has no demonstrably early motte, and reuses pre-existing walls: it may, therefore, have been built originally as a ring-work fortification, with a ditch cutting off an angle of the walls.

The York castles are not central to the urban area, but placed, as were so many other castles, on the southern perimeter, one each side of the river Ouse. The chronicler records that in 1068 the king entered York and raised a castle in the city.[49] This description best fits the castle now known as Old Baile, which lay in the south-west angle of the later medieval city walls. It is possible that these walls represent the wall of the Roman *colonia*, reused in the Anglian and Danish city. In Peter Chassereau's eighteenth-century map of York the line from the walls to the river, protecting the castle in the angle, is marked by a large ditch, partly excavated in the 1960s, which still leaves its mark on the late twentieth-century townscape by causing subsidence in pavements and walls.[50] The combination of angle defence and ditch running down to the river to create the Old Baile exactly parallels the primary fortification of the Tower of London. The castle to the east, now Clifford's Tower, appears not to depend upon earlier fortifications, but to be making use of the defences provided by the junction of the two rivers, the Ouse and the Foss.[51]

Both these castles were constructed, destroyed and reconstructed in a remarkably short period; so quickly that the *Anglo-Saxon Chronicle* refers to them as being built at the same time.[52] The clearest account of the rise, fall and resurrection of the York castles comes from Orderic.[53] The Conqueror arrived at York in the summer of 1068.[54] He received the submission of the citizens, and built a castle. After he had left, the castle was unsuccessfully besieged, early in 1069, drawing him back to York again.[55] He remained eight days in the city and built a second castle, returning to Winchester for Easter, which fell that year on 12 April. After Easter 1069 the northerners made a further attack on both castles, but were unsuccessful, the castellan and his men engaging them in a '*vallum*', the word used in connection with the first castles at Pevensey and Hastings, killing and capturing many.[56] In the late summer of 1069 the castles were attacked again, and on 19 September the garrison, fearing that nearby houses would be used by the attackers as material to fill in the castles' ditches ('*ad implendas fossas*'), set the houses alight and started a fire which destroyed most of York. The Normans left their fortifications to attack their enemies, but were defeated within the city walls.[57] The castles were broken and cast down (*tobraecon* and *towurpan*) by the northerners.[58] The king returned again, retook the city, and ordered the castles to be rebuilt; he spent Christmas at York, and both were restored by January 1070.

The York motte that now carries Clifford's Tower is 15 metres above ground with a diameter at the base varying from 67 metres to 71 metres; Baile Hill, the other motte, is 12 metres high with a diameter at the base of 55 metres. Both were increased in height, Clifford's Tower by about four metres after 1190 and Baile Hill by an unspecified amount in the post-medieval period. Each of these mottes, according to Holden and McNeill's calculations, would have taken 50 men around 120 days to build in reasonable weather. Is it possible that these two considerable mottes were both made between summer 1068 and Easter 1069; that between late September and Christmas 1069 the two mottes were demolished; and between Christmas 1069 and January 1070 the two mottes were rebuilt? Is it not much more probable that these first castles were not mottes, but timber buildings within ring-works, defended by ditch and rampart, quickly created and quickly thrown down: indeed the word '*vallum*', and the defenders' fear that the ditches might be filled in, suggests such a structure.

If the Conqueror's midland and northern urban castles seem to fit the pattern of those built before 1068 in the south, it might be profitable to re-examine the Conqueror's castles in other towns. Other castles that apparently began as ring-works, with mottes added subsequently, include Bristol, Oxford, Carisbrooke in the Isle of Wight, Rochester and possibly Gloucester and Newcastle upon Tyne.[59] Reassessment of the evidence or excavation may reveal further examples.

The first Norman king planted castles within certain towns because of their political importance, and because it was faster to use existing defences than to construct a castle on a green-field site. It seems probable that the first urban castles were ring-works, perhaps of small size, built as quickly as possible in difficult military circumstances. This model provides a more likely explanation of the chronology of early castle-building than any alternative. The early urban castles were usually set within an angle of former town defences: the amount of Anglo-Saxon property destroyed in those areas would vary according to the area of the castle and the density of the housing. In the period between 1066 and 1086, the urban castles were extended, sometimes moved, and almost always rebuilt as mottes or stone towers. The primary fortification is, however, unlikely to have been a motte: and the image of the 'eight-day' motte should be re-examined, in view of the increasing amount of evidence about the nature of early castles.

Notes

1 .   H.M. Colvin, ed, *The History of the King's Works,* 6 vols (London, 1963-82), I, p 22, fig. 5, shows castles built by William I or with his sanction, including those in the major towns of Cambridge, Canterbury, Chester, Colchester, Durham, Exeter, Gloucester, Hereford, Lincoln, London, Newcastle upon Tyne, Norwich, Nottingham, Old Sarum, Oxford, Rochester, Shrewsbury, Stafford (built and destroyed by 1086), Wallingford, Warwick, Winchester, Worcester and York (two castles). Eales reviewed different estimates and suggested that a total of around 500 castles of all types existed in England and Wales by 1086: R. Eales, 'Royal power and castles in Norman England', in C. Harper-Bill and R. Harvey, eds, *The Ideals and Practice of Medieval Knighthood III* (Woodbridge, 1990), pp 54–63.

2 .   As well as Domesday Middlesex and Hampshire, space was left at the head of the Sussex entries (probably for Hastings and Lewes), Somerset and Cornwall. Little Domesday included towns in Norfolk and Suffolk among

the king's lands, and in Essex the entry for Colchester came after encroachments on the king's lands.

3 . *The Ecclesiastical History of Orderic Vitalis*, ed M. Chibnall, 6 vols (Oxford, 1969–80), II, pp 218–9. This passage, and all Orderic's narrative to early 1071, are based on the lost section of William de Poitiers, written before 1077.

4 . N.J.G. Pounds, *The Medieval Castle in England and Wales: A Social and Political History* (Cambridge, 1990), pp 207–8, gives many examples of peripheral locations and reuse of fortifications, and in his fig. 8.5, p 208, illustrates early urban castles in relation to the walls of former Roman towns. For a useful discussion of Anglo-Saxon defences see C.A.R. Radford, 'The pre-conquest boroughs of England, ninth to eleventh centuries', *Proceedings of the British Academy* 64 (1978), pp 131–53. For the towns see *RCHM: Essex*, 4 vols (London, 1916-23), III, pp 50–54; P.J. Drury, 'Aspects of the origin and development of Colchester castle', *Archaeological Journal* 139 (1982), pp 302–419; J. Campbell, 'Norwich', in M.D. Lobel, ed, *The Atlas of Historic Towns* (London, 1975); T.G. Hassall, 'Excavations at Oxford castle, 1965–1973', *Oxoniensia* 41 (1976), pp 232–308; C.M. Mahaney and D.R. Roffe, 'Stamford: the development of an Anglo-Scandinavian borough', *Anglo-Norman Studies* 5 (1983), pp 199–219; D.R. Roffe and C.M. Mahaney, 'Stamford and the Norman conquest', *Lincolnshire History and Archaeology* 21 (1986), pp 5–10.

5 . C.G. Harfield, 'A hand-list of castles recorded in the Domesday Book', *EHR* 106 (1991), p 373, numbers based on H.C. Darby, *Domesday England* (Cambridge, 1977), pp 364–8.

6 . See table on p 47.

7 . For instance, waste properties recorded in Domesday at Barnstaple, Lydford and Exeter in Devon, Dorchester, Shaftesbury and Wareham in Dorset, Leicester, Northampton, Oxford and Worcester. The evidence is discussed in E.S. Armitage, *The Early Norman Castles of the British Isles* (London, 1912); D. Renn, *Norman Castles in Britain*, 2nd edn (London, 1973); D.J.C. King, *Castellarium Anglicanum: An Index and Bibliography of the Castles in England, Wales and the Islands* (New York, 1983); R.A. Brown, 'The castles of the conquest', in A. Williams and R.W.H. Erskine, eds, *Domesday Book Studies* (London, 1987), pp 69–74.

8 . For churches see below note 29 below. Street patterns were disrupted at Bedford: C. Drage, 'Urban castles' in J. Schofield and R. Leech, eds, *Urban Archaeology in Britain*, CBA Research Report no. 61 (London, 1987), pp 117–32; and possibly at Wallingford: M. Airs, K. Rodwell and H. Turner, 'Wallingford', in K. Rodwell, ed, *Historic Towns of Oxfordshire* (Oxford Archaeological Unit, Oxford, 1975), pp 155–8.

9 . Harfield, 'Hand-list of castles', p 374.

10 . *Mansio* and *ma(n)sura* are closely related terms, with links to the French *maison* and the English legal term messuage; the term is used in Domesday for a plot of land, a group of buildings or a house. *Haga* is found only in Domesday circuit one (except for a single reference in Huntingdon), but is commonly found before the Conquest, and is an Old English word linked with *haia*, a hedge, the boundary of an enclosure. *Domus*, the word used most

frequently in Domesday Book for any kind of dwelling, occurs in almost all counties; it is normally translated as 'house', and is the least ambiguous of the terms. While it is tempting to treat these property descriptors as interchangeable, there are awkward passages such as the Nottinghamshire entry which records that there are three *mansiones* in which 11 houses (*domus*) are sited. At Wallingford the Domesday scribe used all three terms, *haga*, *domus* and *masura*. In Norwich several men had both *mansure* and *domus*, which implies the scribes of Little Domesday saw a distinction: but on the other hand, while Exon Domesday distinguishes between *domus* and *mansura* in one man's holding in Bath, the Exchequer Domesday conflates these into two *domus*. *Domesday Book: Shropshire*, ed F. Thorn and C. Thorn (Chichester, 1986), unpaginated notes C14; S. Reynolds, 'Domesday towns', in J.C. Holt, ed, *Domesday Studies* (Woodbridge, 1987), p 304, note 25.

11 .   Acreages of castle sites measured *c*. 1900 are given by Armitage, *Early Norman Castles*, pp 396–9.

12 .   Late Saxon houses were found under the castle at Northampton: Renn, *Norman Castles*, p 258; Anglo-Saxon buildings at Norwich: B. Ayers, *Excavations Within the North-East Bailey of Norwich castle, 1979*, East Anglian Archaeology 28 (Norfolk archaeological unit, Dereham, 1985); B. Ayers, J. Brown and J. Reeve, *Digging Ditches: Archaeology and Development in Norwich* (Norfolk archaeological unit, Norwich, 1992); at Oxford: Hassall, 'Excavations at Oxford castle, 1965–1973', pp 232–308; and at Winchester: M. Biddle, 'Early Norman Winchester', in J.C. Holt, ed, *Domesday Studies* (Woodbridge, 1987), p 314.

13 .   There were variants: some mottes were formed from wooden towers with earth banked up around their foundations, and some ring-works had mottes added to them subsequently.

14 .   D.J.C. King and L. Alcock, 'Ringworks of England and Wales', *Château Gaillard: European Castle Studies* 3 (1969), pp 90–127; J.R. Kenyon, *Medieval Fortifications* (Leicester, 1990), p 5.

15 .   Kenyon, *Medieval Fortifications*, p 7; Pounds, *Medieval Castle*, pp 12–14.

16 .   B.K. Davison, 'Early earthwork castles: a new model', *Château Gaillard: European Castle Studies* 3 (1969), pp 37–47, a paper delivered in 1966. Davison gave a further paper the following year: 'The origins of the castle in England: the Institute's research project', delivered to the Royal Archaeological Institute on 11 October 1967, and published in *Archaeological Journal* 124 (1968 for 1967), pp 202–11. R.A. Brown took issue with Davison in 'A historian's approach to the origins of the castle in England', delivered on 8 January 1969 and published, with a reply by Davison, in *Archaeological Journal* 126 (1970 for 1969), pp 131–48. The debate is summarized by Eales, 'Royal power and castles in Norman England', pp 49–78. Evidence from excavations at Sulgrave and 'Goltho' has been cited in this connection. A revisionist article by Everson convincingly moves 'Goltho' to Bullington, and questions the chronological sequence of the excavated buildings: P. Everson, 'What's in a name? "Goltho", Goltho and Bullington', *Lincolnshire History and Archaeology* 23 (1988), pp 93–9.

17 . Davison, 'Early earthwork castles', p 45; Pounds, *Medieval Castle*, p 15, follows Davison.

18 . William of Jumièges, *Gesta Normannorum ducum*, ed J. Marx, Société de l'histoire de Normandie, (Rouen, 1914), p 134. According to William de Poitiers they built a first fortification (*munitio*) at Pevensey and another at Hastings, as places for themselves and shelters for their ships: Guillaume de Poitiers, *Histoire de Guillaume le Conquérant*, ed R. Foreville (Paris, 1952), pp 168–9. Armitage, *Early Norman Castles*, pp 383–4, published a useful discussion of Latin words used for castles as did Chibnall in *Ecclesiastical History of Orderic Vitalis*, I, pp 244–386 (*Index verborum*); II, p xxxvi; see also J.F. Verbruggen, 'Note sur le sens des mots *castrum, castellum* et quelques autres expressions qui désignent des fortifications', *Revue belge de philologie et d'histoire* 28 (1950), pp 147–55.

19 . A.J. Taylor, 'Evidence for a pre-Conquest origin for the chapels in Hastings and Pevensey castles', *Château Gaillard: European Castle Studies* 3 (1969), pp 150–51; R.A. Brown, *Castles from the Air* (Cambridge, 1989), pp 179–81. Renn, *Norman Castles*, pp 276–9 suggested that the earthwork either enclosed the square area of the present inner bailey or ran across the whole enclosure to form an oval ring-work.

20 . D. Whitelock, D.C. Douglas and S.I. Tucker, eds, *Anglo-Saxon Chronicle* (London, 1961), p 143: text 'D' s.a. 1066.

21 . The phrase was translated by Wormald as 'to be thrown up', but *fodire* means to dig out or excavate, and is related to *fossa*: F.L. Wormald, 'The inscriptions', in F.M. Stenton, ed, *The Bayeux Tapestry* (London 1957), p 179.

22 . *Carmen de Hastingae Proelio of Guy, Bishop of Amiens*, ed C. Morton and H. Muntz (Oxford, 1972), pp 10–11.

23 . Guillaume de Poitiers, *Histoire*, pp 170–71.

24 . *Anglo-Saxon Chronicle*, p 144: text 'D' s.a. 1066, recorded that William went back to Hastings after the battle and waited there to see whether submission would be made to him. Humphrey of Tilleul was given charge of Hastings castle: *Ecclesiastical History of Orderic Vitalis*, II, pp 220–21; J.F.A. Mason, *William I and the Sussex Rapes* (Bexhill, 1966), p 7.

25 . Davison, 'The origins of the castle in England', pp 209–11; P.A. Barker and K.J. Barton, 'Excavations at Hastings castle, 1968', *Archaeological Journal* 134 (1977), pp 80–100. There has been a suggestion that the first Hastings castle was built elsewhere: Renn, *Norman Castles*, p 201. Brown disagreed: 'there is really no doubt that the site of the Conqueror's castle is the present one on Castle Hill nor that his motte, much mutilated, is the core of the present castle mound': *Castles from the Air*, p 126. See also Taylor, 'Evidence for a pre-Conquest origin for the chapels in Hastings and Pevensey castles', pp 144–5.

26 . Guillaume de Poitiers, *Histoire*, pp 212–13.

27 . R.A. Brown, *English Castles*, 3rd edn (London, 1976), pp 44–6, and R.A. Brown, 'The Norman Conquest and the genesis of English castles', *Château Gaillard: European Castle Studies* 3 (1969), pp 1–14. Brown's conclusions are based partly on Martin Biddle's excavation of the so-called 'Harold's earthwork'. See also Brown, 'The castles of the conquest', pp 69–74, and his article 'A historian's approach to the origins of the castle in England'.

28 . Brown, 'The Norman Conquest and the genesis of English castles', p 11. Encroachment on churches and churchyards was recorded at Worcester: William of Malmesbury, *De gestis pontificum Anglorum*, ed N.E.S.A. Hamilton, Rolls Ser. (London, 1870), p 253; and has been found by excavation at Cambridge, Hereford, Norwich and Castle Rising where the twelfth-century castle rampart covered the eleventh-century church.

29 . *Carmen de Hastingae Proelio*, p 38. The burning of the house in the Bayeux Tapestry and flight of the inhabitants may be a clearance of this sort.

30 . Drage, 'Urban castles', believes that the first Canterbury castle was outside the city walls, but a more probable Anglo-Saxon boundary is provided by T. Tatton-Brown, 'The Anglo-Saxon towns of Kent', in D. Hooke, ed, *Anglo-Saxon Settlements* (Oxford, 1988), which puts the site within the walls. See also R. Eales, 'Introduction', *The Kent Domesday*, Alecto edn (London, 1992), pp 1–49.

31 . Domesday Book, fo. 2r. Like *vallum, fossa* can mean a ditch or a bank. Some of the houses were destroyed for the city ditch, but the St Augustine's abbey version of Domesday calls this the castle ditch: A. Ballard, ed, *An Eleventh-Century Inquisition of St Augustine's, Canterbury* (London, 1920), p 9. Early medieval Canterbury has been well described by Urry and others: W. Urry, 'The Normans in Canterbury', *Annales de Normandie* 8 (1958), pp 119–38; W. Urry, *Canterbury under the Angevin Kings* (London, 1967); T. Tatton-Brown, *Canterbury in Domesday Book* (Canterbury, 1987). Around the Dane John a flat-bottomed ditch, once 17 metres wide and 3 metres deep, has been excavated: *Medieval Archaeology* 26 (1982), pp 187–8.

32 . Guillaume de Poitiers, *Histoire*, pp 212–13. Renn, *Norman Castles*, pp 28–9 suggests Richborough. A chronology is set out in D.C. Douglas, *William the Conqueror* (London, 1964), appendix D, pp 396–400, but for a more probable timetable, see F.H. Baring, *Domesday Tables* (London, 1909), p 208, note and chapter 1 in this volume.

33 . Douglas, *William the Conqueror*, p 205.

34 . See chapter 1 in this volume.

35 . In 1071 the abbot of Abingdon, Ealdred, was imprisoned in the castle: *Chronicon monasterii de Abingdon*, ed J. Stevenson, Rolls Ser., 2 vols (London, 1858), I, p 486. Brown, *Castles from the Air*, dates Wallingford 'soon after 1066', p 219. John Palmer has noted that William built a camp 'across the river' at Wallingford in 1066. The relationship with the castle site is unclear. Excavations have been carried out at Wallingford by N.P. Brooks: see *Medieval Archaeology* 10 (1966), p 168; 11 (1967), pp 262–3; 'Excavations at Wallingford Castle 1965 – an interim report', *Berkshire Archaeological Journal* 62 (1965–70), pp 17–21; B. Durham *et al*, 'A cutting across the Saxon defences at Wallingford, Berkshire, 1971', *Oxoniensia* 37 (1973), pp 82–5.

36 . Guillaume de Poitiers, *Histoire*, pp 218–19, 236–7.

37 . The four were Baynard's, Montfichet, Ravenger's and the Tower.

38 . *Medieval Archaeology* 8 (1962–3), pp 255–6; Renn, *Norman Castles*, pp 326–30. Davison, 'Early earthwork castles', p 43; plan in Brown, 'Castles of the conquest', p 71.

39 . R. Mortimer, 'The Baynards of Baynard's Castle', in C. Harper-Bill, C.J. Holdsworth and J.L. Nelson, eds, *Studies in Medieval History Presented to R. Allen Brown* (London, 1989), p 252.

40 . M. Biddle, *Winchester in the Early Middle Ages*, Winchester Studies no. 1 (Oxford, 1976), pp 470–88 and fig. 26; Biddle, 'Early Norman Winchester', pp 312–14.

41 . *Ecclesiastical History of Orderic Vitalis*, II, pp 210–15; R.A. Brown, 'Exeter', in Brown, Colvin and Taylor, eds, *The History of the King's Works*, II, pp 647–9. J. Allan, C. Henderson and R. Higham, 'Saxon Exeter', in J. Haslam, ed, *Anglo-Saxon Towns in Southern England* (Chichester, 1984), pp 385–411.

42 . T. McNeill, *Castles* (London, 1992), pp 42, 45; Kenyon, *Medieval Fortifications*, p 7, citing studies of mottes by Holden at Lodsbridge, by Davison at Castle Neroche and by Barton and Holden at Bramber; Pounds, *Medieval Castle*, pp 18–19, fig. 1.6. Hofmann provided similar figures for cubic metres of earth shifted by sections of the German army in the 1930s, to illustrate the man-days required to build lengths of the eighth-century Carolingian canals: H.H. Hofmann, 'Fossa Carolina: versuch einer Zusammenschau', in W. Braunfels and P.E. Schramm, eds, *Karl der Grosse: Lebenswerk und Nachleben*, IV (Düsseldorf, 1967), pp 444–7. I am grateful to Kelly DeVries for this reference.

43 . For Dover, see above; for the second castle at York, see *Ecclesiastical History of Orderic Vitalis*, II, pp 222–3.

44 . *Ecclesiastical History of Orderic Vitalis*, II, pp 218–19. The king also built castles 'everywhere in that district', which is generally thought to include Stamford.

45 . *RCHM: City of Cambridge*, 2 vols (London, 1959), II, pp 304–6; J. Haslam, 'The development and topography of Saxon Cambridge', *Proceedings of the Cambridge Antiquarian Society* 81 (1982–3), pp 13–29; R.E. Glasscock, 'Introduction', *The Cambridgeshire Domesday*, Alecto edn (London, 1990), pp 1–17. For Lincoln and York, see notes below. Little can be said of Huntingdon, except in its relation to the *burh* and the number of houses it destroyed. There has been no extensive excavation at Warwick castle, and the nature and extent of the Saxon *burh* there is unknown: personal communication from the Warwickshire sites and monuments officer.

46 . Davison, 'Early earthwork castles', p 45; C. Drage, *Nottingam Castle: a Place Full Royal*, Transactions of the Thoroton Society of Nottinghamshire, 93 (Nottingham, 1990 for 1989), especially pp 36, 81–3, 104.

47 . J.W.F. Hill, *Medieval Lincoln* (Cambridge, 1948), pp 82–106; Brown, Colvin and Taylor, *The History of the King's Works*, II, p 704.

48 . N. Reynolds, 'Investigations in the Observatory tower, Lincoln castle', *Medieval Archaeology* 19 (1975), pp 201–5.

49 . *Ecclesiastical History of Orderic Vitalis*, II, pp 218–19.

50 . Chaussereau's map is redrawn by Davison, 'The origins of the castle in England', p 210, fig. 4; the ditch is also shown on the plan of the defences of York, in *RCHM: City of York*, 5 vols (London, 1962-81), II, facing p 57. Baile Hill has been partially excavated: P.V. Addyman and J. Priestley, 'Baile Hill, York: a report on the Institute's excavations', *Archaeological*

Journal 134 (1977), pp 115–56. *RCHM: City of York*, I, p 87 shows uncertainty about the south-western extent of the Roman *colonia* walls; see, however, P. Ottaway, '*Colonia Eburacensis*: a review of recent work', in P.V. Addyman and V.E. Black, eds, *Archaeological Papers from York Presented to M.W. Barley* (York, 1984), p 28: 'the settlement on the SW bank was probably enclosed and defined, at a date not yet established archaeologically, by a defensive circuit thought to correspond roughly to that of the medieval defences'. Also, R. Hall, 'The making of Domesday York', in Hooke, ed, *Anglo-Saxon Settlements*, pp 233–47.

51 . York was a polyfocal settlement, and it is possible that the site of Clifford's Tower was related to the Anglian settlement of York, which stretched from the later Fishergate to Walmgate Bar.

52 . *Anglo-Saxon Chronicle*, p 148: text 'D' s.a. 1067.

53 . *Ecclesiastical History of Orderic Vitalis*, II, pp 218–23.

54 . It seems to have taken Harold Godwinson four days to ride from London to York in 1066 and the same time to return, after Stamford Bridge. William did not take the most direct route, but came by Warwick and Nottingham; perhaps he arrived at York in early July?

55 . *Ecclesiastical History of Orderic Vitalis*, II, pp 222–3.

56 . *Ecclesiastical History of Orderic Vitalis*, II, pp 222–3. Chibnall says '*in quadam valle*' is probably a mistake for '*quadam vallo*' and she translates it as 'one of the baileys'.

57 . The reason for the destruction of the houses and the fire was advanced by the Worcester chronicler, who probably took it from a lost copy of the *Anglo-Saxon Chronicle*: Florence of Worcester, *Chronicon ex chronicis*, ed B. Thorpe, English Historical Society, 2 vols (London, 1848–9), I, p 4.

58 . *Anglo-Saxon Chronicle*, p 150: text 'D' s.a. 1069. There are several possible translations of these two words in J. Bosworth and T.J. Toller, *Anglo-Saxon Dictionary* (London, 1898). The Worcester chronicler (derived from the Anglo-Saxon Chronicle) uses the single word '*fracti*', broken: Florence of Worcester, *Chronicon*, I, p 4. A reference in Domesday Book to the sheriff carrying off a house into the castle, in the first year after the destruction of the castles, suggests building material being reused in reconstruction: Domesday Book, fo. 298r.

59 . Kenyon, *Medieval Fortifications*, pp 29, 31. H. Hurst, 'The archaeology of Gloucester castle: an introduction', *Transactions of the Bristol and Gloucester Archaeological Society* 102 (1984), pp 73–128, suggests that Gloucester castle may have originated as a ring-work in the south-west corner of the Roman walled circuit; see also T. Darvill, 'Excavations at the site of the early Norman castle at Gloucester', *Medieval Archaeology* 32 (1988), pp 1–49; Hassall, 'Excavations at Oxford castle, 1965–1973', pp 232–308. For Rochester, see Brown, *Castles from the Air*, p 9; Brown, 'Castles of the conquest', p 73; Eales, 'Introduction', *The Kent Domesday*, p 44. For Newcastle upon Tyne, *Medieval Archaeology* 27 (1983), p 206.

3. Alms for the Holy Land: The English Templars and their Patrons

John Walker

The order of the Knights Templar was founded in the Holy Land after the First Crusade in about 1119 when a group of knights, including Hugh de Payens and Godfrey de Saint-Omer, banded together to protect pilgrims travelling to the holy places in Jerusalem. At the Council of Troyes in 1129 the order received papal recognition and a rule of life was produced to govern the members of the order, who were soon to become renowned for their military activities. The chronicle and charter evidence which relates to the Templars in the Holy Land shows that the order received a wide range of benefactions from a variety of ecclesiastical and secular donors, and by 1187 the order had established a number of houses, or preceptories, including those at Jerusalem, Acre, Tyre, Beirut, Antioch and Tripoli.[1] Having become established in the Holy Land, the order also began to settle in Europe from the third decade of the twelfth century, developing preceptories in France, England and the Iberian peninsula.[2]

The development of the order in most of Europe was rather different from that in the Holy Land, because instead of concentrating on military functions the main aim of the Templar preceptories was, as Janet Burton and Malcolm Barber have demonstrated, to organize the collection of revenue and men to supply the needs of the crusader states.[3] This meant that anyone making donations to the order was contributing directly to the pursuit of warfare against the Muslims in the Holy Land. What is less clear is whether the donors were aware of the vital role they were playing, and particularly whether their donations were influenced by the desire to aid the Christian cause in the Holy Land or by other factors. It has long been recognized that questions of motivation can cause terrible problems for historians, largely because donors showed an apparent reluctance to explain their motives in anything other than terms of religious piety. It is accepted that the patronage of the Templars and other military orders was, in part at least, due to the upsurge of religious patronage which was a feature of the eleventh, twelfth and thirteenth centuries, but it is also clear that further investigation is required if the specific reasons for the patronage of the Templars are to be discovered.

Despite the potential hazards, it is the intention of this chapter to analyse the motivations behind the patronage of the English Templars in order to try to understand the reasons for the development of the order in the twelfth and thirteenth centuries. This involves a consideration of the evidence relating specifically to the English Templars and a brief survey of the growth of the order. There then follows an examination of potential influences on patronage, ranging from the impact of the Crusades, and the associations that lay people established with the order, to ties of kinship and lordship, and political and geographical factors.[4]

The study of the English Templars is facilitated by the relative abundance of primary source material. In addition to the many references contained in governmental records and chronicle accounts, there are three major pieces of evidence which are particularly useful when considering the patronage of the order. These are the Inquest of 1185–c.1190, the cartulary of Sandford priory in Oxfordshire and the Hospitaller cartulary. The Inquest was a survey of the Templars' possessions in England which was undertaken after the appointment of Geoffrey fitz Stephen as master of the English order, possibly to calculate the finances of the English order with a view to sending resources to the Holy Land.[5] The document contains information relating to the order's possessions, patrons and the management of their estates, county by county, beginning with a survey of Essex and followed by similar accounts of London and Middlesex, Kent, Warwickshire, Oxfordshire, Gloucestershire, Berkshire, Wiltshire, Herefordshire, Bedfordshire, Sussex, Lincolnshire, Derbyshire and Yorkshire. In the degree of detail which it presents, the Inquest is an invaluable piece of evidence which has yet to be fully analysed. The Sandford cartulary is the only document of its kind to survive for any of the English Templar preceptories. Composed in the late thirteenth century, it contains details of many twelfth-century transactions and provides information especially on the order's possessions in Oxfordshire, Wiltshire, Berkshire, Buckinghamshire and Hampshire.[6] The Hospitaller cartulary was begun in 1442 and includes details of the possessions of the Templars that had passed into the hands of the Hospitallers after the suppression of the Templars in the early fourteenth century. The cartulary, which is in two parts, includes charters concerning the Templars' lands in London, Berkshire, Buckinghamhire, Essex, Oxfordshire, Sussex, Staffordshire, Kent, Leicestershire and Cambridgeshire. It also includes surveys of Templar properties taken in the early fourteenth century, which are particularly useful in providing valuations of their possessions.[7] These pieces of source material are augmented by several other documents including details of the order's lands in Cambridgeshire which were removed from the main Hospitaller cartulary and kept in a separate manuscript; an inventory compiled in 1396–7 for the preceptory of Temple Combe in Somerset which comprises over a hundred deeds with details of possessions and names of patrons; a collection of documents relating to the preceptory of Ribston in Yorkshire; and the *Liber Johannis Stillingflete*, which was produced in the early fifteenth century and records Hospitaller benefactions and, in a similar way to the Hospitaller cartulary, information on the patrons and possessions of the Templars.[8]

The exact process which led to the establishment of the Templars in England is incompletely understood, but what is more certain is that the first mission by the Templars was led by Hugh de Payens and came to England in 1128. This mission succeeded in persuading men either to join or to make donations to the order. It is highly probable that three preceptories were founded at about this time, the most important of which was the Old Temple at Holborn in London, the chief centre of the Templars in England until the establishment of the New Temple, also at Holborn, in 1161.

However, it was not until the reign of King Stephen that the order really began to develop, with the receipt of lands, mills, churches, rents and other possessions, and the establishment of preceptories for their administration.[9] Studies have already demonstrated that the foundation of preceptories, and other religious houses, was a complicated and sometimes long and drawn-out process, with exact foundation dates being impossible to ascertain.[10] However, it seems reasonably clear that by the end of Stephen's reign the Templars had established at least ten preceptories, including that at Holborn. Other important foundations were Cowley in Oxfordshire, Cressing and Witham in Essex, Balsall in Warwickshire and possibly Eagle in Lincolnshire. By the end of Henry II's reign new foundations included the New Temple, Holborn, Temple Newsham and Temple Hirst in Yorkshire, Temple Bruer in Lincolnshire, Temple Guiting in Gloucestershire and Temple Ewell in Kent.

The reign of Henry II was also an important period for the development of the Templars in England because the king began to make use of members of the order in his government, and it is from this period that

Templars are recorded as acting as governmental envoys, as custodians of forts and as bankers, with the New Temple being used as a bank after the 1180s.[11] By *c.* 1200 the Templars had become firmly established in England with over 30 preceptories having been founded, together with large landed estates in the northern counties of Yorkshire and Lincolnshire, in the west Midlands in Warwickshire, the south midlands in Oxfordshire, as well as the south-east in Essex, Kent and Sussex. During the thirteenth century the popularity of the order was maintained, particularly during the reign of Henry III, with new foundations being established at Ribston after 1226, Rothley *c.* 1231, Sandford *c.* 1240 and donations to the order continuing into the last decades of the century.[12]

In England the Templars benefited from the patronage of over 800 largely secular and male donors who, as in the rest of Europe, came from a variety of social ranks. At the highest level they included members of the royal families of Blois and Anjou, most notably King Stephen and his wife Matilda, Henry II and Henry III; over 30 earls, including William III de Warenne, earl of Surrey, Simon II de Senlis, earl of Northampton, Gilbert de Clare, earl of Pembroke, and Robert II, earl of Derby; and members of the lesser baronial ranks including Roger I de Mowbray, Gilbert de Lacy, and Reginald de St Valéry, the lord of Tutbury. Beneath these ranks the order received donations from important county families such as the Caux family in Lincolnshire and the Sandford family in Oxfordshire; from members of lesser county families including the Lincolnshire donor William of Ashby de la Launde and Peter of Stoke Talmage in Oxfordshire. Thereafter, patronage of the order came from the knightly classes including people like Thomas de Coleville, Hugh II de Malebisse and members of the Esse family in Oxfordshire.[13]

A more difficult problem than the identification of the order's patrons is an analysis of why these people chose the Templars to be the recipients of their generosity. Part of the answer lies in a consideration of the impact of the Crusades in England. Several writers have noted the effect that the crusading movement had on the patronage of the military orders.[14] Indeed a few examples from charters to the order reveal a rare concern to stress motive for particular donations. Reginald de St Valéry made three grants to the Templars in the mid-twelfth century. The most important was that made *c.* 1146, when crusading fortunes in the east were at a low ebb, giving the advowson of Beckley church in Oxfordshire to the order. Reginald's apparent concern for the situation in the Holy Land was expressed when he stated that the donation was 'pro omnibus illis qui mecum Iherosolimam contendre cupiunt'.[15] There is no evidence that the donor was a participant in the Second Crusade, but he did travel to the Holy Land before the Third Crusade.[16] In 1226 Robert de Ros, having already given the order the vill of Hunsingore and lands at Cathal, granted his manor of Ribston, the advowson of the church there, and the hamlet of Walshford with its mills, clearly stating that the donation was made 'ad sustentationem sancte terre orientalis'.[17] Again, there is some evidence to connect Robert with the crusading movement, as in 1206 he appears to have been on the point of taking the cross.[18] A final charter reference of this kind comes from Thomas II of Sandford's grant of the manor of Sandford c. 1240, which like Robert of Ros's grant was made, in part, 'ad subsidium terre sancte'.[19] Although Thomas was not a crusader himself his uncle Hugh was recorded as preparing to go on Crusade in 1218 and as a minor patron of the Templars.[20] Although these few examples do not suggest a great concern among donors for events in the Holy Land, they do show that some benefactors did have an awareness of the need to provide aid for the Christian forces there and that this awareness was probably founded on some form of personal experience with the crusading movement. In order fully to understand the impact of this movement on the patronage of the Templars, it is therefore necessary to consider how many other patrons of the order had similar connections, and in particular how many have been identified as crusaders.

Of the twelfth-century crusaders who were also patrons of the English Templars the most important was Roger I de Mowbray. He may have gone to the Holy Land on four occasions, including the Second Crusade, and he was ransomed by the Templars and Hospitallers after his capture by the Muslims at the battle of Hattin in 1187.[21] Roger made large-scale grants in Warwickshire, Lincolnshire and Yorkshire. In Warwickshire these included over 300 acres at Balsall, where a preceptory was later established, in Lincolnshire 240 acres on the Isle of Axholme, and in Yorkshire large estates at Weedley, South Cave, and materials which helped in the foundation of three houses at Penhill, East Cowton and Stanghow.[22] Other twelfth-century crusader-patrons included Gilbert de Lacy, who gave the order a large estate at Guiting in Gloucestershire, comprising 12 hides, a mill and the advowson of the church, which formed the basis of the preceptory later established there; Hugh II de Malebisse, who gave over two and a half carucates in Great Broughton and Scawton in Yorkshire; John fitz Eustace de Lacy, the constable of Chester, who died at Tyre on 11 October 1190, having given the advowson of the church of Marnham in Nottinghamshire;[23] and King Richard I, who confirmed the donations of his father and may have made small donations in several counties including Warwickshire, Suffolk and Pembroke.[24]

In total over 20 patrons of the order were crusaders in the twelfth century and in the thirteenth century a further 16 patrons are recorded as going on crusade. These included John Harcourt, whose grant of £10 worth of land at Rockley in Leicestershire was evidently made while he was actually on the Fifth Crusade. Evidence from the Close Rolls shows that he had received the land from King John and that he made the donation to the Templars 'in extremis agens in exercitu Damete', where he died.[25] Emery de Sacy's grant of half a carucate and a mill at Sellburn, Hampshire, seems to have been made in similar circumstances. The Close Rolls again record that the Templars had full seisin of the land, 'qua Emericus de Sacy in extremis agens eis legavit in obsidione Damietta'.[26] Several patrons of the order are recorded on the crusade of Richard of Cornwall in 1239 and on that of the Lord Edward between 1270 and 1272.[27] One of the most important patrons on the latter expedition was David of Strathbogie, the earl of Atholl, who let his manor of Chingford in Essex to the Templars for 18 years in April 1270 before he left for the Holy Land, where he died in August of the same year.[28]

Janet Burton has argued that 'there does not ... appear to be much correlation [in Yorkshire] between those who went on Crusade and those who endowed the military orders', noting that the only Yorkshire crusader to found any houses was Roger de Mowbray.[29] In England as a whole this is certainly true in terms of the number of patrons who went on crusade. Out of a total of over 800 patrons fewer than 40, or 5 per cent, have been identified as crusaders and only a small number of these founded houses. Nevertheless the significance of the movement as an influence for the development of the order cannot be ignored for two reasons. Firstly, although few of the crusader-patrons who have been identified were founders of Templar houses, their number does include some of the most generous patrons of estates and other gifts to the English order, most notably Roger de Mowbray and Gilbert de Lacy. Secondly, as Burton and others have shown, the patronage of crusaders brought other people into contact with, or at least made them aware of, the work of the Templars, leading in the end to further donations to the order.[30]

One of the crusader-patrons, Gilbert de Lacy, had closer connections with the Templars than simply those of a patron. The son of Roger de Lacy, he may have joined the Templars after 1158 (when he was still in possession of his father's lands),[31] and by 1160 as *frater* Gilbert de Lacy he was among a number of Templars who witnessed the peace treaty between Henry II and Louis VII of France. He went to the Holy Land some time after this, when he became the preceptor of the Templar house at Tripoli, and his last appearance (but not necessarily his death) was in 1163, when William of Tyre refers to him as being one of the leaders of a crusader force which defeated Nur-ad-Din.[32] Gilbert's extensive patronage of the Templars made him one of the most generous supporters of the English order; but, because it is not possible to date his donations with any accuracy, it is difficult to know whether he made them before he became a Templar, when he joined the order, or after he had left for the Holy Land. There are certainly few other examples from England of full members of the order acting as patrons.[33] However, there are numerous cases of lay associates acting in this way, and the nature and importance of this type of membership on the patronage of the order can now be considered.

The Templars, in common with other types of religious orders, had different degrees of membership, ranging from full membership to lay association.[34] Full members of the Templars can be defined as those knights, sergeants and chaplains who were subject to the rules and customs of the order and to the ultimate authority of the Grand Master of the Templars in the Holy Land. Lay associates, or confraters, can be defined as those individuals who were connected with a religious order, in such a way as to receive either spiritual or temporal benefits (or both), in return for some kind of commitment to the order which would be less burdensome than that made by a full member. This might involve a material grant of land or other donation. Malcolm Barber has noted that this type of relationship was made easier from a very early stage in the order's history, 'by arrangements of considerable flexibility which enabled [lay] knights to share in the benefits of association with the Temple'.[35] There is, however, some degree of uncertainty about the actual nature of Templar associates and some writers, including S.S. Rovik, have suggested that, unlike other religious orders, the Templars did not make great distinctions between their lay associates: that the only distinction that could be made was between active and passive associates or confraters.[36] Despite Rovik's claims, it is clear that the rule of the Temple does, in theory at least, make provision for several distinct categories of lay associates. It thus distinguishes between *milites ad terminum*, lay knights who joined the order for a limited period of time; *fratres coniugati*, married couples who would have been closely involved in the community, while still remaining a distinct group; and men who joined the order on their death-bed.[37]

Part of the problem in making distinctions between lay associates, and between lay associates and full members, lies in the fact that the term *frater* was often used to describe all types of member. Furthermore, the problem is made more difficult in England (and most of Europe) because of the nature of the order as a non-military organization restricted to alms-collecting and other administrative tasks. Aside from chaplains conducting religious services in Templar houses, it was probably difficult to distinguish many 'full members' from their secular counterparts administering lay estates. It would have been even more difficult to make distinctions between those members of lay society who wished to be associated with the order, without necessarily being involved in the minutiae of its workings.

Despite these problems of definition, the English evidence suggests that two types of lay associate can be identified, and that in both cases the form of association led directly to the patronage of the order. The first category comprised those people who made a commitment to the Templars which would affect them during their lives. These associates were distinguished by reference in their charters to *fraternitatem* of the Templars. One such associate was William de Bosco from Oxfordshire, who gave four acres of land to the order, together with pasturage for 20 animals, 100 sheep and 60 pigs, in a charter of *c.* 1195 which stated that 'fratres receperunt dominum et fratrem meum Ricardum filium Johannes et me in sua fraternitate et in beneficiis domus Templi'.[38] Other men similarly associated with the order included William of Ashby de la Launde who before 1169 conceded waste land at Bruer in Lincolnshire which became the basis for the preceptory of Temple Bruer. In his charter of donation he referred to the fact that the Templars, 'me in fraternitatem receperunt ... et in curam et custodiam suam'.[39] Finally, Henry de Neyre Pel made a contract with the Templars *c.* 1200, whereby he promised them sixpence every year and one third of his chattels at his death, 'ut sim in orationibus et beneficiis similiter et in fraternitate Templi particeps'. His charter further stipulated that his heirs would continue to pay the annual rent after his death, and one-third of their chattels would pass to the order at their deaths.[40] Association in life with the Templars was characterized by individual arrangements which rewarded the associates with unspecified benefits of the *fraternitatem* of the Templars.[41]

The second category of lay association in England seems to have been connected with the agreement to allow the associate to be buried in one of the order's cemeteries. Two famous patrons, Henry III and William I Marshal, both expressed the desire for burial in a Templar house, although only the latter had his wish fulfilled.[42] In general this form of association followed a grant being made to the particular order, which included the body of the associate, as in the case of Thomas I de Sandford who gave the order a mill at Sandford before 1219 and Richard Foliot who gave the Templars over 100 acres of land and his grange at Warpsgrove in Oxfordshire.[43] Some associates clearly specified the burial right as in the case of Peter de Stoke Talmage who gave half a hide of land at Stoke Talmage 'cum corpore meo ad sepeliendum in cimiterio eorundem fratrum'.[44]

A final example of lay association shows how it may have been possible to combine the two types of membership which have been outlined. Robert de Ros has already been considered as a crusader and patron, but as with Gilbert de Lacy there is another side to his career which is relevant to his patronage of the order. In 1212 Robert was recorded as taking the habit of religion but in the following year he was also acting as the sheriff of Cumberland and it is clear that he was particularly involved in political affairs at the end of John's reign. However, in 1226 Robert gave the order the important estate at Ribston and on 23 December 1226 his son did homage for his lands, before Robert's death the next year. The explanation for this apparently confusing scenario may lie in the fact that in 1212, by which time Robert had made his first donation to the order, he became an associate in life of the Templars and in 1226, when he gave Ribston manor and his body to the order, he became an associate in death.[45] While bringing benefits to the lay associates themselves, lay association was obviously of great importance in terms of the patronage of the Templars. Both the methods that have been considered involved donations of lands or money to the order, and, even if relatives were not specifically involved in the contracts of association, there is evidence to suggest that they did make their own donations to the order, thus increasing the importance of this form of membership.[46]

The influences of the crusading movement and lay association indicate that a number of patrons were directly involved either in the affairs of the Templars or in matters which concerned the order. From this, it is plausible to suggest that their donations were based on the knowledge of their significance to the development of the order. However, important as these influences were, there is another side to the patronage of the English Templars which has already been suggested, involving a consideration of family and feudal ties. The importance of family connections for the patronage of religious orders has been noted by a number of historians.[47] In the case of the Templars' patrons, notable examples of the influence of family connections are to be found in the English royal houses of Blois and Anjou and baronial families including the earls of Warwick.[48]

Such ties are also identifiable at a lower social level as the following examples will illustrate. The family of Caux comprised a small but significant family group whose patronage of the Templars in Lincolnshire included donations made in the later twelfth and early thirteenth century.[49] The first patrons of the order were the two brothers Robert III and Geoffrey de Caux, descendants of the Robert de Caux who had over four and a half carucates in Wragby by 1118.[50] Robert III and Geoffrey, through their mother Isabella, were nephews of Robert II, earl of Derby, the founder of the Templar preceptory of Bisham[51] and it may have been this connection which led to the patronage of the Caux brothers before c. 1177. Robert was the more generous of the two brothers, granting the advowson of Rowston church and over two carucates in Brauncewell, Rauceby, Toynton St Peter and Stubton, while Geoffrey gave half a carucate in Grantham.[52] Further family donations came from Robert's daughter Matilda, who gave the town of Rowston, and from her two husbands Adam fitz Peter (d. c. 1184) and Rannulf fitz Stephen.[53]

The Port family from Basing in Hampshire provided four relatively small-scale patrons of the order. The family was descended from the Domesday tenant Hugh de Port, who became a monk of Winchester abbey. His son Henry founded the priory of Monk Sherborne and it was his wife, Hawise, who was the first member of the family to patronize the Templars.[54] Although her charter to the order does not survive, we know of her grant of the land of Ahemund of Fawley from the two confirmatory charters of her son John, who before c. 1170 also gave the order a mill at Warnford.[55] John's son Adam gave the order the services of Robert fitz William Blund and Robert fitz Sewlfi and their heirs, and his grandson William de St John, who had taken his mother's surname, granted in 1235 pasture rights at Great Shefford and Fawley in Berkshire.[56]

A larger family grouping of patrons is the Sandford family in Oxfordshire, descendants of Robert de Sandford, the founder of the Benedictine priory of Sandford, later known as Littlemore, near Oxford.[57] Robert was also the first member of the family to make a donation to the Templars, giving four acres of land in Sandford c. 1150, a donation in which his son Jordan was also associated.[58] Jordan's son Thomas I, who became a lay associate of the Templars in 1219, donated a mill and a fishery at Sandford, and his son Thomas II maintained the family connections with the order c. 1240 by granting the manor of Sandford and the advowson of the church of Blewbury in Berkshire.[59] This donation was not only the most important grant made to the order by a member of his family, but also constituted one of the most important grants to the order in England during the thirteenth century, as it provided the basis for the important preceptory established by the Templars at Sandford. Further donations to the order were made by Thomas II's brothers Hugh, the crusader, and Richard, the latter donating meadows in Sandford to augment the lands of the mill donated by his father.[60]

The evidence provided by the Caux, Port and Sandford families shows that the Templars owed a great deal to the family connections which helped to continue the patronage of the order over several generations, either in the form of confirmations of earlier charters made by relatives or in new grants. It is true that in some cases, such as that of Hugh de Sandford, other motivations may have played their part, but the fact that the evidence from the three families that have been considered can be repeated among many other family groupings shows that the overriding influence of the family on patronage should not be underestimated.

Ties of lordship, by which is meant both feudal ties and those of social association, also appear to have been of some significance in the patronage of the Templars. Evidence from the reign of Stephen suggests that there were close links between royal lordship and patronage of the order. From the 67 known charters made during Stephen's reign, a total of 19 (by far the largest number by any one patron in the period) were given by the king himself, and a further four were added by his wife, Queen Matilda, who gave the manor and advowson of the church of Cressing in 1137 and the manor of Cowley in 1139. Stephen's grants included land, mills and liberties in Dinsley, Shotover, Witham and Cressing, and he may have also been responsible for the foundation of the preceptory of Eagle in Lincolnshire.[61]

The patronage of the house of Blois was undoubtedly significant not only in terms of the donations made by Stephen and Matilda but also because of the influence that this royal patronage may have had on members of the royal court. Among the patrons of the Templars at court was Stephen's chancellor, Philip de Harcourt, whose most notable gift comprised the town and advowson of the church of Shipley, given in 1139 before he defected to the Angevin party.[62] Of Stephen's constables, Robert de Vere, Henry of Essex and Robert II d'Oilli were all patrons.[63] Aside from Stephen's immediate household officials, it is clear that a number of Templar patrons were also frequent attenders at court. Members of the higher nobility who fall into the category of frequent attenders include men like Simon II de Senlis, earl of Northampton, and William III de Warenne, earl of Surrey, who gave seven hides of land in Merton and a rent of 40 shillings in Lewes respectively.[64] Another consistent supporter was Robert

II de Ferrers, earl of Derby. In addition, Gilbert de Clare, a generous patron in Weston, Baldock and Rannock, and Roger I de Mowbray were both apparently Stephen's supporters when they made their donations, although evidence for their donations comes from the Inquest of 1185 rather than from surviving charter material.[65] Stephen and his supporters were, therefore, particularly generous to the Templars, and indeed the available evidence suggests that they were more generous than the supporters of the Angevin party in England.[66]

It is also possible to trace the influence of lordship on the patronage of the Templars among the great baronial patrons of the Templars, including Rannulf III, earl of Chester, William I Marshal and the earls of Pembroke, and Simon II and III de Senlis, earls of Northampton and Huntingdon.[67] Emma Mason has noted the prolific patronage of the Templars, mainly in Warwickshire, by the earls of Warwick and their tenants and associates.[68] During the twelfth century Roger I de Beaumont (d. 1153) founded the preceptory of Warwick, his mother Margaret gave the manor of Llanmadoc in Wales, and Roger's son William I (d. 1184) gave lands in two Warwickshire villages. In addition, the Inquest of 1185–c. 1190 provides evidence of donations made by the earls of Warwick, including an estate of over one and a half carucates in Sherborne.[69] Tenants of William I, recorded in his *carta* of 1166, included five patrons of the Templars, most notably Robert de Harcourt, who gave a mill at Market Bosworth in Leicestershire, and Robert II de Marmion, who gave two and a half carucates and a mill in Barston.[70] Among the lesser baronage similar evidence is also forthcoming. Roger de Mowbray's tenants in 1166 included eight patrons of the Templars, of whom the most generous were Hugh II de Malebisse, the crusader and donor in Great Broughton, and William de Vescy, who gave the advowson of the Lincolnshire churches of Normanton and Caythorpe.[71] Among the witnesses of Roger's charters who were not Mowbray tenants are a dozen patrons of the Templars, the most frequent attestor being Robert de Bussy, the donor of four carucates in Willoughton, Yorkshire, who attested on 55 occasions.[72]

Evidence from the charters of Roger I and Nigel de Mowbray also shows the importance of social association as a factor affecting the patronage of the Templars. The idea that people who associated socially with each other might follow each other in patronizing the same religious orders is suggested by the fact that among the attestors are patrons including Hugh II de Malebisse, Roger de Cundy, Robert de Bussy and Thomas de Coleville, who frequently attested charters either in pairs or in larger groups. For example, Hugh II de Malebisse, an attestor on 63 occasions, witnessed 28 times with Robert de Bussy, 21 times with Thomas de Coleville, and 11 times with Roger de Cundy, while Robert de Bussy attested on 12 occasions with Thomas de Coleville and six times with Roger de Cundy.[73] As with family influences, there are obviously problems of interpretation when considering the influence of lordship and social association on the patronage of the English Templars. However, once again the large number of available examples suggests that these factors were of some influence, particularly because they show how the patronage of the order was exercised through different social levels.

Two final influences on the patronage of the Templars can be noted, political and geographical factors. Writing about the civil war of King Stephen's reign, Elizabeth Hallam emphasized the political significance of monastic patronage. She suggested that both sides in the war recognized the important role that religious houses could play if they happened to have powerful abbots and were established on strategic sites. This led both sides to become involved in politically motivated patronage.[74] Although the Templars were not involved in political quarrels at a high level, in contrast to the Cistercians and Cluniacs, it is evident that patronage of the order did have a political dimension, in the granting and confirming of charters in politically sensitive areas. In particular, Stephen does seem to have been concerned to make grants, and to confirm grants, either in areas which were strongholds of the house of Blois, such as Essex, or in areas where there was some uncertainty as to who held power, as in Berkshire, Oxfordshire and other parts of the Thames valley. In both cases these actions would have aided Stephen in the assertion of his rights in particular areas, while in the second case alone it would have been to the advantage of the Templars to have Stephen's confirmation of their charters, in case he was ultimately successful in the wars of succession. This fact appeared to be more likely after 1141, when the majority of Stephen's confirmations were made.[75]

Finally, there is some evidence of the importance of geographical association on the patronage of the Templars. The Sandford cartulary provides evidence of possessions granted to the Templar houses in Oxfordshire, which show a definite concentration in the Cowley and Sandford area where the order had established preceptories. In the area within five miles the order held and received possessions from benefactors who came from towns and villages including Sandford, Cowley, Littlemore, Horspath, Garsington and Oxford. Within ten miles they held and received possessions from benefactors in places which included Warpsgrove, Easington, Stoke Talmage and Merton.[76]

The establishment of a network of Templar preceptories and the estates which they administered in England was the result of the generosity of a large number of individuals making donations to the order from the 1120s onwards, a generosity which only began to wane in the second half of the thirteenth century. These donations enabled the English order to fulfil its role, as a recruiting and fund-raising organization, in a similar way to the other branches of the order on the European mainland. Although the motivations behind the patronage of the order are clearly open to varying interpretations, it is possible to come to some conclusions. In the first place a study of the importance of the crusading movement on patronage reveals that a small but important minority of the order's patrons were evidently aware of the problems faced by the Christian forces in the east. Similarly, the connection between lay association and patronage shows that a body of patrons were involved in the activities of the order. For that reason it is possible to suggest that the patronage of the English Templars was, in part at least, a result of the desire to help the order in the performance of its role.

It is true that other factors were involved in the patronage of the order, most notably ties of family and lordship, but also in some cases political and geographical factors; and it is clear, moreover, that these factors were influential in their own way and that they did help to maintain the patronage of the order beyond the first waves of enthusiasm that it experienced in the mid-twelfth century, as has been shown to be the case with the order of St Lazarus. However, while accepting that they played their part, often in conjunction with each other, it would be wrong to see the patronage of the English Templars as being motivated by nothing more than blind family or feudal loyalties or by accidents of politics and geography. The Templars owed a great deal to the fact that some of their patrons at least had a wider view of the order's importance outside England.

Notes

1 . M. Barber, *The New Knighthood: A History of the Order of the Temple* (Cambridge, 1994), especially chapter one. This is the only modern account in English of the history of the Templars. For the order in the Holy Land see, S.S. Rovik, 'The Templars in the Holy Land during the twelfth century', unpublished DPhil thesis, University of Oxford, 1986.
2 . Barber, *New Knighthood*, p 19.
3 . J.E. Burton, 'The Knights Templar in Yorkshire in the twelfth century: a reassessment', *Northern History* 27 (1991), pp 26–40, especially 26–7; M. Barber, 'Supplying the crusader states: the role of the Templars', in B.Z.

Kedar, ed, *The Horns of Hattin* (Jerusalem and London, 1992), pp 314–26; Barber, *New Knighthood*, chapter seven.

4 . For a comparable study of the order of St Lazarus see John Walker, 'The motives of patrons of the order of St Lazarus in England in the twelfth and thirteenth centuries', in J. Loades, ed, *Monastic Studies: the Continuity of Tradition* (Bangor, 1990), pp 171–81.

5 . *Records of the Templars in England in the Twelfth Century. The Inquest of 1185*, ed B.A. Lees, British Academy Records of the Social and Economic History of England and Wales, 9 (London, 1935); Barber, *New Knighthood*, pp 251 and 381, note 95.

6 . *The Sandford Cartulary*, ed A.M. Leys, Oxfordshire Record Soc., 19 and 22 (1937, 1941 for 1940).

7 . BL, Cotton MS, Nero E.VI. See also M. Gervers, *The Hospitaller Cartulary in the British Library Cotton MS Nero E. VI* (Toronto, 1981) and M. Gervers, *The Cartulary of the Knights of St John of Jerusalem in England* (Oxford, 1982).

8 . BL, Cotton MS, Nero C.IX; R.A. Bartelot, 'Calendar of all the charters and muniments of Templecombe', *Somerset and Dorset Notes and Queries* 21 (1935), pp 86–92; W. Dugdale, *Monasticon Anglicanum*, ed J. Caley, H. Ellis and B. Bandinel, 6 vols in 8 (London, 1817–30), VI (ii), pp 831–9; R.V. Taylor, 'Ribston and the Knights Templars', *Yorkshire Archaeological and Topographical Journal* 7 (1881–2), pp 429–52; 8 (1883–4), pp 259–99; 9 (1884–5), pp 71–98.

9 . Barber, *New Knighthood*, p 14; for foundation dates see D. Knowles and R.N. Hadcock, *Medieval Religious Houses: England and Wales,* 2nd edn (London, 1971), pp 292–7. The only modern account of the Templars in England is provided by T.W. Parker, *The Knights Templars in England* (Tucson, 1963).

10 . V.H. Galbraith, 'Monastic foundation charters of the eleventh and twelfth centuries', *Cambridge Historical Journal* 4 (1934), pp 214–15; Burton, 'Knights Templar in Yorkshire', pp 27–31.

11 . E.M. Hallam, 'Aspects of the monastic patronage of the English and French royal houses, *c.* 1130–1270', unpublished PhD thesis, University of London, 1976, p 125.

12 . *Sandford Cartulary*, *passim*; Burton, 'Knights Templar in Yorkshire', pp 38–9; Walker, 'Patronage of the order of St Lazarus and the Templars', pp 253–68.

13 . Documentary references relating to these individuals and families are provided below.

14 . Burton, 'Knights Templar in Yorkshire', pp 31–5; H. Nicholson, *Templars, Hospitallers and Teutonic Knights. Images of the Military Orders, 1128–1291* (Leicester, 1993), pp 60–61. John Walker, 'Crusaders and patrons: the impact of the Crusades on the patronage of the order of St Lazarus in England', in M. Barber, ed, *The Military Orders. Fighting for the Faith and Caring for the Sick* (London, forthcoming).

15 . *Records of the Templars in England*, p 49; *Sandford Cartulary*, nos. 89, 295.

16 . B. Siedschlag, *English Participation in the Crusades, 1150–1220* (Bryn Mawr, 1939), pp 110–11.

17 . *Early Yorkshire Charters*, ed C.T. Clay, Yorkshire Archaeological Soc., Records Ser., Extra Ser., 10 vols (Wakefield, 1935–65), X, nos. 13–14.

18 . Burton, 'Knights Templar in Yorkshire', pp 38–9; Siedschlag, *English Participation*, p 135.

19 . *Sandford Cartulary*, no. 1.

20 . Siedschlag, *English Participation*, p 139.

21 . *Charters of the Honour of Mowbray, 1107–1191*, ed D.E. Greenway (London, 1972), pp xxxi–xxxii; A. de Marsy, 'Fragment d'un cartulaire de l'ordre de Saint Lazare, en Terre-Sainte', *Archives de l'orient Latin* 2 (1884), pp 121–57, at 140.

22 . *Charters of the Honour of Mowbray*, nos. 270–6; *Records of the Templars in England*, pp 33–5, 78–9, 111, 125, 132, 254–8, 269–70; Burton, 'Knights Templar in Yorkshire', pp 29–31.

23 . *Records of the Templars in England*, pp 47–8, 50, 80; Siedschlag, *English Participation*, p 118; *Early Yorkshire Charters*, ed W Farrer, Yorkshire Archaeological Soc., Record Ser., Extra Ser., 3 vols (Edinburgh, 1914–16), III, p 457.

24 . *Records of the Templars in England*, pp 139–44; Hallam, 'Aspects of monastic patronage', pp 128–9.

25 . *Calendar of Charter Rolls, 1226–57* (London, 1903), p 51; *Rotuli litterarum clausarum in Turri Londinensi asservati, 1204–27*, 2 vols (Record Commission, London, 1833–44), I, p 402; Siedschlag, *English Participation*, p 140.

26 . *CIPM*, I, p 269; *Rotuli litterarum clausarum*, I, p 401; Siedschlag, *English Participation*, p 138.

27 . Dugdale, *Monasticon Anglicanum*, VI (ii), p 836; F.M. Powicke, *King Henry III and the Lord Edward* (Oxford, 1947), p 205; S. Lloyd, *English Society and the Crusade, 1216–1307* (Oxford, 1988), appendix 4.

28 . *CPR, 1266–72*, p 423; A.A.M. Duncan, 'The earldom of Atholl in the thirteenth century', *Scottish Geneaologist* 7 (1961), pp 2–10.

29 . Burton, 'Knights Templar in Yorkshire', p 34.

30 . *Ibid*, pp 34–5; Walker, 'Crusaders and patrons'.

31 . W.E. Wightman, *The Lacy Family in England and Normandy 1066–1194* (Oxford, 1966), pp 184–90.

32 . *Recueil des actes de Henri II*, ed L. Delisle and E. Berger, 4 vols (Paris, 1909–27), I, no. cxli; *Records of the Templars in England*, p cxxiv; E.A. Babcock and A.C. Krey, eds, *William Archbishop of Tyre*, 2 vols (New York, 1976), II, p 306.

33 . *Records of the Templars in England*, p 70; Walker, 'Patronage of the order of St Lazarus and the Templars', pp 61–4.

34 . Walker, 'Patronage of the order of St Lazarus and the Templars', pp 67–89.

35 . M. Barber, 'The social context of the Templars', *TRHS* 34 (1984), pp 27–46, at 41.

36 . Rovik, 'The Templars in the Holy Land', p 129.

37 . J.M. Upton-Ward, ed, *The Rule of the Templars. The French Text of the Rule of the Order of the Knights Templar* (Woodbridge, 1992), nos. 66, 69, 632. For further discussion of this subject see E. Magnou, 'Oblature, classe chevaleresque et servage dans les maisons méridionales du Temple au XIIme siècle', *Annales du Midi* 73 (1961), pp 377–97.

38 . *Sandford Cartulary*, no. 454.

39 . *Records of the Templars in England*, p 250.

40 . *Sandford Cartulary*, no. 407.

41 . A.J. Forey, *The Templars in the Corona de Aragón* (London, 1973), pp 42–3.

42 . *Calendar of Charter Rolls, 1226–57*, pp 135, 210–11; Barber, *New Knighthood*, pp 215–17.

43 . *Sandford Cartulary*, nos. 6, 162.

44 . *Ibid*, no. 208.

45 . *Rotuli litterarum clausarum*, I, p 116.

46 . Walker, 'Patronage of the order of St Lazarus and the Templars', pp 80, 88.

47 . R.V. Turner, 'Religious patronage of Angevin royal administrators *c*. 1170–1239', *Albion* 18 (1986), pp 1–21, 8; R. Mortimer, 'Religious and secular motives for some English monastic foundations', in D. Baker, ed, *Studies in Church History* 15 (1978), pp 75–85, 81; Walker, 'Motives of patrons of the order of St Lazarus', pp 175–6.

48 . Walker, 'Patronage of the order of St Lazarus and the Templars', pp 94–8, 157–8, 180.

49 . *Ibid*, pp 101–5.

50 . *The Lincolnshire Domesday and Lindsey Survey*, ed C.W. Foster and T. Longley, Lincoln Record Soc., 19 (1924), p 250.

51 . BL, Cotton MS, Nero E.VI, fo. 92r; *Records of the Templars in England*, pp 147, note 13, 203.

52 . *Records of the Templars in England*, pp 79, 87, 90–91, 93, 98, 109.

53 . *Records of the Templars in England*, pp 101, 134, 261–2; *Early Yorkshire Charters*, ed Farrer, III, p 358.

54 . J.H. Round, 'The families of St John and of Port', *The Genealogist*, new ser., 16 (1899–1900), pp 1–13; *VCH: Hampshire*, ii (London, 1903), p 226, and iv (London, 1911), pp 115–16; Walker, 'Patronage of the order of St Lazarus and the Templars', pp 98–101.

55 . *Records of the Templars in England*, p 52; *Sandford Cartulary*, nos. 329–30.

56 . *Records of the Templars in England*, p 52; *Sandford Cartulary*, nos. 331–3; Dugdale, *Monasticon Anglicanum*, IV, p. 646; *VCH: Hampshire*, iv, pp 115–16.

57 . Walker, 'Patronage of the order of St Lazarus and the Templars', pp 105–9.

58 . *Sandford Cartulary*, no. 16.

59 . *Ibid*, nos. 1, 6, 8.

60 . *Sandford Cartulary*, nos. 12–13.

61 . BL, Cotton MS, Nero E.VI, fos 52r, 92r, 133v, 134r, 137r, 289r, 289v; *Rotuli hundredorum temp. Hen. III and Edw. I in Turr. Lond' et curia receptae scaccarii Westm. asservati*, ed W. Illingworth, 2 vols (Record Commission, London, 1812–18), I, 284; *Sandford Cartulary*, nos. 39, 40, 41, 42; Walker, 'Patronage of the order of St Lazarus and the Templars', pp 156–71, 278–87.

62 . BL, Cotton MS, Nero E.VI, fo. 148r.

63 . *Records of the Templars in England*, pp 24, 78; *Sandford Cartulary*, nos. 62, 127.

64 . *Records of the Templars in England*, p 44; *Sandford Cartulary*, no. 424; Clay, ed, *Early Yorkshire Charters*, VIII, p 94.

65 . *Records of the Templars in England*, pp 63–5, 65–9, 77–8; BL, Cotton MS, Nero E.VI, fo. 135v.

66 . Walker, 'Patronage of the order of St Lazarus and the Templars', pp 278–87.

67 . *Ibid*, pp 180–201.

68 . E. Mason, 'Fact and fiction in the English crusading tradition: the earls of Warwick in the twelfth century', *Journal of Medieval History* 14 (1988), pp 83–4.

69 . *Ibid*, p 83; *Records of the Templars in England*, pp 26–7, 81, 113–14; W. Dugdale, *The Antiquities of Warwickshire Illustrated* (Coventry, 1765), p 380.

70 . *The Red Book of the Exchequer*, ed H. Hall, Rolls Ser., 3 vols (London, 1896), I, pp 324–7; *Records of the Templars in England*, pp 26, 35; Walker, 'Patronage of the order of St Lazarus and the Templars', pp 181–2.

71 . *The Red Book of the Exchequer*, I, pp 418–21; *Records of the Templars in England*, p 79; Walker, 'Patronage of the order of St Lazarus and the Templars', pp 206–7.

72 . *Records of the Templars in England*, p 100; Walker, 'Patronage of the order of St Lazarus and the Templars', pp 213–15.

73 . Walker, 'Patronage of the order of St Lazarus and the Templars', pp 222–4.

74 . Hallam, 'Aspects of monastic patronage', pp 61–6. See also M. Chibnall, 'The Empress Matilda and church reform', *TRHS*, 5th ser., 38 (1988), pp 108–13.

75 . Walker, 'Patronage of the order of St Lazarus and the Templars', pp 159–60.

76 . *Ibid*, pp 238–9, 299.

4. Knights, Esquires and Military Service: The Evidence of the Armorial Cases before the Court of Chivalry

Andrew Ayton

The later medieval period, particularly the fourteenth century, was a time of opportunities and challenges for the English gentry. For centuries the secular landholding aristocracy had been a military class, their possession of land being directly associated with the performance of an elite military function, but by the fourteenth century there was a great deal more to aristocratic life than war and chivalric culture. Military service, along with combat training on the tournament field and such thinly disguised substitutes for war as the chase, had to compete with other responsibilities arising from landholding: active participation in shire administration and involvement in the political life of the kingdom.

Such distractions from the martial calling were admittedly not new. It has long been recognized that 'by the end of the twelfth century knights were training themselves in the arts of local government'.[1] Yet the fourteenth century witnessed, for the gentry, an increasing participation in shire administration: by 1400 there may have been twice as many men actively involved as there had been a hundred years earlier.[2] This is not to suggest that a process of demilitarization was taking place; it was more a matter of diversification of function. War was not so easily to be excluded, particularly since the Edwardian period witnessed what has recently been characterized as 'the triumph of chivalric knighthood';[3] and any tendency to set aside the sword in favour of peaceful pursuits was interrupted, from the 1290s, by the heavy manpower demands of the Anglo-Scottish and Anglo-French conflicts, and put into reverse in the mid-fourteenth century by the positive attractions of Edward III's large-scale war in France.[4]

At a time of intensified martial and administrative responsibilities, the gentry found also that its traditional status as a warrior class was being challenged. This was a consequence of those changes in military organization, in the composition of armies and in the conduct of war which some historians have seen as amounting to an English 'military revolution'.[5] The knightly warrior now found himself serving alongside archers, either as a combined mounted force on *chevauchée* or in dismounted tactical formations on the field of battle. Since the archer was essential to the successful operation of what soon became widely known as 'English' tactics (and given that the characteristic mark of chivalric status, the warhorse, was now usually a spectator from the baggage park), the genteel combatant can hardly have avoided the conclusion that his role as elite warrior had, to some extent, been undermined. What is more, he could well find himself fighting shoulder to shoulder with men-at-arms of decidedly sub-genteel origin, *parvenus* who had benefited from the profits of campaigning. No doubt many shared Sir Thomas Gray's evident distaste at the spectacle of hordes of 'young fellows who hitherto had been of small account' taking advantage of the opportunities offered by the French war: some 'became exceedingly rich ... many of them beginning as archers and then becoming knights, some captains'.[6] War was no longer a distinctive activity that allowed the minor aristocrat to stand apart from his social inferiors. That the gulf separating the armies which had fought at Falkirk and Bannockburn from those which carried the day at Crécy and Poitiers was profound can have been only too apparent to those few men whose careers in arms straddled the first half of the fourteenth century.

The nature of the gentry's response to these developments, to the expanding opportunities offered by administrative service in the shires and to the genteel warrior's diminished status in war, is as yet imperfectly understood. To determine the extent of the gentry's involvement in war with any precision – to establish what proportion of knights and esquires took up arms, and how regularly – would require a major research effort. That, hitherto, this subject has been left largely unexplored can probably be explained by reference to the documentary sources for military service, which are voluminous, yet, even when fully gathered and collated for a particular campaign, still frustratingly incomplete.[7] Consequently, while a great many of those who served as knights of the shire, sheriffs or peace commissioners can be identified without difficulty, such a degree of completeness cannot be achieved in the study of the thousands of individuals in the genteel military community. The prosopography of fourteenth-century military service is, then, a subject very much in its infancy (and always likely to remain something of a poor relation, overshadowed by wealthier siblings);[8] but since payrolls recording personnel numbers have survived for many of the royal armies of this period, we can at least trace the general pattern of the gentry's fluctuating commitment to the king's war without too much difficulty.[9] Perhaps the most striking development in this respect was the temporary 'remilitarization' of the traditional warrior class in the middle of the fourteenth century, stimulated, it would seem, by a combination of factors: the possibilities offered by paid, contractual service; government pressure through an experimental military assessment based on landed wealth; encouragement of chivalric *esprit de corps*, most notably by the adoption of the soldier martyr St George as patron of the Order of the Garter;[10] and the extraordinary military successes of the French war. For the gentry, a social group consisting of about 9000–10,000 families,[11] the recruitment peaks were the siege of Calais (1346–7), where there were perhaps 4000 English men-at-arms, the Reims campaign of 1359–60, which involved well over 3000, and Richard II's Scottish expedition of 1385, in which perhaps as many as 4500 men-at-arms served. So much can be established from the pay records. Although there remains the problem of *identifying* the men behind these numerical totals, the payroll data do at least suggest an enduring commitment to the martial calling among the English gentry, despite the pressures and challenges they faced during this period.

Of the sources that can illuminate both the martial ethos of the later medieval English aristocracy and the military role that they performed – both *mentalité* and actual service – the records of the Court of Chivalry, the court of the Constable of England and the Earl Marshal, occupy a place of particular importance. Reflecting the breadth of the Court's jurisdiction in affairs relating to 'deeds of arms and of war',[12] the surviving records embrace such diverse matters as ransom disputes, appeals of treason and safe conducts;[13] but perhaps the most familiar records of this court are those arising from disputes between aristocratic families over the right to particular armorial bearings. These disputes were pursued with the utmost vigour and determination because armorial bearings were at the heart of an aristocrat's sense of identity, at once marks of social status and symbols of family honour. As Richard, Lord Scrope put it in 1391, 'the highest and most sovereign things a knight ought to guard in defence of his estate are his troth and his arms'.[14]

The bulk of the surviving records of the armorial disputes before the Court of Chivalry consists of the depositions of witnesses selected by the protagonists to give evidence concerning possession of the contested arms. Naturally enough, a large proportion of the evidence focuses on occasions when the plaintiff and defendant, or members of their families, had been seen on active service bearing the arms in question. We learn a good deal, therefore, about the military service performed by the contestants in these disputes and their kinsmen, but also much about the martial experience of the witnesses themselves. Indeed, it is this revealing autobiographical material that is of primary interest to the historian of military service, for many of the witnesses are otherwise little known to history, faceless men who acquire a degree of identity through their testimony.

Armorial disputes before the Court of Chivalry were fairly common during the mid- to late fourteenth century, probably because the mobilization of contract armies brought together, from all over England, an armigerous community whose ranks were now swelled by the inclusion of esquires. However, extensive records have survived for only three cases.[15] The most celebrated is that between the Yorkshireman, Richard, Lord Scrope of Bolton and Sir Robert Grosvenor of Cheshire over the right to the arms *azure a bend or*. The extensive records of this case, published *in extenso* in the 1830s,[16] have proved a rich source of information on the social networks that bound together magnate affinities and regional military communities, and a revealing guide to the the nuances of four-teenth-century chivalric society.[17] As for the other two collections of records, that concerned with the case between Reginald, Lord Grey of Ruthyn and Sir Edward Hastings, dating from the first decade of the fifteenth century, has recently been analysed in an article by Maurice Keen.[18]

This chapter focuses primarily on the third collection, documenting the 'cause of arms' between John, Lord Lovel and Thomas, Lord Morley,[19] materials which hitherto have escaped systematic study. The dispute arose when both men bore the arms *argent a lion rampant sable crowned and armed or* during the Scottish campaign of 1385. Lovel claimed these arms by descent from the Burnell family through his grandmother,[20] while Morley sought to demonstrate that they had long been the possession of his family in unbroken succession. Lovel's bid may have been connected as much with the larger objective of securing the Burnell-Haudlo estates as with the upholding of his family's honour.[21] So, although the evidence does not appear to support Morley's cause unequivocally,[22] it was prob-ably a fair result that he was allowed to retain the arms which his grandfather and father had borne in war with such distinction, and which he himself was to bear again when, in the presence of John, Lord Lovel, he served in Richard II's Irish expedition of 1399.[23]

The neglect by modern historians of the depositions from the Lovel–Morley case is perhaps a little surprising since their attractions are considerable. Dating from the mid-1380s, they are contemporaneous with the corresponding records of the Scrope–Grosvenor case, thus allowing comparisons to be drawn. Lovel–Morley is admittedly the less extensive of the two collections and perhaps less rich in colourful campaigning stories, but it is certainly not overshadowed by Scrope–Grosvenor. Nor, in the surviving depositions, is there much duplicated material: only nine men, all of them knights, gave evidence in both cases.[24] Moreover, as a group, the Lovel–Morley deponents offer an impression of the genteel military community which, in some important respects, is refreshingly different from that provided by the witnesses in the Scrope–Grosvenor case. In the latter cause of arms, we find, on the one hand, the mobilization of the military community of Cheshire behind Grosvenor's claim and, on the other, the weighty support of John of Gaunt's extended military affinity for Scrope.[25] Under the influence of the lordship of Edward the Black Prince, Cheshire society had become highly militarized, with a particular focus on the war in Aquitaine. Gaunt's retainers were, as Simon Walker has recently reminded us, tied to their lord by an 'emphatically military commitment'.[26] Neither could be regarded as representative subsets of the wider military community of England. The Lovel–Morley witnesses appear to offer a more subtle picture of the martial experience of the English gentry. Morley, whose family was rooted in Norfolk,[27] drew his supporters, in the main, from East Anglia and neighbouring areas. Lovel's estates were more scattered, but many of his supporters were drawn from the counties around his principal power bases in Oxfordshire and Wiltshire.[28] These regions were not noted for exceptional military commitment: Norfolk is a far cry from Cheshire.[29] Neither Morley nor Lovel was close to John of Gaunt and few of their supporters were men of the front rank. Indeed, one of the attractions of the Lovel–Morley records is that they carry us into the world of relatively obscure genteel combatants. If it would be misleading to present them as a more *representative* sample of the military community at large, these men certainly possess characteristics sufficiently distinctive to warrant separate analysis.

The surviving records of the Lovel–Morley case consist of two rolls which are now to be found at the Public Record Office, London. These are not the original documents of the Court of Chivalry's registrar but contemporary transcripts from his registers, drawn up after the case went to appeal to the king in Chancery.[30] The rolls are largely filled with the depositions of witnesses, but they also contain the questions that were put to each of the deponents and miscellaneous details concerning the personalia and proceedings of the peripatetic court. The roll focusing on Morley's case provides information about sittings from Thursday 13 April 1386 until Saturday 27 April 1387. The court assembled on 46 days in almost as many different locations, from the main centres in Norwich, Westminster and London, to out of the way manors, religious houses and parish churches in Norfolk, Suffolk and Essex. The itinerary documented on the roll concerned with Lovel's case spans a much shorter period, little more than a month from late March to the end of April 1386. Once again, the locations range from religious institutions, like the Benedictine abbey at Malmesbury and the priory of the Austin friars, Oxford, to parish churches and 'la sale de la manoir' of Sir John de Ipre at 'Poole' in Berkshire. Neither of the rolls has been preserved in its entirety. It would appear that Lovel's roll has lost a great deal of material, since the surviving portion begins with deposition number 157.[31] Morley's roll is also incomplete: apart from a gap in the proceedings from mid-April to mid-August 1386, some of the witnesses named in the court's itinerary do not appear among the surviving depositions.[32]

Taking the two rolls together, we have a total of 239 depositions. Of these, 177 are on the Morley roll (including three which are recoverable only from an abbreviated summary) and since 17 men gave evidence on two separate occasions, we have the testimony of 160 individuals. Fifty-eight were churchmen, a significantly larger proportion than we find on the rolls of the Scrope–Grosvenor case.[33] Most of the rest were knights or esquires, but with the earl of Salisbury at one end of the social spectrum and 11 men of lesser gentry status, who called themselves 'gentlemen' or men 'of gentle blood', at the other. Turning to the 52 laymen whose evidence in support of Lovel's cause has survived, as a group they have a couple of striking characteristics: first, that they include only ten knights (a point to which we will return); and, second, that they were predominantly old men, only nine declaring themselves to be under 60. The ages of the lay witnesses in the Lovel–Morley case ranged from 19 to 96, but while Morley supporters were, on average, a little over 50 years of age, the mean age of those supporting Lovel was over 65.[34] This contrasts sharply with the laymen who spoke in support of Sir Robert Grosvenor's cause – they were aged about 40 on average – but the advanced years of so many of the Lovel–Morley witnesses is easy enough to explain. With the outcome of the dispute depending to some extent on the terms of the Court of Chivalry's judgment in the Burnell–Morley case during the siege of Calais (1346–7), both Lovel and Morley needed as many men as they could find who could recall the events of 40 years earlier.

The depositions, in the form that we have them, are a very mixed bag. Some are bland and perfunctory; others are scrupulously precise or, breaking free from stereotyped responses to the prescribed questions of the court, offer distinctive, colourful evidence. Some of the most detailed depositions focus on heraldic evidence located away from the battlefield: arms, identified as being those of the Morley, Burnell or Lovel families, displayed in window glass, on escutcheons, embroidered capes and altarcloths, much of it preserved in parish churches or religious houses.[35] Well might Peter Coss observe that 'English churches seem to have been literally festooned with armorial glass and depictions of donors';[36] and yet heraldic display was, if anything, an even more pervasive presence in aristocratic residences. William Wollaston remembered the contested arms being used 'en lytes, tapitz, bankers, sales, vessealx et autres utensyles' in the home of Lovel's grandparents.[37]

On occasion, these 'heraldic' depositions take the form of detailed word pictures, mingling meticulous descriptions of images in paint or incised brass with comments on their social and genealogical context.[38] Here we see family alliances and the social solidarity of regional genteel communities made tangible in armorial display.[39] Such evidence as this might seem far away indeed from the noise and confusion of the battlefield, but often enough there can be found in it vivid illustration of the pervasiveness of the martial ethos in aristocratic culture. Take, for example, the *petite chivaleret* – the little knightly effigy – in Reydon church, marking the burial of Robert Morley's heart, brought back from Prussia by his companions in arms;[40] or the banners set up in several churches by Thomas Bolyngton to commemorate Robert, Lord Morley following his death during the Reims campaign;[41] or Sir William Morley's *cote armoure* given to the parish church of Somerton.[42]

Heraldic display, moreover, was an essential ingredient of that most martial of pastimes, the tournament. Indeed, Sir Gervase Clifton, a deponent in the Scrope–Grosvenor case, considered tournaments to be 'schools of arms'.[43] Nine of the Lovel–Morley witnesses, including three clergymen,[44] comment on the involvement of the Morleys in such colourful events. Their memories of tourneying and jousting in Bungay, Bury St Edmunds, Dartford, Dunstaple, Norwich and Thetford serve to remind us just how commonplace and widespread these events were,[45] though 'commonplace' would hardly be an apt description of William de Pembridge's vivid recollection of the famous Smithfield tournament of June 1343, when Robert, Lord Morley competed dressed as the Pope, accompanied by 12 cardinals.[46]

Many of the lay witnesses had been selected because their practical campaigning experience enabled them to give first-hand evidence on occasions when the contested arms had been borne on active service; and a large proportion of them had been present at, or were at least aware of, the Burnell–Morley 'cause of arms' during the siege of Calais. But the witnesses' remarks on these matters also serve to bring a spotlight to bear, if fleetingly, on their own martial careers. How far can these fragments of autobiographical detail, if considered *en masse*, contribute to our understanding of the extent and depth of the gentry's involvement in war in the mid- to late fourteenth century? The weight of evidence provided by the Court of Chivalry records is admittedly not that great. Although there are over 500 surviving depositions from laymen in the records of the two armorial cases of the mid-1380s,[47] many are silent about war, unspecific about service performed or, when the deponents were young men, relatively insubstantial. Looking at the Lovel–Morley records in particular, it is important to recognize from the outset that the depositions in support of Lovel's cause offer only very limited evidence of military service. In spite of the fact that 48 of the 52 lay witnesses were clearly men with long military careers behind them – none claiming less than 40 years in arms – they reveal disappointingly little about their campaigning experience, except (as was required by their support of the Lovel cause) their involvement in the Crécy-Calais campaign. But even here, while nearly all spoke about the siege of Calais, only five mentioned the preceeding *graunde chivauche* from La Hougue to Crécy.[48]

Turning to the 111 lay depositions in support of Morley's cause, we find a very different corpus of information. Of these, about 30 are either focused exclusively on heraldry in churches and other non-military matters,[49] or else imprecise in their treatment of military service.[50] Twenty-four men mentioned only one expedition specifically. This leaves 56 witnesses who claimed two or more discrete spells of service, 17 with four or more, and over 30[51] with declared careers spanning 20 years or longer; and these are certainly minimum figures, since, as we shall see, the Court of Chivalry did not demand complete life stories from those testifying before it.

What contribution can these data make to the compilation of nominal rolls for individual royal armies? There are some unexpected bonuses: two of Lovel's witnesses had been armed since the battle of Bannockburn, over 70 years earlier.[52] But for the early decades of Edward III's reign the depositions rarely yield more than a handful of names for any particular expedition. For example, only three of the Morley deponents claimed to have taken part in the expedition to Brittany in 1342–3, whereas a scan of the Chancery rolls yields 722 recipients of letters of protection for this campaign.[53] No fewer than 23 witnesses proudly remembered the triumph at Crécy, and if we add the deponents from the Scrope–Grosvenor case this figure rises to 38;[54] but, once again, other nominal records offer the names of hundreds of Crécy veterans.[55]

Notwithstanding the relatively small yield from the depositions, the quality of the information is often high. Some men throw light on minor military enterprises which otherwise have left little trace in the sources. Thomas Rose, a man whose service in arms displays a striking nautical bent, remembered a raid on the Normandy coast in 1339 in which five towns were burnt.[56] Where major expeditions are concerned, the deposi- tions often reveal the identities of participants who go unmentioned in the more conventional military records. For example, none of the five old men who recalled the battle of Halidon Hill in 1333 has a letter of protection on the Scottish roll of that year.[57] In this particular instance, over 50 years had elapsed since the dramatic events near Berwick; but there would seem, on balance, to be little reason to doubt the reliability of the basic factual information in these depositions. Although the regular appearance of stock phrases might suggest that 'coaching' had taken place, it should be remembered that the depositions were essentially responses to a pre- scribed list of questions, and that the court registrar may well have sought to simplify what must have been a demanding secretarial task by employ- ing simple, shorthand phrases whenever possible. That being said, the depositions do contain a great deal of distinctive detail, clearly based upon personal experience. Moreover, the testimony was delivered under oath and, often, in the presence of other well-informed retired soldiers. A few of the witnesses admitted to family or retaining ties with either Lovel or Morley,[58] and some made reference to failing memories,[59] but it is doubtful whether many lied.

What we have in these depositions, therefore, is a source of informa- tion on military service which, although not voluminous, is both reliable and rich in high-grade material. Although the Lovel witnesses reveal comparatively little about their military careers, some of them do offer nice touches of detail. Sir Maurice Bruyn recalled how, on the point of death during the Reims campaign, Robert, Lord Morley ordered that the disputed arms should be returned '*sanz delay*' to Lord Burnell.[60] Sir Thomas Blount told how he had missed the adjudication in the Burnell–Morley case during the siege of Calais, because, having being wounded in the leg by a *forcelet* near Thérouanne, he was obliged to rest in his tent.[61] Among the host of reminiscences about the Burnell–Morley case – the conflicting stories and the details concerning who was, or was not, at the judgment in St Peters church outside Calais – are to be found some genuine insights into court procedure.[62] Edmund Seint Omer, a Morley supporter, recalled how he had been present at an examination of witnesses at Sir Hugh Hastings' manor of Elsing in Norfolk, and that their depositions, with their seals attached, had been taken to the king in the siege camp outside Calais.[63] According to William Kyng, the judgment in the crowded church had been announced by Henry of Lancaster himself '*en Engleis*'.[64]

As a group, Morley's witnesses reveal a good deal more about their military experience than their counterparts on the Lovel roll. Repeatedly we find that a window is opened on to a career on which the conventional military records cast little or no light. Some men, like John Raven *esquier* – a veteran of Sluys, Crécy, the sea-battle off Winchelsea and the Reims campaign – would be wholly unknown to history were it not for their depositions in support of the Morley cause.[65] Even when a witness is a well-known figure of his time, we often find that his testimony tells us something new about his earliest experiences of war.[66] From the historian's point of view, the ideal witness stated clearly when he first took up arms and (if appropriate) when he finally hung up his sword. Although only four of Morley's witnesses specified the number of years since they had first been armed,[67] the majority of those supporting Lovel (and, indeed, many of those involved in the Scrope–Grosvenor case) did provide this information. Even when the precise start and finish of a martial career are not made clear, a deposition will often, nevertheless, offer a skeletal profile of the deponent's life in arms. Such evidence, coming from the mouth of the man himself, is to be particularly prized,[68] since it makes the task of nominal record linkage, that most demanding aspect of prosopographical research, a good deal easier. With a reliable chronological framework of a man's military career already established by his deposition, it is altogether more straightforward to assign to him further fragments of information as they become available.

The Court of Chivalry depositions do not provide complete career profiles and we should not expect them to do so, since the witnesses were not asked to tell the whole story of their lives in arms. Rather, they were requested to comment on specific topics: a particular event, such as the Burnell–Morley armorial dispute, or those expeditions in which the parties to the current dispute, or their kinsmen, had been seen armed. It is clear that many of the witnesses duly confined themselves to such directly relevant matters. A strictly minimalist approach is particularly evident with Lovel's supporters. Although obviously men of military experience, they were not required to state *'en quelx voiages'* the Lovels had seen service, since, as some of the Morley witnesses were only too keen to point out, this service had not been performed with the contested arms.[69]

The Morley witnesses were given a looser rein; indeed, the third of the questions put to them actually invited more general comments on their own careers. But detailed responses to this question are to be found only in some of the earliest depositions;[70] and most witnesses focused on those campaigns when a Morley, bearing the disputed arms, entire or differenced, was present. This probably explains why William de Thweyt *esquier* furnished an impressive list of six expeditions, but failed to mention the service which he is known to have performed in three other theatres of war.[71] The selectivity of witnesses' remarks can be seen particularly clearly with those nine men for whom depositions survive from both the Lovel–Morley and Scrope–Grosvenor cases. Both Sir John de Brewes and Sir John Lakyngheth claimed to have seen a Scrope at Mauron in 1352, but saw no reason to mention this most memorable, hard-fought battle in their testimony in support of Thomas, Lord Morley.[72]

One consequence of this selectivity is that the overall pattern of military experience revealed by the Lovel–Morley depositions has a decidedly distorted shape. Twenty men recalled seeing Robert, Lord Morley at the sea-battle off Winchelsea in 1350 and as many as 15 witnessed him leading the attack at Sluys ten years earlier. By contrast, only one man mentioned either the confrontation at Buironfosse in 1339 or the battle of Auberoche in 1345, the reason apparently being that there had not been a Morley at either notable event. Similarly, while 27 men said that they had seen Sir William Morley serving in John of Gaunt's army in 1369, only one man bothered to mention Gaunt's Great *Chevauchée* across France in 1373. But the bias towards certain events has not served altogether to distort the general picture of aristocratic military service emerging from the Lovel–Morley rolls, since two of the events which were central to this armorial dispute – the clash between Burnell and Morley at the siege of Calais and Robert, Lord Morley's death in 1360 – occurred during expeditions which witnessed exceptional turnouts of English knights and esquires. Forty-one of Morley's witnesses, half of his 'military' supporters, had fought on Edward III's last great expedition to France in 1359–60, while no fewer than 76 of the men giving evidence in the Lovel–Morley dispute revealed that they had taken part in the investment of Calais 40 years earlier.[73]

Even allowing for the limitations of the Lovel–Morley depositions, the evidence of over 130 witnesses, including two churchmen, who drew upon their own experience of war in their testimony nevertheless provides a distinctive and instructive body of data. As we have seen, the Morley witnesses include over 30 men who had served intermittently (often, no doubt, more regularly than their evidence reveals) in the king's armies for a period of at least 20 years.[74] A handful of them, indeed, had served for over 35 years. The Lovel roll rarely offers any indication of the length of active careers, but nearly all the men claiming military experience remembered the siege of Calais 40 years earlier. Since the testimony of long-serving veterans was particularly prized by the contesting parties in armorial disputes, we should perhaps be wary of assuming that 20 years of regular campaigning was necessarily the norm amongst the fourteenth-century country gentry. Nevertheless, such men as these may help to cast a little light on several of the most important issues relating to military service.

The Morley roll suggests that the royal armies which achieved the extraordinary English military successes of the mid-fourteenth century included a sizeable contingent of seasoned warriors, men who had accumulated a good deal of practical campaigning experience through repeated spells of service. For many of those testifying in the Court of Chivalry in the 1380s this practical experience of war had begun at the age of 14 or 15: over a dozen of the Lovel witnesses were 'first armed' before the age of 20.[75] When campaigning opportunities had presented themselves, as they often did during the mid-fourteenth century, men had served proper apprenticeships in arms. They had learned their profession in the field rather than from books,[76] and the accumulated tactical experience paid dividends on the battlefields of France. Thus, in the Morley depositions we see veterans of the Scottish wars following their king's ambitions as they were redirected towards the continent. The tactical continuity from Halidon Hill to Sluys and Crécy, which can easily be recognized at the highest levels, existed at the lowest in such men-at-arms as William de Thweyt and Henry de Hoo.[77] Standing back from the depositions, we can see how the personnel of an army brought with them overlapping accumulations of personal experience: alongside the Halidon Hill veterans at Crécy were greybeards like William Wollaston who could remember the débâcle at Bannockburn,[78] and much younger men like Hugh Coursoun de Carleton, who less than a year before had been involved in Henry of Lancaster's triumph at Auberoche.[79]

It is often argued that the driving force behind much of the regular military service by knights and esquires in the fourteenth century lay in the stipulations of indentures of retinue, that regular soldiers were often retainers.[80] To what extent is this borne out by the testimony of the Lovel–Morley witnesses in 1386–7? There are few direct references to retaining or ties of affinity;[81] but it is one of the most distinctive features of this collection of depositions that many of Morley's supporters (and some of Lovel's) name the captains with whom they had served,[82] and these data allow us to trace patterns of martial allegiance upon which can be based some tentative conclusions on the role of retaining in military recruitment. A wide range of captains are mentioned (as many as 15 different individuals for the Reims campaign, for example), from the king's principal lieutenants to minor company commanders who are not usually perceptible in the payrolls.

This attention to detail, particularly by Morley's witnesses, allows us to distinguish the restless, near-professional soldier from the man with more permanent ties of allegiance. In this respect the pattern of service displayed by knightly warriors appears to be somewhat different from that of esquires. The knights, although often lifetime acquaintances of the Morleys and in two cases related to them, rarely served under their banner: only three state explicitly that they had done so.[83] The knightly deponents who supported Morley's case in 1386–7 were much more likely to have campaigned with the earl of Suffolk or with other captains of comital status. Some displayed loyalty to a particular magnate captain, perhaps suggesting the existance of a formal retaining bond. Sir Robert Marny served regularly with the earl of Northampton from the 1330s until the siege of Calais and then switched to the service of Henry of Lancaster;[84] Sir Richard Sutton campaigned with Sir Bartholomew Burgherssh senior and then with his son; Sir William de Wingfield was regularly armed in the Prince of Wales' retinue.[85] But the Lovel–Morley depositions suggest that inconstancy was common and, perhaps, more usual: that many of the regularly serving knights avoided a permanent commitment to a single magnate, preferring to enlist in a series of different war retinues during their careers in arms. Changes were sometimes prompted by the death or retirement of captains, but as often, it seems, by restlessness, ambition and a willingness to fight in a variety of theatres of war. A good example is Sir Nicholas de Goushill's wide-ranging martial career, which lasted more than 35 years and which took him to Scotland, Ireland and all over France in the retinues of at least seven different captains.[86]

Taken as a group, the deponents who were esquires at the time of giving their testimony in 1386–7 present a slightly different pattern of service. No fewer than 17 of them had served at least once with one of the Morleys, and half a dozen of these men appear to have been regular soldiers under the Morley banner.[87] One of them, Oliver de Mendham, admitted that he was a feed servant of Thomas, Lord Morley, but the others, including Henry de Hoo, a man of *gentil sanc*, who had been accompanying Morleys to war since Halidon Hill, denied that they were bound by any formal retaining ties. Rather, it seems to have been informal ties, based perhaps upon friendship, perhaps upon the shared circumstances and interests of a genteel regional community, that brought men intermittently into the war retinues of the Morleys and, indeed, into the service of other captains with significant landed interests in East Anglia: most notably the earls of Suffolk and their Ufford kinsmen, the dukes of Lancaster, Henry of Grosmont and John of Gaunt, and baronial figures like Willoughby and Scales.[88] William de Erpyingham was one of several esquires who claimed in 1386–7 to have campaigned more than once under the Ufford banner.[89] But given the independence of the Norfolk gentry – an attitude based upon the prosperity of the county and the absence of a pre-eminent magnate – it should occasion no surprise to find regular soldiers, whether knights or esquires, being prepared to look much further afield when choosing a captain. Erpyingham was with the earl of Arundel at Crécy, while John Raven sketched a picture of martial experience gained in the service of captains who were not influential figures in East Anglia.[90] On the other hand, the career of William de Thweyt, a younger son of a minor Norfolk gentry family, was based very largely on service under three members of the Ufford family and Sir John de Norwich: service which carried him far away from his East Anglian roots to Scotland, Gascony, Brittany and northern France, and to positions of military responsibility in Ireland and on the south coast of England.[91]

Men like Erpyngham, Raven and Thweyt – men who fought regularly, but never became knights – formed the backbone of Edwardian armies, yet the military importance of esquires could hardly be said to be matched by their visibility in 'conventional' military records. It is not that army payrolls fail to indicate their numbers: at the start of the French war, 75–80 per cent of men-at-arms in royal armies were esquires, and by the last decades of the century this figure was typically over 90 per cent.[92] The problem lies with the nominal records for military service in the mid- to late fourteenth century, for these tend, by and large, to leave the ordinary men-at-arms in the shadows. With comparatively few army muster rolls surviving from this period, it is necessary to rely heavily on enrolled letters of protection for information on the gentry's military service. Protections tell us a great deal about knightly combatants – those with landed property requiring protection in the courts, the topmost levels in the genteel military community – but much less about the role of landless men-at-arms, thereby leaving the unwary prosopographer of military service with a distorted impression of the composition of royal armies.

Given this fundamentally limiting bias in our primary source of evidence, it is refreshing to find, as we do, in the Lovel–Morley depositions a record which offers far more than occasional glimpses of esquires, those otherwise shadowy men who were forming an increasingly large proportion of the genteel military community. Two-thirds of Morley's 102 lay witnesses were esquires or 'gentlemen',[93] while of the 52 laymen speaking for Lovel no fewer than 42 were men who had not received the accolade of knighthood. We will never know whether Lovel and Morley would have preferred larger numbers of knights among their witnesses;[94] but even if this were so, the prominence accorded to the testimony of esquires in the Lovel–Morley proceedings speaks for itself. It was not only that they had acquired the right to possess distinctive armorial bearings during the course of the fourteenth century, that they now occupied a place in the armigerous aristocracy,[95] but also that their knowledge and experience of war and its usages carried great weight. In the later fourteenth century, then, a man did not have to be a knight to be a respected member of the genteel military community. Indeed, as is shown by the evidence of ten deponents in support of Morley's cause, that community embraced *gentils hommes* as well: men like the venerable old soldiers Henry de Hoo, Philip Warenner and William de Sutton, men of *gentil sanc*.[96] They may not yet have been accepted within armigerous society,[97] but their knowledge and experience of war were certainly deemed worthy of note in armorial disputes.

Through the personal reminiscences of numerous individuals, the records of the Lovel–Morley case highlight the central role of esquires in the genteel military community. The payrolls might reveal the numerical significance of esquires, but nominal data are required if the numbers are to be brought to life. The Lovel–Morley depositions do this particularly well. By presenting skeletal career profiles, they minimize the difficulties posed by nominal record linkage; and what these profiles show more than anything is that behind the numerical totals of 'esquires' in the payrolls were not only young men serving their apprenticeships before becoming knights, but also a good many veterans: younger sons from knightly families and members of lesser or 'parish' gentry families who, despite much service, remained esquires throughout their careers in arms. In short, the active warrior aristocracy extended well down the social hierarchy, beyond the knightly community, to rest squarely in ranks of the lesser gentry.

To recognise that the lesser, or 'parish', gentry performed a crucial role, quantitatively and qualitatively, in the functioning of English royal armies represents a valuable corrective, for it has been usual for historians, following the impression given in many of the military records, to portray the higher levels of the aristocracy – 'the substantial, knightly families' and above – as the most heavily committed to war service. As one distinguished historian has put it recently: 'the higher one looks in the scales of the estate of gentility, the sharper the mark of its martial tradition'.[98] Perhaps, proportionately, there was indeed, among the relatively small number of comital, baronial and substantial knightly families, a higher level of military participation than among the thousands of lesser knightly and 'parish' gentry families. But there can be no doubt that this impression has been reinforced unduly by the bias towards the knightly combatant in many of the surviving military records; and we should be wary of assuming that the commitment to military service was significantly less marked at the lower levels of the lay landholding community.

The Lovel roll, for all its limitations, lends weight to this interpretation. While 42 (80 per cent) of the surviving depositions supporting Lovel were provided by men of sub-knightly status, only four of these men made no mention of a military career.[99] Turning to the depositions supporting Morley's cause, we find unequivocal evidence of the depth of military involvement among the lesser gentry of East Anglia. While ten of Morley's knightly witnesses had martial careers spanning 20 years or more, no fewer than 20 of the esquires testified to at least two decades of martial service; and a larger proportion of the esquires mentioned more than two discrete spells of service. Admittedly, most of the laymen who provided only 'non-military' evidence were of sub-knightly status, but of the 66 esquires and gentlemen supporting Morley only 17 made no reference to personal military service in their depositions. None sought to distance himself from the military calling as explicitly as some of the witnesses in the Grey v. Hastings case of 1408–10. Perhaps, as Maurice Keen has suggested, 'the seeds of that cooling of bellicose ardour, among gentlemen, that had become noticeable by the 1440s, had been sown a generation earlier'.[100] But there was no sign of this in the mid-1380s. Despite the challenges facing the gentry – adverse economic conditions,[101] the greater demands of shire administration and the diminished status of the genteel warrior – the last quarter of the fourteenth century does not witness a significant trend of demilitarization among the gentle-born. Decades of campaigning, requiring heavy, if intermittent, recruitment, and a decidedly more intensive phase of warfare after 1369, had focused the attention of the gentry on the wars in France and Scotland – wars in which esquires and other men of sub-knightly status played an important, if too rarely recognized, part.

Notes

1. A.L. Poole, *Obligations of Society in the Twelfth and Thirteenth Centuries* (Oxford, 1946), pp 53–6. Unless otherwise stated, all documents cited in the notes are in the custody of the Public Record Office, London.

2. J. Gillingham, 'Crisis or continuity? The structure of royal authority in England, 1369–1422', in R. Schneider, ed, *Das spätmittelalterliche Königtum im europäischen Vergleich* (Sigmaringen, 1987), pp 71–2.

3. P. Coss, *The Knight in Medieval England, 1000–1400* (Gloucester, 1993), chapters 4 and 5.

4. For a contrary view, see S. Walker, *The Lancastrian Affinity, 1369–1399* (Oxford, 1990), pp 45, 80; cf. N. Saul, *Knights and Esquires: The Gloucestershire Gentry in the Fourteenth Century* (Oxford, 1981), pp 52–3.

5. On the Edwardian military revolution, see A. Ayton, 'English armies in the fourteenth century', in A. Curry and M. Hughes, eds, *Arms, Armies and Fortifications in the Hundred Years War* (Woodbridge, 1994), pp 21–38.

6. *Scalacronica*, ed and trans. Sir H. Maxwell (Glasgow, 1907), pp 131, 134.

7. On the sources, see A. Ayton, *Knights and Warhorses. Military Service and the English Aristocracy under Edward III* (Woodbridge, 1994), chapter 5.

8. Cf. J.S. Roskell, L. Clark and C. Rawcliffe, eds, *The History of Parliament: the House of Commons, 1386–1421*, 4 vols (Stroud, 1993), which offers exhaustively researched biographies of well over 3000 men.

9. For a brief discussion, see Ayton, 'English armies in the fourteenth century', pp 27–31.

10. Edward III's establishment of the order might be regarded as the 'high-water mark' of 'chivalric knighthood' in England: cf. P. Coss, *The Knight in Medieval England, 1000–1400*, chapter 5.

11. C. Given-Wilson, *The English Nobility in the Late Middle Ages* (London, 1987), pp 69–72.

12. On the Court of Chivalry, see M. Keen, 'The jurisdiction and origins of the Constable's court', in J. Gillingham and J.C. Holt, eds, *War and Government in the Middle Ages* (Woodbridge, 1984), pp 159–69, which adds substantially to, and corrects in some respects, the treatment of the medieval period in G.D. Squibb, *The High Court of Chivalry: a Study of the Civil Law in England* (Oxford, 1959). My debt to Dr Keen's work will be apparent from these notes; I should also like to thank him for allowing me to consult his current 'work in progress' on the Court of Chivalry.

13. See, for example, A. Rogers, 'Hoton versus Shakell: a ransom case in the court of chivalry, 1390–5', *Nottingham Medieval Studies* 6 (1962), pp 74–

108; 7 (1963), pp 53–78; J.G. Bellamy, 'Sir John de Annesley and the Chandos inheritance', *Nottingham Medieval Studies* 10 (1966), pp 94–105; M. Jones, 'Roches contre Hawley: la cour anglaise de chevalerie et un cas de piraterie à Brest 1386–1402', *Mémoires de la société d'histoire et d'archéologie de Bretagne* 64 (1987), pp 53–64.

14 .   *CCR, 1389–92*, p 518.

15 .   Other 'causes of arms' have left no more than traces in the surviving records: e.g. Thomas Baude v. Nicholas de Singleton, *gules, three chevrons argent* (*CPR, 1391–96*, pp 332, 576; *CPR, 1396–99*, p 89); and Sir William de Aton's dispute with Sir Robert de Boynton over possession of *or, on a cross sable, five bull's heads caboshed*, which was settled in 1375 when both men agreed to accept the judgment of Henry, Lord Percy (A.S. Ellis, 'On the arms of de Aton', *Yorkshire Archaeological Journal* 12 (1893), pp 263–6).

16 .   N.H. Nicolas, ed, *The Scrope and Grosvenor Controversy*, 2 vols (London, 1832).

17 .   M. Keen, 'Chivalrous culture in fourteenth-century England', *Historical Studies* 10 (1976), pp 14–22; cf. B. Vale, 'The Scropes of Bolton and Masham, *c.* 1300–1450', unpublished DPhil thesis, University of York, 1987, pp 95–105. On Grosvenor's case and supporters, see R. Stewart–Brown, 'The Scrope and Grosvenor controversy, 1385–1391', *Transactions of the Historic Society of Lancashire and Cheshire* 89 (1938 for 1937), pp 1–22.

18 .   M. Keen, 'English military experience and the Court of Chivalry: the case of Grey v. Hastings', in P. Contamine, C. Giry-Deloison and M. Keen, eds, *Guerre et société en France, en Angleterre et en Bourgogne, XIVe–XVe siècle* (Lille, 1992), pp 123–42.

19 .   For the records of this case, see note 30 below. For Lovel's career, see *GEC*, VIII, pp 219–221; for Morley, see *GEC*, IX, pp 216–17 and C. Richmond, 'Thomas, Lord Morley (d. 1416) and the Morleys of Hingham', *Norfolk Archaeology* 38 (1984), pp 1–12. Morley was involved in a further Court of Chivalry case in 1399: see SP9/10, fos 3r–44v.

20 .   The sister and heir of Edward, Lord Burnell (d. 1315), Maud, had taken Lovel's grandfather, John, as her first husband (*GEC*, II, pp 434–5), but she had subsequently married Sir John de Haudlo and their son Nicholas (who assumed the name of Burnell) received the Burnell inheritance in Shropshire. This Nicholas died in early 1383 and it is quite likely that Lovel's bid to secure the Burnell arms was the first step in a plan to gain control of the Burnell–Haudlo lands that had passed to the heirs of his grandmother Maud's second marriage (see *CIPM*, XV, nos. 719–29). Lovel had some experience of the workings of the Court of Chivalry, having been appointed a commissioner of the court in May 1385: *CPR, 1381–85*, p 598.

21 .   Hildebrand Barre stressed that Lovel held land and rents in Somerset, Hampshire and Cheshire by descent from the marriage of Maud Burnell and John, Lord Lovel (d. 1314): PRO30/26/69, no. 227.

22 .   Much of the debate revolved around the outcome of an earlier dispute over these arms, during the siege of Calais in 1346–7, between Robert, Lord Morley and Nicholas de Burnell. Since there were apparently no extant records of the Burnell–Morley case, it was necessary in 1386–7 to rely upon

the memories of surviving eye-witnesses. According to Morley's deponents, Lord Robert had received the judgment in his favour without qualification; a couple of men added that Burnell was allowed to bear the arms with a difference: *a bordure azure* (C47/6/1, nos. 10, 96). Sir John de Breux claimed to have seen Burnell serving in '*divers lieux*' with *argent ove une lion rampaunt darme degonte dore* (C47/6/1, no. 102). Lovel's witnesses offered a quite different story. According to them, the king had '*prist la cause a ses maynz*' and ordered that the arms should be awarded to Lord Morley because of his distinguished military record, but only for the duration of his life. Thereafter they should revert to the Burnells. Several witnesses added that Morley had put pressure on the king: he vowed 'by goddesflash' that if the arms were judged not to be his, he would never fight in the king's war, or on crusade, again (PRO30/26/69, nos. 169, 186, 204). William Moreys and Hildebrand Barre claimed that Lord Robert was the first Morley to bear the disputed arms (PRO30/26/69, nos. 175, 227), but no one stated specifically that the Morleys had used the contested arms with a difference – a forked tail – during Edward II's reign, as is suggested by the Parliamentary Roll of Arms: *A Roll of Arms of the Reign of Edward the Second*, ed N.H. Nicolas (London, 1829), p 45; cf. p 8. By the 1330s the Morleys were bearing the arms without the forked tail: *Rolls of Arms of the Reigns of Henry III and Edward III*, ed N.H. Nicolas (London, 1829), p 7; Bodleian Library, Oxford, Ashmole MS 15A (Ashmolean Roll of Arms); see also F. Blomefield, *An Essay Towards a Topographical History of the County of Norfolk*, 2nd edn, 11 vols (London, 1805–10), II, p 439. The expert testimony of heralds was little used in the great armorial disputes of the 1380s.

23 . *CPR, 1396–99*, pp 525, 538, 545.

24 . All nine men were supporters of Scrope's cause; of these, eight also spoke in support of Morley's claim and one, Sir Maurice de Bruyn, backed Lovel's.

25 . On Grosvenor's supporters from Cheshire, see P. Morgan, *War and Society in Medieval Cheshire, 1277–1403* (Manchester, 1987), pp 128–30; M.J. Bennett, *Community, Class and Careerism: Cheshire and Lancashire Society in the Age of Sir Gawain and the Green Knight* (Cambridge, 1983), p 166.

26 . Walker, *The Lancastrian Affinity, p* 43.

27 . For the Morley lands, see *CIPM*, X, no. 634; XI, no. 365; XV, nos. 124–9; C138/29, no. 57. Morley served regularly on commissions in Norfolk during the 1380s: e.g. *CPR, 1381–85*, pp 254, 496, 589; *CPR, 1385–89*, pp 82, 85, 167, 173, 264, 545, 547.

28 . *CIPM*, XIX, nos. 404–17; for the holdings of Lovel's widow and sons in Wiltshire, Dorset and Devon in 1412, see K.B. McFarlane, *England in the Fifteenth Century* (London, 1981), p 262. Lovel was regularly appointed to commissions in Oxfordshire and Berkshire, and after 1393 built a new castle at Wardour in Wiltshire (licence to crenellate: *CPR, 1391–96*, p 261). The majority of the surviving depositions in support of Lovel suggest a connection with either Somerset-Dorset, Oxfordshire or neighbouring counties.

29 . On the character of the shire community of late-fourteenth-century Norfolk, a county lacking a pre-eminent magnate, see R. Virgoe, 'The crown and local government: East Anglia under Richard II', in F.R.H. Du Boulay and C.M.

Barron, eds, *The Reign of Richard II* (London, 1971), pp 218–41; R. Virgoe, 'The crown, magnates and local government in fifteenth-century East Anglia', in J.R.L. Highfield and R. Jeffs, eds, *The Crown and Local Communities in England and France in the Fifteenth Century* (Gloucester, 1981), pp 72–87; Walker, *The Lancastrian Affinity*, pp 182–209.

30 . C47/6/1 (a roll of materials relating to Morley's case, including depositions in support of his cause); PRO30/26/69 (a similar, incomplete roll concerning Lovel's case). I am grateful to Dr Maurice Keen for drawing my attention to the second of these rolls, a document presented to the Public Record Office in 1928. The lost portion of Lovel's roll may be the document which John Anstis owned and quoted brief extracts from: see A.R. Wagner, *Heralds and Heraldry in the Middle Ages*, 2nd edn (Oxford, 1956), pp 22–3, where Anstis' date of 1395 is accepted. For a seventeenth-century copy of the PRO documents, see College of Arms MS, *Processus in Curia Marescalli*.

31 . The first membrane contains four faded depositions, only partly legible; m. 2 begins with deposition no. 161. The sequence ends with no. 228, but contains a gap, probably due to clerical error, from 190 to 199 inclusive. For extracts from a selection of these depositions, including the faded ones at the head of the roll, see Blomefield, *An Essay Towards a Topographical History of the County of Norfolk*, II, pp 437–9.

32 . For example, 12 of those named as being witnesses on 16 August 1386 are not included among those with depositions.

33 . 31 per cent (75) of the Lovel–Morley depositions were made by churchmen, as compared with 7 per cent (31) of those on the Scrope–Grosvenor rolls.

34 . The witnesses were frequently imprecise about their ages, qualifying the number of years with '*et plus*', '*et outre*' or '*ou entour*'; moreover, it is likely that many of them were actually older than they claimed: cf. K.B. McFarlane, *Lancastrian Kings and Lollard Knights* (Oxford, 1972), p 161.

35 . For example, a chasuble, an amice and other vestments bearing the Burnell arms: evidence gathered on 27 April 1386 at the Austin friary, London (PRO30/26/69, nos. 218–20). Cf. similar evidence in support of Grosvenor's case, summarized in R. Stewart-Brown, 'The Scrope and Grosvenor controversy', pp 17–19.

36 . Coss, *The Knight in Medieval England*, p 89.

37 . PRO30/26/69, no. 186; cf. nos. 210, 223.

38 . For example, the painted images of the Burnells in the Austin friary, Oxford (PRO30/26/69, m. 7). Cf. from the records of the Grey v. Hastings case: A.R. Wagner, 'A fifteenth-century description of the brass of Sir Hugh Hastings at Elsing, Norfolk, *The Antiquaries Journal* 19 (1939), pp 421–8.

39 . For example, the *table*, on which were depicted the *ymages* of Philip, Lord Burnell and his wife, examined in the church of Stratfield Mortimer on 18 April 1386. Two witnesses described the history of the *table*, ending in its deposit in the chapel of Aldermarston manor: PRO30/26/69, nos. 216–17.

40 . C47/6/1, nos. 151–7.

41 . C47/6/1, nos. 158–64. Cf. the banner in Osney abbey, placed there by Sir Robert Fitz Elys in memory of Sir Philip Burnell: PRO30/26/69, nos. 214–15.

42 . C47/6/1, no. 82.

43 . Nicolas, ed, *The Scrope and Grosvenor Controversy*, I, 152.

44 . C47/6/1, nos. 2, 7, 14, 15, 19, 71–3, 92.

45 . Cf. J. Vale, *Edward III and Chivalry* (Woodbridge, 1982), appendix 12: 'Provisional list of the tournaments of Edward III, 1327–55'.

46 . C47/6/1, no. 7; cf. Adam Murimuth, *Continuatio chronicarum*, and Robert de Avesbury, *De gestis mirabilibus regis Edwardi tertii*, ed E.M. Thompson, Rolls Ser. (London, 1889), pp 146, 230–31.

47 . Five hundred and twenty-seven in all, including imperfect and abbreviated depositions.

48 . PRO30/26/69, nos. 167, 175, 176, 183, 186.

49 . Six men also provided a second 'military' deposition at another time, while three witnesses have left two separate 'non-military' depositions.

50 . E.g. Edmund Seint Omer's 30-year career in France, Scotland and '*autre lieus diverses*': C47/6/1, no. 103; see also nos. 28, 98.

51 . Thirty-three, if we include the earl of Salisbury and Edmund Seint Omer, whose testimony was imprecise.

52 . William de Wollaston, aged 96 *et plus*, and Reynaud Fyfide. aged 85 *et plus*; both claimed to have seen Edward, Lord Burnell at Bannockburn: PRO30/26/69, nos. 186, 210.

53 . C47/6/1, nos. 20, 27, 29; C76/17; C76/18; C61/54.

54 . Eighteen of the Crécy veterans supported Morley, five backed Lovel's claim. One man, Sir Richard de Sutton, gave evidence in both the Lovel–Morley and the Scrope–Grosvenor cases.

55 . See A. Ayton, 'The English army and the Normandy campaign of 1346', in D. Bates and A. Curry, eds, *England and Normandy in the Middle Ages* (London, 1994), pp 253–68.

56 . C47/6/1, no. 20; he appears to have misremembered the date: cf. J. Sumption, *The Hundred Years War: Trial by Battle* (London, 1990), p 266; *Chronicon Henrici Knighton*, ed J.R. Lumby, Rolls Ser., 2 vols (London, 1889–95), II, p 10.

57 . C47/6/1, nos. 10, 29, 92, 97 and 106; cf. C71/13. In the Scrope–Grosvenor case, the prior of Marton mentioned that his church possessed an embroidered coat of arms worn by Sir Alexander de Neville at this battle: Nicolas, ed, *The Scrope and Grosvenor Controversy*, I, pp 139–40.

58 . Related to Morley: C47/6/1, nos. 28, 30, 41; to Lovel: C47/6/1, no. 46; PRO30/26/69, no. 188.

59 . E.g. C47/6/1, nos. 28, 29, 97, 98; see note 34 above for doubts about the ages data.

60 . PRO30/26/69, no. 221. This was not how Morley's supporters remembered it: Henry de Hoo stated that Lord Robert's last wish was that his son, William – and not the Burnell heirs – should have his arms (C47/6/1, no. 10).

61 . PRO30/26/69, no. 176; the outcome of the dispute was reported to him by Sir Thomas West. Blount also mentioned that there had been '*plusours autres chalenges darmes*' during the Crécy campaign and that the king, presumably concerned about the disruption they were causing, had ordered them to stop. For similar evidence, cf. Robert Trolley's deposition (no. 183) and Wagner, *Heralds and Heraldry*, p 23.

62 . See, for example, PRO30/26/69, no. 160 (John Moulham). While most evidence about previous causes of arms concerns the Burnell–Morley case, John de Rothyng offered a tantalizing glimpse of a *grande controversye* involving Sir John de Morley (bearing the disputed arms with a label) that arose during the Black Prince's Iberian adventure of 1366–7: C47/6/1, no. 32; cf. no. 35.

63 . C47/6/1, no. 103.

64 . C47/6/1, no. 96. William Moreys suggested that Henry of Lancaster had spoken in favour of Burnell, while John Broyn recalled that the crush of people in the church had made it difficult to hear everything and that the judgment had subsequently been proclaimed by *un heraud nome Lancastre* (PRO30/26/69, nos. 167, 175).

65 . C47/6/1, no. 6.

66 . For example, Sir Guy de Brian recalled that he had been first armed at Stanhope Park in 1327: Nicolas, ed, *The Scrope and Grosvenor Controversy*, I, p 76.

67 . C47/6/1, nos. 59, 99, 101, 106.

68 . Cf. Henry Tilleman: C.T. Allmand and C.A.J. Armstrong, eds, *English Suits Before the Parlement of Paris, 1420–1436*, Camden Soc., 4th ser., 26 (London, 1982), p 104.

69 . E.g. C47/6/1, nos. 23, 24, 25, 26, 102. For the circumstances affecting the evidence given in another armorial dispute, see Keen, 'English military experience and the Court of Chivalry', pp 125 ff.

70 . E.g. C47/6/1, nos. 99 and 101.

71 . Gascony, 1337–9 (C61/49, m. 17); Brittany, 1342–3 (C76/18, m. 9); Ireland, 1344–6 (C260/57, m. 28). Cf. his deposition: C47/6/1, no. 92.

72 . Nicolas, ed, *The Scrope and Grosvenor Controversy*, I, pp 63, 208–9; C47/6/1, nos. 45, 102. Cf. Sir Maurice de Bruyn's contrasting depositions for Lovel (PRO30/26/69, no. 221) and Scrope (Nicolas, ed, *The Scrope and Grosvenor Controversy*, I, pp 161–2).

73 . Morley: 31; Lovel: 45. The Lovel depositions also mention, in addition to the constable and marshal, 33 men who were at the judgment in St Peter's church outside the walls of Calais. Only one of Lovel's supporters claimed involvement in the Reims campaign.

74 . There are fewer mentions of crusading than we find in the Scrope–Grosvenor case: C47/6/1/, nos. 102, 151. Cf. M. Keen, 'Chaucer's knight, the English aristocracy and the crusade', in V.J. Scattergood and J.W. Sherborne, eds, *English Court Culture in the Later Middle Ages* (London, 1983), pp 45–61.

75 . Cf. Keen, 'English military experience and the Court of Chivalry', pp 131–2; N. Orme, *From Childhood to Chivalry: the Education of the English Kings and Aristocracy, 1066–1530* (London, 1984), pp 190–91.

76 . Cf. Orme, *From Childhood to Chivalry*, pp 185–9, which discusses the influence of Vegetius' *Epitoma de re militari*; P. Contamine, *War in the Middle Ages* (London, 1985), pp 210–18.

77 . C47/6/1, nos. 10, 92.

78 . PRO30/26/69, no. 186.

79 . C47/6/1, no. 99.

80 .   E.g. Saul, *Knights and Esquires*, pp 53–4; Walker, *The Lancastrian Affinity*, pp 42–50.

81 .   Two deponents were *servants* of the Morleys; Sir John le Straunge was '*de l'alliance*' of Thomas, Lord Morley: C47/6/1, nos. 26, 46, 100.

82 .   Such information is rarely supplied in the Scrope–Grosvenor records.

83 .   C47/6/1, nos. 31, 40, 64. The depositions of four militarily active knights omit the names of captains (nos. 102, 104, 105, 106), and they may well have been serving for part of their careers under the Morley banner. For men related to the Morleys, see C47/6/1, nos. 28, 30.

84 .   C47/6/1, no. 27. Letters of protection confirm Marny's claim of regular service, first with Northampton and then with Lancaster: *Treaty Rolls, 1337–39*, ed J. Ferguson (London, 1972), nos. 291, 733; C76/15, m. 20; C76/17, m. 36; C76/33, m. 9; C76/34, mm. 5, 16, 18; C76/37, m. 3; C76/38, m. 16.

85 .   C47/6/1, nos. 8, 38.

86 .   C47/6/1, no. 29; Goushill's career, as presented in his deposition, can be filled out by reference to other records: see Ayton, *Knights and Warhorses*, p 236 and notes 189–91.

87 .   C47/6/1, nos. 5, 10, 11, 20, 26, 59.

88 .   On the principal landholders in late-fourteenth-century Norfolk, see Virgoe, 'The crown and local government: East Anglia under Richard II', pp 225–8; Walker, *The Lancastrian Affinity*, pp 183–6.

89 .   C47/6/1, nos. 13, 39, 42, 92.

90 .   C47/6/1, no. 6; cf. nos. 22, 44, 52.

91 .   See A. Ayton, 'William de Thweyt, esquire: deputy constable of Corfe Castle in the 1340s', *Notes and Queries for Somerset and Dorset* 32 (1989), pp 731–8. By 1386–7 Thweyt had known the Morleys for over 60 years, yet his service with William, Lord Morley in France in 1369 was the one and only time that he had campaigned under them.

92 .   Ayton, *Knights and Warhorses*, pp 228–9. The declining contribution of knights to royal armies was a reflection of a more general decline in the numbers of knights in society: from being as many as 1500 knights in 1300, there appear to have been no more than a few hundred by the 1430s.

93 .   Sixty-six esquires and 'gentlemen', 36 knights.

94 .   Three-quarters of the deponents supporting Richard, Lord Scrope's cause were knights, but he had the extended military affinity of John of Gaunt to draw upon.

95 .   Saul, *Knights and Esquires*, pp 20–5; D. Crouch, *The Image of Aristocracy in Britain, 1000–1300* (London, 1992), pp 235–6; Coss, *The Knight in Medieval England*, pp 127–31.

96 .   C47/6/1, nos. 5, 10, 11.

97 .   Coss, *The Knight in Medieval England*, p 133. On the emergence of the self-styled 'gentleman', see D.A.L. Morgan, 'The individual style of the English gentleman', in M. Jones, ed, *Gentry and Lesser Nobility in Late Medieval Europe* (Gloucester, 1986), pp 15–35.

98 .   M. Keen, *English Society in the Later Middle Ages* (Harmondsworth, 1990), pp 136; cf. M. Powicke, *Military Obligation in Medieval England* (Oxford, 1962), p 171, for a similar view.

99 . PRO30/26/69, nos. 201, 206, 207, 216; the second of these men, Thomas Fretewell, said that his father, Ralph, aged 106 at the time of his death, had seen Philip, Lord Burnell '*en un viage fait en Escoce*'.

100 . Keen, 'English military experience and the Court of Chivalry', p 135.

101 . A.R. Bridbury, 'The Black Death', *EcHR*, 2nd ser., 26 (1973), pp 577–92.

5. Town Defences in Medieval England and Wales

D.M. Palliser

'Town walls,' wrote Hilary Turner in introducing her pioneering study of the subject, 'are a neglected branch of military architecture.'[1] However, in the quarter-century since then the subject has been given much more attention, thanks not least to her example. Her gazetteer of towns has been amended and amplified in surveys by M.W. Barley and C.J. Bond, while the surviving walls of York have had a whole volume devoted to them.[2] Numerous town defences have been investigated architecturally and archaeologically, and major urban archaeology programmes have usually included the study of defences as a key element. Nor is it only the physical remains that have been studied: there have been welcome projects integrating the archaeology with analysis of the relevant documents, while the murage tax, which Turner was almost the first to study, has been analysed further by C. Allmand.[3] Given all this work, most of it helpfully accessible through the bibliographies and survey of J.R. Kenyon,[4] it is unnecessary to review the whole field here. It is now possible to begin to answer specific questions of motive and opportunity, of cost and constraint. In particular, there is the challenge recently put by Bond: 'The whole rationale of town defences is still imperfectly understood. Why were some towns provided with defences while others of similar size in similar situations were not?'[5]

There is a widespread and understandable tendency to assume that almost all towns of any importance were once walled. One standard textbook can note of the fifteenth century that 'even small towns had their walls, for the country was weakly policed'.[6] It is true that although few stone circuits survive more or less intact – York and Chester, Conway and Caernarvon – many others still retain gates, towers or substantial stretches of walling. Among the more impressive are Canterbury, Colchester, Denbigh, Exeter, Newcastle upon Tyne, Norwich, Southampton, Winchester and Yarmouth. Turner, who counted 108 English and Welsh towns which were once walled, has noted remains surviving at 84 of them. 'Few towns of importance,' she concludes, 'were without walls by the end of the fifteenth century.'[7] It is known from documentary evidence, for instance, that many town defences were demolished in the post-medieval period, often for 'improvements' or industrial expansion in the eighteenth and nineteenth centuries; even the walls of York were nearly demolished by the corporation. There are also continuing archaeological discoveries of defences, with no, or almost no, documentary record. Thus, for example, several points of the thirteenth-century defences of Saffron Walden have now been identified, one as recently as 1992.[8]

It is therefore scarcely surprising that 'one of the most significant achievements of the last few decades has been a steady increase in the number of towns where post-Roman defences have been recognized'. Barley increased Turner's total of 108 to 146 with 'defences of some kind' for the period 1066–1500, while Bond has counted 211 English and 55 Welsh towns with 'some sort of communal defences' in use at some time over the longer period 500–1600.[9] Nevertheless, these totals need to be kept in perspective. There were some 640 boroughs in medieval England alone, and more than a thousand other places with markets, many of which were towns rather than villages.[10] In other words, although no agreed total of medieval towns exists, those with defences were in the minority. Furthermore, Bond's relatively high figures depend, as he points out, on chronological and typological definitions. They include all recorded pre-Conquest communal defences of the type called *burh*, not all of them urban and not all of them fortified after 1066; while for the post-Conquest period they include towns with gates or earthen defences but no masonry walls.

There were broadly two periods of English urban defences. Between the eighth and twelfth centuries old Roman defences were reused, and new ones built, but the latter were almost all of earth and timber, although a few, including Hereford, employed stone even before the Conquest. From the thirteenth century onwards, however, new circuits wholly or partly in stone, with stone gates and mural towers, were built around the larger towns and some smaller towns. Occasionally after 1300 brick was employed instead of stone, notably at Kingston upon Hull, where the entire circuit was of brick from 1321. The walls might be completely new defences, as at Hull, or they might form a replacement for, or an addition to, an earlier circuit of earthen defences. In many instances a new stone circuit took in a larger area than the old earthworks, and in a few cases such as Bristol stone circuits were themselves enlarged as the town grew, although the continental model of successive concentric rings of stone walls was rare, probably because 'most stone walls were built between 1250 and 1350, at the time of maximum urban expansion'.[11] The following analysis concentrates on the period from the thirteenth century onwards, and the basic question posed is a reformulation of Bond's. Why were some towns provided with full circuits of stone (or brick) and some with earthworks, while others remained completely undefended?

It should be added that all such communal defences for townsfolk were distinct from the post-Conquest private defences called castles, which have been separately studied for towns by Drage.[12] The first urban castles were those constructed by William I to dominate the shire towns, and thereafter both kings and private lords built castles which could protect as well as overawe the townsmen. Where the town was walled, the defences were usually connected to the castle, which played a part in the defensive circuit, as at London and York; cases like Norwich, where the castle is sited in the middle of the intramural area, were always exceptional. Drage suggests that 'urban castles' should be properly used to describe those established within existing towns, while 'castle boroughs' might be used for the very different cases where the castle was the primary feature and the town came later.[13] The former category includes most royal castles in towns, while many seigneurial boroughs started with a fortress to which the lord added or encouraged an urban settlement outside the gate. In some cases lords built extensive defences which could enclose the townspeople as well as the castle garrison; towns like Castle Acre, Clare, Devizes, Pleshey and Trematon were settled in what were really outer baileys of castles. In most cases, the town developed outside the castle, sometimes with defences of its own linked to the castle, as at Ludlow or Richmond, but often with no walls at all. Beresford, who has analysed post-Conquest town plantations in full, finds that of 125 castle towns in England and Wales, 45 were walled in stone or brick, 18 had other defences, but half (62) were undefended except for the castle.[14]

Those places which never acquired stone walls were generally among the less important towns, but this was by no means invariable. Towns with only earthen banks and ditches included Beverley, Boston(?), Cambridge, Derby(?), Devizes, Ipswich, Lichfield, Salisbury, Taunton and Tonbridge, though some had gates if not walls. Leland noted of Beverley that 'the town is not walled', but that it possessed three 'fair gates of brick', one of which still survives.[15] Towns which apparently possessed no communal defences at all after the Norman Conquest included Aylesbury, Bedford, Buckingham, Ely, Hertford, Reading and Wells, while other significant towns which possessed bars or gates but no other defences included Banbury, Chesterfield and Tewkesbury. These examples, which are only a selection, include seven shire towns and four cathedral cities; while the vast majority of smaller towns were also completely undefended.

This patchy picture of urban fortification can be paralleled in Scotland, but it is in sharp contrast to Ireland, where Avril Thomas's recent gazetteer shows that all the larger towns, and about half of the middling and smaller ones, were walled in stone.[16] It contrasts also with most of continental western Europe. 'The image of the medieval town,' wrote P. Dollinger with particular reference to France, 'is for us inseparable from its stone *enceinte*, crenellated, flanked by towers, and pierced by massive gates'; while C. Meckseper can from a German perspective define a town as 'a fortified (*befestigten*) and permanently occupied place' with trading functions.[17] These generalizations could certainly not extend to England. Dr Brodt has recently compared the towns of Westphalia and East Anglia in the fourteenth century, and what strikes her especially is that most Westphalian towns were created by their lords as strongpoints, whereas 'one of the most striking phenomena of East Anglia ... is that of towns without walls'.[18]

The contrast might have been less sharp if some other regions had been compared to Westphalia, for walled towns were distributed very unequally. Although the great majority of important towns lay in the southeastern half of the country – east of a line joining York to Exeter – the largest concentration of walled towns was in Wales and the Welsh Marches. This understandably reflects the military situation, with intermittent but widespread border warfare, and the piecemeal conquest of Wales. Yet military determinism is not a sufficient explanation, for endemic warfare on the Scottish border from the 1290s to the 1550s did not produce similar results. It is true that Carlisle, Durham, Newcastle and York already had stone walls, and that between 1313 and 1321 Berwick, Hartlepool, Hull, Lancaster and Richmond also received murage grants.[19] Nevertheless, although the North was widely raided by the Scots – as far south as York in 1319 and Beverley in 1321 – 'towns like Kendal, Hexham, Darlington, Barnard Castle and Appleby seem never to have made the least attempt to acquire their own defences', while two others which did so, Alnwick and Warkworth, waited until the fifteenth century.[20]

From the 1290s to the 1450s another broad zone vulnerable to hostile military action was the south and east coasts. The French raided and sacked many ports, including Southampton in 1338, Rye in 1339 and 1376, Winchelsea in 1359 and 1380 and Plymouth and Dartmouth in 1377. As a result, not only did some of these towns strengthen their defences in response, but so did other ports which felt threatened – Exeter, Yarmouth and Lynn, for example. Furthermore, important towns situated near the coast also sought to improve their defences, or were ordered to do so by the king – Canterbury and Rochester, Colchester and Norwich, and even Gloucester and Bath. Significantly, Norwich, despite its size and importance, possessed no defences except ditches (and the royal castle) until the walls were begun in or shortly after 1297. 'It is certain that the major urban fortifications of East Anglia, those of Norwich and Great Yarmouth, were built in response to that [French] threat.'[21] In general, however, East Anglia, like the central and eastern Midlands, had few stone-walled towns. This rarity of serious defences in much of England was a source of comment and surprise to continental writers. Pierre Grégoire, for example, noted in the sixteenth century that 'nations which do not have walled and fortified cities are exposed to the plunder of foreigners, as is evident from England'.[22]

However, if only a minority of towns had stone circuits, they did include nearly all the very large and wealthy towns (that is, large and wealthy by medieval English standards, if not by the standards of Italy, Flanders or Germany). Taking the 20 largest and wealthiest towns as measured by the 1334 lay subsidy and by the 1377 poll tax, which yields a combined list of 23 towns,[23] 18 out of 23 enjoyed, or were currently building, full stone circuits. Admittedly Norwich had, as we have seen, begun its circuit only in the 1290s, while Coventry, which was rapidly rising into the leading rank of English towns, started its stone walls as late as the 1350s. In contrast, many middling and smaller towns had no defences at all, or earthworks at best.

Size and wealth, however, like geographical position, were not everything: there was also the matter of lordship. At least half the English boroughs were not royal but seigneurial, and 'broadly, it was the privileged royal borough that was defended, and the seigneurial borough that frequently went unwalled'.[24] Admittedly, royal boroughs were usually larger and more important than seigneurial towns, so that the distinction overlaps with that of size: but that is not the whole story. Of the 23 largest and wealthiest towns in the fourteenth century, five had no stone walls, and only one of those was royal – Ipswich, which seems to have intended stone walls but never built them, though it did build its West Gate in stone.[25] The other four were all seigneurial; Boston's lord was the earl of Richmond, Bury St Edmunds was subject to its abbey, and Salisbury to its bishop, while Beverley's lord was the archbishop of York. Ecclesiastical lords may have been as unwilling to permit their urban subjects communal walls as they were to allow them communal self-government. On Turner's figures, 'of the forty-six towns owned by the Church only eight were walled',[26] and those eight included towns with only earthwork defences (Beverley and Salisbury) as well as those with stone walls. It is noteworthy that when Edward III temporarily freed Wells from the power of its bishop in 1341, one of the privileges he granted the burgesses was to let them have a stone wall, crenellated and surrounded by a moat.'[27] (This was never built, presumably because once the bishop regained power he would not permit it, though in 1340 he had himself obtained a royal licence to build a defensive wall round the cathedral close 'for the security and quiet of the canons and ministers resident there'.)[28] It is probably also no coincidence that Coventry, long divided between seigneurial lordships, began its stone circuit in, or just after, the year it achieved full autonomy under the Tripartite Indenture of 1355, with a victory by the corporation and the queen mother over Coventry priory.[29]

Underlying the varied patterns of urban defences were considerations of cost. Constructing earth-and-timber defences around an entire town was costly enough in time and labour, if not in materials; the more durable and formidable stone or brick circuits needed expensive materials and skilled labour on a large scale. Permission, or requirement, to build defences was usually granted or imposed by the crown, partly because shire towns and other major centres were usually in royal hands, but over and above that because power was strongly centralized from late Saxon times, and royal permission was often sought even for defending seigneurial towns. It was also linked with the matter of resources; most towns could not afford to construct serious defences, and only the king could authorize or command special resources for that purpose.

Kings very early developed and maintained a close interest in fortified towns as a vital element in national defence, to be erected and maintained by the population as a whole. The original method was to require all the landholders of a district or shire to find the labour to construct, repair and man them. The three 'common burdens' (*trimoda necessitas*) of army service, bridgework and boroughwork were normally specified as incumbent on all estates granted by royal charter, certainly from the later eighth century in Mercia and Kent, and from the mid-ninth century in Wessex; and the kings of united England in the tenth and eleventh centuries reiterated this threefold obligation in charters and lawcodes.[30] Many Domesday entries for shire towns concern such common obligations, entries which gave rise to F.W. Maitland's 'garrison theory', a theory which this is not the place to pursue, but which may yet prove to be nearer the truth than some of its critics have allowed.[31] Records are scanty for the twelfth century, but enough survive to suggest that the system of 'boroughwork' remained normal. The abbot of Bury St Edmunds (1121–38) assumed that the moat or rampart (*fossatum*) surrounding the town would be constructed or maintained jointly by the abbey's knights, sokemen and burgesses, while in 1204 King John ordered defences to be dug round Ipswich 'with the aid of the whole neighbourhood and of the county of Cambridge'.[32] In 1227 repair of the walls of Oxford was still being demanded from the 'mural mansions' in the town, which represent houses being kept up by the great landholders of Oxfordshire for that purpose.[33]

In the late twelfth and early thirteenth centuries, the crown began to replace such common obligations on the labour of the district by the levying of tolls to be applied to the upkeep of the defences, the earliest known case being a royal charter to Hereford in 1189.[34] Within a generation this was systematized into a tax called murage, a special tax on specific goods authorized by the king for a particular town for a specified period of time, the proceeds to be applied solely to the town's defences. The crown's permission was essential, for, as Maitland pointed out, townsmen had no general right to levy local taxes. 'If the burgesses wished to repair their walls, their bridges, their streets, they had to apply to the king for a grant of murage, pontage or pavage; and such grants were not to be had as matters of course.'[35] The history of the murage tax has now been studied by Turner and Allmand,[36] although more remains to be done in municipal archives. Between 1216 and 1220 Henry III authorized such grants to three Marcher towns, Hereford (again), Bridgnorth and Shrewsbury;[37] they quickly became the usual means of levying money for town walls, and remained so for the rest of the Middle Ages, though the old system did not disappear at once. In thirteenth-century Lincolnshire 'murage', in the sense of a tax for labour, was levied on the rural wapentakes, and as late as 1275 each knight's fee of the barony of Lewes paid £5 towards walling the town.[38]

The shift from 'boroughwork' to murage requires explanation. Partly, perhaps, the old levy of manpower needed replacing by money, in much the same way that military service was being commuted, and especially once skilled masons were needed rather than semi-skilled diggers. This could, however, have happened without disturbing the principle of county assessment, as Lincolnshire and Lewes demonstrate. The shift from county assessment to urban tolls may reflect rather the growth of commerce and of borough autonomy, persuading the king that the fairest system would be one operated by the townsmen themselves and levied on those trading there. The construction of walls was perceived by the crown and the towns as beneficial not only to the townspeople but to their hinterland and, indeed, the realm as a whole. The 1218 murage grant to Shrewsbury stated that the new wall was for the greater security both of the burgesses and for the districts around, while in 1253 the citizens of Norwich petitioned the king for the right to build a wall 'to the benefit of the king and for the greater security of the town'.[39] This was just the period when the larger royal towns were being granted more powers of self-government, and they probably wished to have a tax under their own control.

Although murage continued to be levied well beyond 1500, its most useful period was over by about 1350. It proved complex to collect, as at Shrewsbury where the collectors could change weekly, and embezzlement was a common problem.[40] Murage grants became longer and incorporated very specific lists of goods and rates.[41] Furthermore, merchants were as anxious to acquire exemption from murage in other towns as they were to levy it in their own. In 1233 the men of Carmarthen were exempted from paying murage at Bristol, the first of many such concessions by the crown to townsmen, foreign merchants, churchmen and others. In other cases towns negotiated reciprocal agreements directly, as when in 1260 York and Lincoln agreed not to levy tolls (including murage, presumably) on each other's citizens.[42]

By the mid-fourteenth century murage grants were inadequate for their purpose, and thereafter with the crown's permission sources of revenue for defences became more varied, including customs duties, fee-farms and the profits from judicial fines, as well as property taxes on the burgesses themselves.[43] Richard II, for instance, was concerned that the walls of Coventry had been begun but were being left unfinished. To encourage the work, he ordered in 1385 that all merchants and inhabitants were to be assessed according to their means, while in 1391 he granted £24 a year for five years from all crown fees on woollen cloth sold in Warwickshire, Shropshire and Leicestershire.[44] Nevertheless, public resources were often insufficient, and by the fifteenth century it was becoming regarded as a meritorious work of charity to give money for the repair of town defences. In 1487 the mayor of York personally paid for 60 yards of wall, and in the same year John Colins left £10 in his will for the building and repair of the walls.[45]

In short, it was a matter not only of whether king or townsmen wanted defences, but of how they were to be paid for. Writing of some stone circuits never completed, and of others on which workmanship progressively deteriorated, Professor Platt notes that 'it was not so much that the burgesses lost their enthusiasm for walls, as that they could not generally afford them'.[46] Salisbury, for instance, despite its size and wealth in the fourteenth century, 'showed some reluctance to provide itself with adequate fortifications'. The reluctant bishop, under threat of war in 1367, authorized a stone wall, four stone gates, and a ditch eight perches wide. The task proved too heavy, the citizens arguing that the great circumference made it impossible without compulsory labour or taxes, even though a licence was obtained to impress workmen and labourers. In 1387 the citizens petitioned parliament to order that all with tenements and rents in Salisbury should contribute to the cost of the 'great ditches', and the idea of a stone wall was apparently abandoned, while apparently only two of the four gates were built.[47]

Given these conflicting pressures of royal and seigneurial power, of urban autonomy, and of financial constraints, what motives were uppermost in building expensive and time-consuming defences, and whose was usually the initiative? It was taken as axiomatic by Turner 'that the primary purpose of a wall was defensive, that it was built for this purpose and was regarded principally in this light', and although some subsequent work has stressed purposes like prestige and status, T.P. Smith has recently re-emphasized the primacy of defence.[48] Evidence is sparse from the twelfth century, but from the early thirteenth century charters, murage grants and royal orders multiply; and it is possible in some cases to establish motive and initiative. Of 51 murage grants issued for English and Welsh towns in the thirteenth century, over half (27) were for towns in Wales and the Welsh Marches, and that figure excludes the impressive fortress-towns of Edward I in north Wales, which were financed directly by the crown.[49] That reflects the zone of insecurity, just as the northern towns fortified between 1315 and 1321, and the coastal towns fortified against the French in the fourteenth century, reflect other wars.

Some of these murage grants may have been issued in response to local pressure, but in others the king was clearly the prime mover. In 1218 Henry III brusquely ordered the men of Shrewsbury to fortify their town in case enemies should enter through lack of fortification ('*pro defectu firmacionis*'), and his grants of murage to them in 1218 and 1220 were presumably to ensure the means of having his order obeyed. The 1218 order, modelled on a writ of King John to Limoges in 1215, was apparently the first of its kind in England,[50] and it reflected the fact that there were now autonomous groups of townsmen on whom responsibility could be devolved. Shrewsbury may have been exceptional, however; once murage grants became frequent, the implications often are that the townsmen themselves wanted the defences.[51]

The threat of civil war or invasion was often a spur to either king or townsmen into ordering, or requesting, walls. In 1267 Henry III personally supervised the digging of ditches round Cambridge, and according to one chronicler he intended to wall the town in stone, but had to leave suddenly when London was threatened.[52] At the same time he was ordering the archbishop of York and the men of Beverley to apply murage money already collected to improve the defences of Beverley, though there is no evidence of action taken.[53] In a later emergency, that of the Scots' harrying of northern England under Edward II, it may have been townsmen who took the initiative. Certainly the men of Hull petitioned the king in 1321 for permission to wall their town, while neighbouring Beverley, which had to be ransomed from the Scots in 1322, immediately afterwards asked the king for the right to a wall and ditch.[54]

Similarly, many of the coastal and inland ports fortified in the fourteenth century were responding to invasion crises or panics. In 1339 Edward III, provoked by the French raid on Southampton the year before (the town had walls to landward but not along the shore), overrode the town's liberties, and ordered the county sheriff to improve the defences. In 1360 he ordered the men of Gloucester to repair their walls without delay, on hearing that because of the recent truce with the French they were neglecting them, 'whereat the King is much surprised; and because it is advisable that the town should be well fortified in time of peace as of war'.[55] In 1377 Richard II's government, facing the prospect of a French raid on Exeter, ordered its mayor and bailiffs to strengthen the defences, and to 'compel by distraint all persons residing therein, and having lands and goods there, to contribute to their repair.' And in 1387 it ordered the men of Canterbury to re-elect two bailiffs who had been vigorous in improving the city's defences, and who would, the king believed, continue the work because of French threats.[56]

Whether the initiative came from the towns or the crown, major programmes were not always begun in times of military threat. That is, perhaps, unsurprising: times of war or threatened war were also times when supplies of labour and materials were most likely to be disrupted, while stable conditions were more likely to generate surplus wealth for expensive projects. 'The considerable expenditure on town walls during the later thirteenth century in places like Nottingham, Leicester, Oxford and Winchester, remote from the sources of any predictable threats, suggests that there were other motives beyond the purely military need.'[57] Security was in any case often seen in terms of protection from criminals and from outlaws rather than from armies. Henry III allowed the bishop of Salisbury to fortify his new cathedral city with ramparts or ditches (*fossatis*) 'for fear of robbers', while the jurors of Northampton testified in 1278 that the purpose of night watches on their walls was against 'malefactors' entering and leaving the town.[58] Security of trade was sometimes an explicit consideration: the petition of the men of Hull in 1321 for walling their town cited the need for security to encourage native and overseas traders, as well as defence against the Scots.[59]

There was also, in less defensive terms, a common desire by urban authorities to control entry so as to levy tolls on incoming traders. From that point of view, gates or even wooden bars might be just as effective as a circuit of walls, and that may be why some towns like Beverley and Salisbury completed stone or brick gatehouses but never built walls. In 1228 the archbishop of York was entitled to the customs and dues of merchants passing through York's Micklegate Bar, tolls from the other city gates being presumably levied by the citizens.[60] In London the gates were similarly used for levying tolls, and on a large scale: in 1305 the collector of murage at Newgate was said to receive tolls from over 200 carts of grain a day, though the figure is probably much exaggerated.[61] Control of the gates could also be helpful in arresting suspects or excluding undesirables. It was common even in peacetime for gates to be locked at night, and by the fifteenth and sixteenth centuries, and probably earlier, they were often manned by day to screen against beggars and suspected carriers of infectious disease.

Perhaps the chief motive for major towns, next to defence, was in enhancing the communal image. M.O.H. Carver has emphasized in a continental context that town walls may give a misleading picture of permanent warfare, and that walls 'above all were surely understood as a sign of independent government ... worth having, even if purely as a token. Settlements can have walls therefore as much to say "town", as to ward off a foe.'[62] Of course, English towns lacked the independence of many imperial and Italian cities, owing to the power of the crown, but considerations of prestige could well have weighed heavily with the larger towns of the thirteenth and fourteenth centuries. Oxford, for instance, had an elaborate circuit of stone walls praised by a Franciscan poet as one of the town's chief glories, and it is now known to have had, uniquely for England, concentric defences two walls deep around part of its circuit facing north.[63] Yet this does not seem to have been a response to any specific military threat. More certainly, Coventry's long and elaborate defences must represent civic pride rather than military defence; begun with a ceremonial laying of the first stone by the mayor just after full autonomy was acquired from the crown, they were continued in a leisurely way for nearly two centuries. The section around the earl's half was complete by 1400, but the continuation round the prior's half was carried on more slowly, often at an agreed annual length, until final completion of the circuit in the 1530s. C. Platt regards it as an unarguable 'gesture of municipal pride'.[64] Towns which already had walls and gates might well rebuild their main gates in more showy fashion. The early-sixteenth-century Stonebow at Lincoln and South Gate at King's Lynn 'speak more of civic pride than concern for security'.[65] The same might equally be said of York's Micklegate Bar, heightened about 1350–75 and decorated with the royal arms, and Monk Bar, with its imposing upper storey added a century later. These were, after all, points of display as well as defence. In the fifteenth century monarchs approaching York from the south were welcomed by the mayor and aldermen at Micklegate Bar, while the heads of prominent rebels were also displayed there. It is also significant that, although the city's jurisdiction extended well beyond the walls, York's municipal records are careful to distinguish between 'city' (the walled area) and 'suburb', and that mayors during their year of office were required to be physically housed within the walls, even if their permanent homes were suburban.[66]

Whatever the main purposes of defences, other uses could be incorporated from the start. Stone gatehouses could combine ground-floor defence with chambers above and alongside for other purposes. Oxford's eleventh-century stone church tower of St Michael at the Northgate seems to have been from the beginning an integral part of the town's defences, and Oxford was one of a number of towns – including Bristol, Canterbury and Winchester – which possessed groups of churches over or adjacent to gatehouses.[67] No doubt there were often practical reasons for this, doubling up on the use of expensive stone constructions, but spiritual protection was also a consideration. Several such gate-churches were dedicated to St Peter, the doorkeeper of Heaven, and St Michael the guardian archangel. In a very early description of Chester, written about 1195, Lucian describes the four gates in those terms, admittedly distorting the topography to make his point. He has St Werburgh to the north, St John to the east, St Peter to the west (the church is really central), and St Michael, correctly, by the south gate. 'Nothing,' he adds, 'is more true than that scripture, "I have set watchmen upon thy walls, O Jerusalem".'[68]

In time, other uses for gates, towers, walls and moats proliferated. Gatehouses became meeting-halls for guilds, or domestic accommodation; towers became houses or workshops; wet moats could be used for water power, as at Hereford, and dry moats leased out for pasture. At Lincoln the town hall was housed over the Stonebow, and at Southampton above the Bargate. Gates at London, Chester, Durham, Newcastle and Oxford were employed as prisons.[69] At Norwich in the 1290s the prior was fined for pasturing his pigs on the bank or moat, and the dean for planting trees there.[70] Even the use of wall-walks for recreation can be attested long before the age of tourist trails. At Northampton in 1278, when the burgesses objected to a request by the Carmelites to enclose a section of town wall, they affirmed that not only were the walls needed for watchmen, but also other townsmen, especially the sick, often walked on the walls from gate to gate to take the air; while in winter they used the same route to avoid the muddy and unpleasant conditions at ground level.[71] By the fourteenth and fifteenth centuries some towns, including Barnstaple and Shrewsbury, were allowing townspeople to encroach on, and even demolish, sections of the wall for housing.[72]

The pattern is thus a varied one. A combination of strong central authority, limited urban autonomy and powers of taxation, and much internal peace, prevented or made unnecessary the universal adoption of fully defensive walls as in some other countries. Zones of invasion and border warfare were exceptional, and only Edward I's conquest of north Wales produced a magnificent series of planned and fortified towns comparable to the bastides of France. Yet many of the larger towns did build walls, at least in part for self-advertisement; and smaller towns often wanted at least bars, gates and ditches to create obstacles and control-points. Nevertheless, the motivation and the initiative varied considerably from town to town and from decade to decade, and more investigation of the sources is still required. The same country could include major towns which were virtually undefended, like Ipswich and Cambridge, and others bristling with strong fortifications. When Leland visited Newcastle about 1540, he found that 'the strength and magnificence of the walling of this town far passeth all the walls of the cities of England and of most of the towns of Europe'.[73]

Notes

1 .   H.L. Turner, *Town Defences in England and Wales* (London, 1970), p 13.
2 .   M.W. Barley, 'Town defences in England and Wales after 1066', in M.W. Barley, ed, *The Plans and Topography of Medieval Towns in England and Wales*, Council for British Archaeology, Research Report 14 (London, 1976), pp 57–71; M.J. Jones and C.J. Bond, 'Urban defences', in J. Schofield and R. Leech, eds, *Urban Archaeology in Britain*, Council for British Archaeology, Research Report 61 (London, 1987), pp 81–116; *RCHM: City of York*, 5 vols (London, 1962-81), II.
3 .   E.g. J.Z. Juddery *et al*, *Exeter City Defences*, Exeter Museums Archaeological Field Unit, Reports 88.14, 89.09, 89.10 (1988–9); C. Allmand, 'Taxation in medieval England: the example of murage', in M. Bourin, ed, *Villes, bonnes villes, cités et capitales* (Caen, 1993), pp 223–30.
4 .   J.R. Kenyon, *Castles, Town Defences, and Artillery Fortifications in Britain: a Bibliography*, Council for British Archaeology, 2 vols (London, 1978 and 1983); J.R. Kenyon, *Medieval Fortifications* (Leicester, 1990), pp 183–99.
5 .   Jones and Bond, 'Urban defences', p 110.
6 .   A.R. Myers, *England in the Late Middle Ages* (London, 1959), p 53.
7 .   Turner, *Town Defences*, pp 13, 25.
8 .   Reported in *Medieval Archaeology* 37 (1993), p 258.
9 .   Barley, 'Town defences', p 57; Jones and Bond, 'Urban defences', p 92.
10 .   M. Beresford, 'English medieval boroughs', *Urban History Yearbook 1981*, p 59; R.H. Britnell, *The Commercialisation of English Society, 1000–1500* (Cambridge, 1993), p 115.
11 .   Barley, 'Town defences', p 68.
12 .   C. Drage, 'Urban castles', in Schofield and Leech, eds, *Urban Archaeology in Britain*, pp 117–32.
13 .   Drage, 'Urban castles', p 117.
14 .   M. Beresford, *New Towns of the Middle Ages* (London, 1967), p 183.
15 .   L. Toulmin Smith, ed, *The Itinerary of John Leland*, 5 vols (London, 1906–10), I, p 47.
16 .   A. Thomas, *The Walled Towns of Ireland*, 2 vols (Dublin, 1993).
17 .   C.-L. Salch, *L'atlas des villes et villages fortifiées en France* (Strasbourg, 1978), preface by P. Dollinger; C. Meckseper, *Kleine Kunstgeschichte der Deutschen Stadt im Mittelalter* (Darmstadt, 1982), p 3.
18 .   Bärbel Brodt, 'Towns without walls', in *Urbanism: Pre-Printed Papers, Volume 1* (York, 1992), p 231.
19 .   Turner, *Town Defences*, pp 25, 97–109. She also lists Durham, which was not its first fortification.
20 .   Jones and Bond, 'Urban defences', p 110; Turner, *Town Defences*, p 97. However, Kenyon, *Medieval Fortifications*, p 189, lists Barnard castle as one occupying a castle outer bailey.
21 .   Turner, *Town Defences*, pp 81–2, 136–7; Brodt, 'Towns without walls', p 231.

22 . P. Grégoire, *De republica libri sex et viginti* (1596), quoted in. W. Somner, *The Antiquities of Canterbury*, 2nd edn (London, 1703), p 8, note. I am grateful to Professor H.A. Lloyd for verifying the reference.

23 . A.D. Dyer, *Decline and Growth in English Towns, 1400–1640* (London, 1991), pp 64, 70, for ranking tables for both years.

24 . C. Platt, *The English Medieval Town* (London, 1976), p 41.

25 . Turner, *Town Defences*, p 126; Kenyon, *Medieval Fortifications*, pp 185–6.

26 . Turner, *Town Defences*, p 91.

27 . D.G. Shaw, *The Creation of a Community: the City of Wells in the Middle Ages* (Oxford, 1993), p 115.

28 . C. Platt, *The Architecture of Medieval Britain* (New Haven and London, 1991), p 148.

29 . E. Gooder, *Coventry's Town Wall*, revised edn, Historical Association, Coventry branch (1971), p 5.

30 . N. Brooks, 'The development of military obligations in eighth- and ninth-century England', in P. Clemoes and K. Hughes, eds, *England Before the Conquest* (Cambridge, 1971), pp 69–84; N. Brooks, 'Church, crown and community', in T. Reuter, ed, *Warriors and Churchmen in the High Middle Ages* (London, 1992), pp 1, 2.

31 . See e.g. Turner, *Town Defences*, p 29.

32 . A. Ballard, *British Borough Charters, 1042–1216* (Cambridge, 1913), p 93; Turner, *Town Defences*, p 30.

33 . H.L. Turner, 'The mural mansions of Oxford', *Oxoniensia* 55 (1991), pp 73–79.

34 . Turner, *Town Defences*, p 30.

35 . F. Pollock and F.W. Maitland, *The History of English Law Before the Time of Edward I*, 2 vols, 2nd edn (Cambridge, 1898), I, p 662.

36 . Turner, *Town Defences*, pp 30–44; C. Allmand, 'Taxation in medieval England: the example of murage', in Bourin, ed, *Villes, bonnes villes, cités et capitales*, pp 223–30.

37 . Allmand, 'The example of murage', p 225.

38 . W.L. Warren, *The Governance of Norman and Angevin England, 1086–1272* (London, 1987), p 33; Allmand, 'The example of murage', p 226.

39 . Allmand, 'The example of murage', p 225.

40 . Turner, *Town Defences*, pp 36–7; Allmand, 'The example of murage', pp 227–8.

41 . See e.g. the London list of 1315 in Turner, *Town Defences*, pp 227–30.

42 . Turner, *Town Defences*, p 38.

43 . Turner, *Town Defences*, p 40; Allmand, 'The example of murage', pp 228–9.

44 . Gooder, *Coventry's Town Wall*, pp 10, 12.

45 . Francis Drake, *Eboracum* (London, 1736), p 262; P.H. Cullum and P.J.P. Goldberg, 'Charitable provision in late medieval York', *Northern History* 29 (1993), p 38.

46 . Platt, *The English Medieval Town*, p 42.

47 . K.H. Rogers, 'Salisbury', in M.D. Lobel, ed, *Historic Towns* (London, 1969), p 6.

48 . Turner, *Town Defences*, p 87; T.P. Smith; 'Why did medieval towns have walls?', *Current Archaeology* 8 (1985), pp 376–9.

49 . Turner, *Town Defences*, p 25.

50 . A. Ballard and J. Tait, *British Borough Charters, 1216–1307* (Cambridge, 1923), pp lxviii, 120, 347.

51 . Turner, *Town Defences*, p 16.

52 . M.D. Lobel, 'Cambridge', in Lobel, ed, *The Atlas of Historic Towns* (London, 1975), p 12.

53 . BL, Lansdowne MS 402, fo. 60r (letters patent of 10 February 1267, not recorded in *CPR*); York, Borthwick Institute of Historical Research, Reg. 2, fo. 85v.

54 . Turner, *Town Defences*, pp 25, 89; *VCH: Yorkshire. East Riding,* vi, ed K.J. Allison (Oxford, 1989), p 178.

55 . Turner, *Town Defences*, pp 82, 172.

56 . Juddery *et al*, *Exeter City Defences*, p iii; Turner, *Town Defences*, p. 41.

57 . Jones and Bond, 'Urban defences', p 92.

58 . Ballard and Tait, *British Borough Charters, 1216–1307*, p 121; T. Hudson Turner, *Some Account of Domestic Architecture in England, from the Conquest to the end of the Thirteenth Century* (Oxford, 1851), pp 109–10; J.C. Cox, in *VCH: Northamptonshire*, ii (London, 1906), p 148.

59 . Turner, *Town Defences*, p 89.

60 . D.M. Palliser, 'York's west bank', in P.V. Addyman and V.E. Black, eds, *Archaeological Papers from York Presented to M.W. Barley*, York Archaeological Trust (York, 1984), p 106.

61 . B.M.S. Campbell *et al*, *A Medieval Capital and its Grain Supply*, Institute of British Geographers, Historical Geography Research Series 30 (1993), p 31.

62 . M.O.H. Carver, *Arguments in Stone: Archaeological Research and the European Town in the First Millennium* (Oxford, 1993), p 70.

63 . A.G. Rigg, *A History of Anglo-Latin Literature 1066–1422* (Cambridge, 1992), p 273; Kenyon, *Medieval Fortifications*, pp 187–9.

64 . Platt, *The English Medieval Town*, p 95.

65 . Barley, 'Town defences', p 68. For the dating of the South Gate, see Turner, *Town Defences*, p 127.

66 . D.M. Palliser, *Tudor York* (Oxford, 1979), p 104.

67 . R. Morris, *Churches in the Landscape* (London, 1989), pp 214–22.

68 . D.M. Palliser, *Chester: Contemporary Descriptions by Residents and Visitors*, 2nd edn (Chester, 1980), p 7.

69 . *RCHM: City of York*, II, p 4; Jones and Bond, 'Urban defences', p 104.

70 . W. Hudson, ed, *The Leet Jurisdiction in the City of Norwich*, Selden Soc., 5 (1892), pp 37, 44.

71 . Turner, *Domestic Architecture*, p 109; Cox, *VCH: Northamptonshire*, ii, p 148.

72 . Kenyon, *Medieval Fortifications*, pp 184–5.

73 . Smith, ed, *Itinerary of John Leland*, V, p 60.

6. War and Peace in the Works of Erasmus: A Medieval Perspective

Peter Heath

The published interests of medievalists rarely extend to Erasmus, and the modernists familiar with his work seldom probe beyond his own assessment of the Middle Ages. Thus when Léon Halkin avers that 'Le pacifisme d'Érasme est un des aspects les plus originaux de son oeuvre,'[1] the exact extent and nature of that originality is rather assumed than defined. The aim of this chapter, therefore, is not so much to present the reader with new material as to merge, so to speak, two hitherto separate and distinct databanks in order to test more precisely what was new about the Erasmian view of war; to this end the ideas of Erasmus and the English poet John Gower will be juxtaposed.

In a famous colloquy first printed in 1529 Erasmus alludes to his own efforts to promote peace and prevent wars. Charon, whose role is to ferry the shades of the dead across the Styx, is expecting an increase in business because of the imminent wars and has ordered a bigger vessel, a trireme, for the purpose, but he is worried about the effects on his business of 'a certain Polygraphus up there [i.e. on Earth] who's incessantly attacking war with his pen and urging men to peace'; however, Alastor reassures Charon that Polygraphus 'has sung to deaf ears this long while'.[2] That Erasmus was 'incessantly attacking war and urging men to peace' is beyond question, but his most celebrated assaults on warfare and warmongers appeared within the space of three years: in 1515 the adage 'Dulce bellum inexpertis' ('War is sweet to those without experience of it'); in 1516 *Institutio principis christiani* (*The Education of a Christian Prince*); in 1517 *Querela pacis* (*The Complaint of Peace*); and sometime during these years a work to which he never owned but which he undoubtedly wrote, *Julius exclusus*.[3] These were the peaks in a range of attacks which dated from his earliest works almost to his last. In a letter of 1524 he wrote of himself: 'How great a hater of war I am, and what a lover or peace, is made clear in all my books'.[4] A youthful poem, composed *c.* 1491, laments that 'whole ages, alas, we wear away in blind and wicked warfare'.[5] About 30 years later he wrote of 'the world's two most powerful kings locked for so many years now in mortal conflict, in such a way that no part of the world is free from its share of the evil results'.[6] And he was still writing about war in 1529, in the colloquy cited above,[7] and in 1530 in the tract *De bello turcico*.[8]

Erasmus's passionate obsession with war has two particular sources. Firstly, his career took him with dismaying predictability to areas and centres of strife; and secondly, his emphasis upon the love of Christ, the *philosophia Christi*, rendered all war, especially that between Christians, questionable.

As for his experience of war, it began quite early, in the monastery of Steyn, near Gouda. From 1488 to 1492, while he was there, this region around Rotterdam and Gouda was afflicted by a bloody civil war. When later he was in Italy, seeking a doctorate from the University of Bologna, Pope Julius II led most of his cardinals at the head of an army to capture Bologna from the Bentivoglio, its unlawful despots. On that occasion Julius relied upon French assistance to counter the interests of Venice in shoring up the Bentivoglio, but later he opted for Venetian aid against further French ambitions in Italy; Erasmus was in Paris in 1510 when French outrage at this reached its climax. He mercilessly satirized Julius not only in bitter poems[9] – little known and one of them unpublished until much later – but also in *Julius exclusus*; while he never admitted to publishing this, his poems, as well as the religious sentiments with which it concludes, confirm his authorship.[10] By 1514 Erasmus was in England, just as Henry VIII was preparing for war against the French and the Scots. A decade later the long conflict between Francis I and Charles V had begun; entwined with the Reformation and the Turkish threat, it was to provide the backdrop to the rest of Erasmus's life.

As for the *philosophia Christi*, this was fully expounded as early as 1503 in the *Enchiridion militis christiani* (or *The Handbook of the Militant Christian*), which Erasmus wrote at the request of a wife for the benefit of her impious husband.[11] The work is in form a battle plan against the temptations of the Devil. The philosophy of Christ, the basis for this plan, was the teaching of the Saviour accessible to all in the pages of Scripture, as opposed to the 'philosophy' of the schoolmen, the medieval theologians and scriptural commentators, which was presented as the preserve of clerics and scholars. Whereas they had so elaborated Christian doctrine as to conceal, in Erasmus's eyes, some of its essential truths and to frustrate their implementation, Christ, in contrast, offered a clear message in the Scriptures to the ploughman as much as to the academic, and at the heart of this teaching was the love of God which entailed the love of one's fellow men and women.[12] This love constituted a formidable obstacle to men killing each other, whatever the cause. It was impossible, so Erasmus wrote in *Praise of Folly*, 'for a man to draw a murderous sword and plunge it into his brother's vitals without loss of the supreme charity which in accordance with Christ's teaching every Christian owes to his neighbour'.[13] On several occasions throughout his works Erasmus drew on Plato's view that for Greek to fight Greek is civil war, and he likened war between Christians to civil war,[14] but in 'Dulce bellum inexpertis', he put it even more intimately: 'If one brother kills another, it is called fratricide. But a Christian is nearer allied to another Christian than any brother can be, unless the bonds of nature are closer than those of Christ!'[15] Yet whether this was quite so exclusively a conclusion of the *philosophia Christi* is open to serious doubt, since a long medieval tradition was equally appalled by the paradox of Christians slaughtering each other and attempted by various means to reduce this vile carnage.

The practice, which was so evidently at variance with the *philosophia Christi*, of adducing texts from Greek philosophy and from Roman Law in favour of war, was roundly condemned by Erasmus:

> the whole of Christ's teaching has been so contaminated by writings of the dialecticians, sophists, mathematicians, orators, poets, philosophers and lawyers of the pagan world that a great part of one's life must be spent before one can turn to reading the Scriptures, and the result is that when one does get to them one is so corrupted by all these worldly ideas that the precepts of Christ either seem thoroughly shocking, or are distorted in accordance with the doctrines of these other authorities.[16]

Even the notion that war is sanctioned by the Scriptures and the Fathers of the Church was challenged by Erasmus.[17] The Old Testament examples of Jews fighting their enemies afford no justification for the modern Christian warrior, least of all when he is fighting other Christians: the Jews did not fight Jews, and they fought by divine command, not in response to passion, pride or greed. In any case, why emulate the Jews only on war and neglect their other customs such as circumcision, animal sacrifice and ritually pure food? More than this, the Jewish actions represent the habits of those who are not yet followers of Christ: when St Peter took up his sword he fought 'as a Jew, who had not yet received a truly Christian spirit' – witness how soon afterwards he denied his Lord. By contrast, Christ's 'whole life and teaching speak of nothing but tolerance'. Those who interpret some of his words as approving of war, twist their meaning: 'A doctor who is truly Christian never approves of war; perhaps sometimes he may think it permissible, but with reluctance and sorrow'. When early popes and the Fathers of the Church sanctioned war, it was not the kind of war which was being waged in Erasmus's time. And why prefer the words of men on war to those of Christ on love? 'Why should I be more impressed by the writings of Bernard [of Clairvaux] or the arguments of Thomas [Aquinas] than by the teaching of Christ?' Christ 'repeatedly greeted his disciples with an assurance of peace, saying "Peace be with you"', and at his death he said to them, 'I give you my peace, I leave you peace'.[18]

In the opening years of the sixteenth century, any theories of war had to take account of the threat posed by the Turkish advance into Europe. Of all combat, that to defend Christendom from the pagans seemed least objectionable, and for almost the previous half-century popes had been trying to raise a crusade for that purpose. Even Erasmus thought that it was less culpable to fight Turks: 'if war ... is not wholly avoidable, that kind [i.e. war against the Turks] would be a lesser evil than the present unholy conflicts and clashes between Christians'.[19] Nevertheless, in his view safety from the Turks depended not upon war but upon conversion, since by killing them 'it is more likely that we shall turn into Turks than that our efforts will make them into Christians',[20] a spectacle – of a potential Christian killed by a so-called Christian – which could only give pleasure the Devil.[21] Instead, we should be 'turning as many as we can of those infidels into believers',[22] for 'they [too] are men for whose salvation Christ died'.[23] Furthermore, the bloody divisions between Christians were hardly calculated to impress the Turks with the virtues of the Christian religion, nor were the Turks likely to be awed by the prudence and strength of Christian forces. In the *Institutio* Erasmus asked what Turks and Saracens must make of it when they see that for 'hundreds of years the Christian princes have been utterly unable to agree among themselves?'[24] And militarily, 'What more agreeable spectacle could we set before the Turks ... than the sight of the three most prosperous monarchs of all Europe engaged in suicidal strife?'[25]

In his efforts to dissuade men from war, Erasmus depicted its horrors of scale and detail: 'in war an army of all the evils of tragedy moves like a sea in flood';[26] it is 'so deadly that it sweeps like a plague through the world'.[27] Among its worst effects is the pain it causes individuals, especially those who have least interest in conflict,[28] the poor and lowly, 'those who are involved in war against their will'.[29] 'War, the purveyor of deaths and funerals' is never 'more fearful and cruel than [in] the way it tears apart those who have been tied together by the closest bonds'.[30] Erasmus reminded the Christian prince that war is paid for with 'so much human blood, so many widows, so many grief-stricken households, so many childless old people, so many made undeservedly poor'.[31]

Even for the enthusiastic soldier there is tragedy. In the colloquy 'Military Affairs' Thrasymachus admits that he went to war only for the booty but returned with an empty purse and laden with sins: 'I saw and did more wickedness there than ever I did in my whole life'.[32] In another colloquy, 'The Soldier and the Carthusian', the latter asks, 'Which in truth do you think is more lamentable, to butcher a Christian – who never harmed you – for a little pay or to send yourself body and soul to perdition? ... What kind of soul do you bring back? Rotten with how many diseases? Torn by how many wounds?'[33] One of the most alarming aspects of war for Erasmus was the demoralization it works on individuals and society, 'overwhelming all in waves of disaster and crime'.[34] In the wake of war comes 'damage to individual morals and public discipline';[35] the destruction of towns and villages, the burning of churches and ruin of farmland, robbery, murder, fornication and incest result.[36] War invites into your country 'the criminal dregs of hired mercenaries',[37] 'that accursed tribe ... who batten on the miseries of the human race',[38] 'than whom no class of men is more abject and indeed more damnable'.[39] 'What is war, indeed, but murder shared by many, and brigandage, all the more immoral from being wider spread?'[40] Chastity was particularly at risk: 'Whose virtue is safe in war?'[41] In short, as he wrote in 'Dulce bellum', 'War takes all that is joyous and beautiful and speedily smashes it, quenches it, wipes it out at one blow, and pours out a sludge of evil over the lives of men.'[42]

Not only the lowly and defeated suffer; more than one victor has been forced to conclude that the costs of victory were too great.[43] Louis XII went to the aid of Julius II and 'came home, with all his business, as it seemed, successfully concluded. But what a flood of evils this let loose for the French!'[44] Social disruption is matched by economic destruction: cities are very quickly destroyed, but much more slowly rebuilt.[45] As a result, the price of peace often proves to be ten times lower than the cost of war.[46] Moreover, war begets wars – 'many wars from one'[47] – and the aftermath of war is often almost worse than war itself.[48]

Erasmus declared that war is 'so impious that it is quite alien to Christ',[49] but it is also contrary to man's nature. The Christian prince was urged to weigh the differences between man, 'an animal born for peace and goodwill', on the one hand, and beasts and monsters 'who are born to predatory war', on the other.[50] All other creatures are endowed by nature with weapons of their own – horns, claws, fangs, quills etc – but 'If one considers the outward appearance of the human body, does it not become clear at once that nature, or rather God, created this being not for war but for friendship, not for destruction but for preservation, not for aggressiveness but for kindness?'[51] These arguments serve only to increase the mystery of why man embarks so readily on war, seeing that it is against both his nature and his self-interest and is 'the most disastrous thing there is'.[52] After all, war is an unnecessary addition to the natural misfortunes which so abundantly afflict mankind,[53] and it produces 'more calamities than nature',[54] 'as if too little misfortune came without our seeking'.[55]

Erasmus nowhere presents a coherent or comprehensive answer to this question of why men go to war; he offers instead piecemeal assertions which range from unhelpful generalities to extravagant simplicities, depending in part upon the audience he is addressing. In 'Military Affairs', Thrasymachus, after his bitter experience as a soldier, supposes that people go to fight 'because they are driven by devils';[56] on several occasions Erasmus invokes the classical Furies – devils by another name.[57] At the heart of wars, however, he sees princes, which is no doubt why he addressed so many of his writings about war to them. He was especially concerned that they should not consult their own vanity or lust for grandeur, nor listen to their courtiers and lawyers, but rather consider the wishes of the people whose welfare they were charged by Christian duty to promote; he pointed out that, while martial fame was more spectacular, 'glory in peace is more desirable',[58] reminding the prince that 'nothing is more certain evidence of a truly great spirit than the ability to overlook wrongs suffered' and to accept 'a disadvantageous peace rather than pursue the most advantageous of wars'.[59] In 1526 he blamed the protraction of the war between Francis I and Charles V on their education (that is, indoctrination by their tutors), and on their lawyers who were 'still arguing about boundaries'.[60] In his *Paraphrase of Mark*, he asserted that 'most wars arise out of a few empty words, invented one might think in order to nourish man's vainglory ... These and other things like these are the roots of war'.[61] Among these roots, too, he specified marriage treaties – 'most wars usually originate in these marriages'[62] – though he ignored the extent to which such pacts concluded or averted wars. While princes may have been motivated by dynastic or territorial pride, that disillusioned veteran Thrasymachus maintained that booty was the lure for the ordinary combatants: 'few men go there from any loftier motive'.[63]

Erasmus thus dismisses most wars as the result of princes' overweening folly, vanity or ambition, while for their soldiers greed was the spur. Yet some wars were different in kind. In 'The Soldier and the Carthusian', the soldier claims that it is lawful to kill an enemy, and the monk concedes that 'Maybe it is if he attacks your country. Then it does seem righteous to fight for wife and children, parents and friends, and for civil peace.'[64] And certainly 'men who repel the violent attacks of barbarian invaders by their wholehearted and loyal determination, and protect the peace and security of their country at their own peril' were explicitly spared Erasmus's condemnation in *Querela pacis*.[65] In the *Paraphrase of Mark* he concedes that 'A good prince has perhaps a duty to wage war sometimes, but,' he adds, 'never until he has tried all other courses and is driven to it by ultimate necessity.'[66] There might be some just wars, 'although with the world in its present state, I am not sure that any of that kind could be found ... For these reasons the good Christian prince must be suspicious of all wars, however just.'[67] That Erasmus never quite defined a just war and in the above quotations opted for cautious wording – 'does seem' and 'has perhaps' – reveals his instinctive reluctance to admit or to deny outright that there are just wars. Probably his confidence in them was undermined by the ease with which 'every man thinks his own case most just';[68] 'who does not think his own cause just?'[69] In the colloquies and adages he satirized the absurdity of clergy on both sides claiming divine approval of their cause,[70] as if 'Christ is in both camps fighting against himself'.[71] He was severe on those clergy who either took up arms themselves or counselled others to do so, offering assurances that God is on their side, and proclaiming in sermons on both sides 'that war is just, holy and right'.[72]

Perhaps for this reason he maintained, in *Panegyric for Philip of Austria*, that 'peace however unjust' is preferable to 'the justest of wars'[73] and, in *Parabolae*, that 'it is sometimes better to suffer wrong in silence than to seek revenge at a still higher price, or to accept terms of peace however damaging or unfair than to enter upon a war with all its measureless evils'.[74]

Erasmus repeatedly commended concession and compromise as far better alternatives to conflict, and he regarded the church as the ideal agency for arranging compromise, since it had an obligation, for the love of Christ, always to promote peace above war. He addressed these words to the prince: 'If some dispute arises between princes, why do they not take it to arbitration instead? There are plenty of bishops, abbots, scholars, plenty of grave magistrates whose verdict would settle the matter more satisfactorily than all this carnage, pillaging, and universal calamity'.[75] In a well-known letter of 1514 to the abbot of St Bertin, Erasmus declared that 'It is the proper function of the Roman pontiff, of the cardinals, of bishops, and of abbots to settle disputes between Christian princes; this is where they should wield their authority'.[76] But he lamented the failure of popes – he had Julius in mind again – to use this power, 'second only to Christ's': 'It should surely have been exercised, were its holders not gripped by the same passions as the people'.[77] The people, indeed, were as perverse as the pope: 'When the pontiff calls for war, he is obeyed. If he calls for peace, why is there not the same obedience to his call?'[78] In the colloquy 'Charon', Erasmus noted that 'only the Roman Pontiff [then Leo X] is zealous in urging peace, but his efforts are wasted'.[79]

Erasmus claimed that he did not 'totally condemn war' since he taught 'much moderation in undertaking and waging war'.[80] Although he was loth to admit that just wars could or should ever be waged, he nevertheless prescribed how they should be conducted if they did occur. In the adage 'War without Tears', he deplored those Christian princes who 'fight with machines such as no pagans with all their ferocity and no barbarians invented'.[81] 'How can one believe that artillery is an invention of man?' Peace asks in *Querela pacis*.[82] Elsewhere Erasmus asserted that if war was inescapable then a Christian prince 'will conduct it with as little bloodshed as possible. He will take care that his soldiers have the least possible licence to inflict harm upon innocent victims, and he will try to see that the war spreads over as small an area as possible and that it be not prolonged for any period of time.'[83] A righteous war, for Erasmus, had to be merciful and restrained in its execution as well as being justified by its cause and commenced only as a last resort.

From the tenth century onwards the church took steps to curtail the occasions and effects of war. The Peace of God and Truce of God respectively protected the helpless from hostile attack and defined close seasons during which hostilities were to cease.[84] These measures found their way into the authoritative lawbooks of the church in the twelfth and thirteenth centuries, and they were the subject of decrees at the Second and Third Lateran Councils in 1139 (cap. 12) and 1179 (caps. 21, 22).[85] Moreover, in the 1139 assembly, 'that murderous art of crossbowmen and archers, which is hateful to God' and therefore too horrible for use against Christians, was condemned (cap. 29);[86] the Third Lateran Council (cap.

27) denounced mercenaries.[87] By then, however, the notion of a just war had been revived.[88] Conceived by Aristotle, discussed by Cicero and adapted by St Augustine, it was subjected to intense scrutiny and elaborate definition during the twelfth-century Renaissance. Some commentators, rejecting the principles which lay behind the Peace and Truce of God, took the view that it was entirely permissible to prosecute a just war by any possible means at any time: no less a figure than Aquinas argued that fighting was quite as legitimate on feast days as were surgical operations to save individual life.

The just war *par excellence* was the crusade – undertaken not for vengeance nor greed nor pride (Urban II limited crusading indulgences to those who fought 'out of pure devotion and not for love of glory or gain');[89] intended to defend the church and faith; and commanded by a recognized public authority, the pope. In reality, however, crusades became unruly and bloody affairs which assailed not only pagans and heretics, but even Christians who rebelled against a papal vassal or supported an antipope. The most notorious example of this in English history occurred in 1383, when Bishop Henry Despenser of Norwich led just such a crusade, sponsored by Pope Urban V, to Flanders against England's enemy, the French, who were supporters of the antipope, Clement VII.[90] That the Despenser crusade proved a fiasco damaged the bishop's reputation as much as it undoubtedly fuelled doubts about the morality of a crusade against Christians, and about war in general.[91]

Crusades, however, had two particularly welcome aspects. Firstly, they encouraged popes to mediate between Christian antagonists in preparation for a united crusade against the Saracens or other pagans or heretics. And secondly, they advanced the assimilation of the knight into the Christian ethos, albeit at the constant risk of exposing the church to martial contamination.[92]

With almost Erasmian perception and phrase, Pope Gregory VII wrote in 1075 that 'reason and common interest demand [even more] that we sow seeds of love among the great of the earth, since their love or hate for each other infects many'.[93] One way to accomplish this was for the clergy to avert hostilities by offering their mediation to antagonists, and indeed successive popes sent missions of cardinals and other legates to reconcile monarchs with each other and with their fractious barons and vassals. Very frequently this papal activity for peace was prompted by the needs of an imminent crusade, and sometimes it was spurred by the need to protect Rome or the papal states from invasion or capture, but it would be difficult to explain all papal diplomacy in these selfish or cynical terms; seldom, though, were popes invited to arbitrate, and they usually intervened on their own initiative. How effective these missions were, even how many there were, why they succeeded or failed, and what was their overall contribution to European peace in the later Middle Ages, are questions which still await sustained investigation: warfare rather than peace has preoccupied historians.[94]

Although clergy were forbidden to take up arms or to direct conflicts – the Sixth Commandment applied absolutely to them – it was allowed that in extreme necessity clerics could bear arms and armour for self-defence or for the defence of the church against pagans and heretics.[95] Prelates, who often came from aristocratic families or held their ecclesiastical estates by military tenure, sometimes found the temptations of combat irresistible. Nevertheless, very few of them actually engaged in combat. Henry Despenser, bishop of Norwich (1370–1406), was one of the few: before he became bishop, he had fought in Italy for the pope against Milan; in the suppression of the Peasants Revolt in 1381 he played a vigorous and zestful part; and in 1383 he financed and led his crusade to Flanders.[96] A like-minded contemporary was the abbot of Battle – described by a chronicler as that 'outstanding warrior in monk's habit' – who led the repulse of the French raiders from Winchelsea in 1376 and 1377, though this was more obviously out of necessity and in the cause of defence.[97] The independence of the church must have been compromised and inhibited by the prelates' status in England as tenants-in-chief. Those who did not fight nonetheless espoused and commended royal warfare; bishops gave their overt support to royal campaigns by ordering prayers, processions, masses and sermons to promote them.[98]

Military service, however, was not confined to the occasional prelate; ordinary beneficed clergy and chaplains in England were arrayed, by royal command, with their swords and bows and arrows and pikes on many occasions between 1368 and 1418.[99] For example, by royal writ in 1372 all diocesan clergy aged between 16 and 60 were mustered, each armed according to his estate and means; those with benefices worth more than ten marks were to come as archers with bows and arrows. The practice was discontinued after 1418, apparently in response to clerical complaints about the burden of equipping themselves.

Some clergy found the pen mightier than the sword and used it to good effect to arouse – rather than allay – hatred. In Edward III's reign, for example, English monks were known to compile school books – such as the popular *Invective against the French* – which were laced with a decidedly unchristian chauvinism.[100] Just as remarkable for their cultivation of knightly values were two later secular clerics who edited a handbook of chivalry for aristocratic patrons. In the early fifteenth century Dr Nicholas Upton, a cleric who was to become a canon of Salisbury cathedral, adapted Vegetius's classical treatise on warfare, *De re militari*, for his patron Humphrey, duke of Gloucester.[101] Almost a century later John Blount, Fellow of All Souls College, Oxford, and later vicar of Hempstead in London diocese, translated this same work of Upton's into English for his patron – and possibly his relative – William Blount, Lord Mountjoy.[102] Upton reiterates the protection canonically extended to non-combatants: priests, monks, *conversi*, religious, travelling merchants, husbandmen about their business (as well as their plough beasts and beasts of burden), 'Rome goers' and visitors to holy places were to be exempted from any belligerent action; but he comments that 'thys was not observyd in my tyme in fraunce'.

Defence was the key to Christian warfare: defence against the infidel and the heretic, defence of the church, the community, the kingdom and the defenceless. The first of many accounts of the duties attaching to knight-hood was compiled by Bonizo of Sutri around 1090, and prominent among his and later versions was the defence of the faith and the weak: the knight was 'to fight to the death for the good of the commonwealth, to suppress heretics and schismatics, to defend the poor and widows and orphans'.[103] The dubbing of a knight, though it was conducted by other laymen, took place in church, resembled a kind of ordination and was completed and dignified by an oath which committed the new knight to the defence – *inter alia* – of the church and clergy.[104] In the 1460s Bishop Bekington of Bath and Wells reminded some unruly Somerset knights of this oath.[105] John Mirk recalled in one of his sermons the custom in one Surrey church where, at the reading of the gospel, 'each knight that is in the church draweth out his sword and so holdith it naked in his hand until it be done, thus showing that he is ready to fight any man that will come and challenge anything read in the gospel'.[106] It was thus as defenders of the church that knights were accommodated into Christian ethics.

In late-fourteenth-century England, however, there were voices to be heard which impugned these values and the church's espousal of them.[107] Mostly these were the voices not of schoolmen or of lawyers or even of clergy (at least not orthodox ones), but of laymen, courtiers and poets, and one of the most interesting of these was John Gower. He was born about 1330 and died in 1408. His early manhood thus coincided with the dazzling English victories over the French at Crécy and Poitiers, and over the Scots at Neville's Cross. In his middle age there were no victories of note, but a succession of costly and catastrophic humiliations which accompanied the cumulative effects of the plague visitations and the political twilight of Edward III's dotage and Richard II's minority. It was at this stage of his life that Gower began work on three formidably long poems – each in a different language – exploring the failures of that gloomy time when, on top of everything else, the church in England was riven by heresy and in Europe generally by chronic schism. This is the background to Gower's views on war and peace which seem to have been not a lifelong conviction but the result of mature reflection or simply of disillusion.

These poems which examine the social, political and moral collapse of England are *Vox clamantis* (over 10,000 lines in Latin, *c*. 1377–81); *Mirroir de l'omme* (over 30,000 lines in French, *c*. 1376–9); and *Confessio amantis* (more than 33,000 lines in English, *c*. 1386–93). Although some relevant material is to be found in the first two, it is particularly in the last that his views on war are laid out. Extant in some 50 manuscripts, the *Confessio* was printed by Caxton and twice in early Tudor times; it continued to be read into the seventeenth century and provided a source for Shakespeare's *Pericles, Prince of Tyre*; by the fifteenth century it had been translated into Spanish and Portuguese.[108] The poem was dedicated originally to Richard II, then in a revised form to Henry of Bolingbroke, and finally to the latter as king after he had ousted Richard in 1399; the dedication to Henry IV is a lengthy prayer for peace, in verse and in the tradition of the *Speculum regis*. After a Prologue, the poem itself is arranged in eight books; the Prologue, Book III and the Dedication or 'In Praise of Peace' contain Gower's views on war. The poem is in the form of a confessional, in which – inverting the usual practice – the penitent, Amans, interrogates the confessor, Genius, on each of the deadly sins. It is a voyage of self-discovery for Amans which allows ample room for comment upon the contemporary world, the troubles of which are used to illuminate his personal crisis, while the dialogue form allows the author, through the voice of the confessor, freedom for frank criticism of *inter alia* the church, knighthood and war. Although the subject of war occupies fewer than a thousand lines of this long poem, it is no minor theme for Gower, as its emphatic reiteration in the dedication to Henry IV makes clear. No doubt the poet's views on war were those of only a small minority in England, let alone in Europe, but so too were those elaborated by Erasmus just over a century later.

Amans asks three leading questions of Genius: whether it is ever lawful to kill a man; whether it is lawful to kill men in a worldly cause; and whether it is lawful 'To werre and sle the Sarazin'.[109] It is in the answers to these questions that Gower's thoughts on war are disclosed. He maintains that war is a defiance of biblical teaching and of Christ's own words: Moses, in the Sixth Commandment, and the angels, by their salutation to the shepherds ('Pes to the men of welwillinge'), outlaw homicide, and Christ himself 'hath comanded love and pes'.[110] In the Dedication, Gower makes two points which remarkably anticipate the words of Erasmus: 'Pes was the ferste thing he let do crie'; and at his ascension Christ 'yaf his pes, which is the fondement of charite'.[111] War is indeed against charity, for, as the apostle says, there is no good life which is not grounded upon charity and

> ... charite ne schedde nevere blod,
> So hath the werre as ther no propite.[112]

Genius tells Amans that war 'In worldes cause' violates charity:

> After the lawe of charite,
> Ther schal no dedly werre be.[113]

His treatment of war arises from and is a corollary of his treatment of murder, for he was asked by Amans whether it is lawful to kill men. But killing is not just contrary to scripture and charity, it is also unnatural: 'ek nature it hath defended'.[114] No more is said about this; the reader has to listen attentively to Gower's laconic utterances.

Nevertheless, it is conceded that war in defence of oneself, or the faith or the helpless and weak may be just. Amans asks the confessor in what circumstances one can kill a man without committing a sin, and Genius replies by citing the duty of a king to

> ... defende
> His trewe poeple and make an ende
> Of suche as wolden hem devoure.
> Lo thus, my sone, to socoure
> The lawe and comun riht to winne,
> A man mai sle withoute sinne.

More than that, by such defence he may

> ... do therof a gret almesse,
> So forto kepe rihtwinesse.[115]

The poet here is writing about individual killings, but he then goes on to talk of war:

> ... for his contre
> In time of werre a man is fre
> Himself, his hous and ek his lond
> Defende with his oghne hond,
> And, slen, if that he mai no bet,
> After the lawe which is set.[116]

The general sense of the passage suggests that canon and divine law are to be understood here, rather than simply the law of the land. A just defence, involving killing, is permitted if no alternative is possible – 'if that he mai no bet': there is an implied duty to exhaust every other way first.

War is to be avoided not only because it conflicts with Christian teaching and with man's nature, but also because it is harmful in so many ways. It brings with it, as Erasmus remarked, a sea of troubles:

> ... dedly werre hath his covine
> Of pestilence and of famine,
> Of poverte and of alle wo.[117]

Gower reminded Henry IV, in the dedication, that 'werre bringth in poverte at hise hieles'.[118] Along with the economic consequences, 'poverte of worldes good',[119] were political ones:

> ... thurgh lacke of love
> Where as the lond divided is,
> It mot algate fare amis.[120]

Above all these evils are the moral corruption and anarchy which accompany war:

> For alle thing which god hath wroght
> In erthe, werre it bringht to noght:
> The cherche is brent, the priest is slain,
> The wif, the maide is ek forlain,
> The lawe is lore and god unserved.[121]

The first two lines here anticipate Erasmus's statement about war extinguishing all that is joyous and beautiful, pouring out a sludge of evil over the lives of men; the third line can be matched by his lament of the church's sufferings, and the fourth line by his comment that in war chastity is particularly at risk; the fifth line parallels the humanist's observation that war disrupts the good order of society.

The similarities between Gower and Erasmus become especially striking when Gower tells the story of the pirate who defended himself before Alexander the Great by asserting that

> Oure dedes ben of o colour
> And in effect of o decerte,
> Bot thi richesse and my poverte
> Tho ben noght taken even liche.[122]

This story of Alexander's piracy found its way from Augustine's *City of God* (Bk. IV, Cap. iv) into medieval sermon aids such as the *Gesta Romanorum*; it was a commonplace that could hardly have been unknown to Erasmus when he declared that all war was brigandage. Gower and he share a common source here, as in so much else.

Nor was Erasmus saying very much new when he pointed out that wars were often more costly than even the victors could welcome. Gower, though, measured cost by the numbers of dead whereas Erasmus – perhaps gauging his audience's susceptibility more shrewdly – measured it in political and economic terms. Even so, their views are nearer than at first appears, since Erasmus is at pains to remind the ruler of his obligation to consult the wellbeing and preservation of his subjects. Gower thought that war brought the prince no worthwhile victory:

> As to the worldes rekeninge
> Ther schal he finde no winninge.[123]

Martial fame is vanity, even for Alexander, Joshua, Charlemagne and Arthur, among others, because in the end there is only death, 'which hath the werres under fote'.[124]

There is no certainty that more idealistic campaigns fought in the hope 'to pourchace The hevene mede' – evidently meaning crusades – are any more rewarding:

> Crist hath comanded love and pes,
> And who that worcheth the revers,
> I trow his mede is ful divers.[125]

When answering the question whether it is lawful to slay Saracens, Genius savagely points out that Christ's example, and that of his apostles, was to die for the faith, not kill for it; and he goes on to say that, as one can read in the chronicles, imposing truth by force brings only insecure gains to Christendom. The Gospel teaches that we should preach and suffer for the faith, 'Bot forto slee, that hiere I noght.'[126] Yet that Gower was condemning crusades has been challenged in an important article by Elizabeth Siberry.[127] Her case is that he was hardly likely to denounce them in a poem addressed to Bolingbroke, a celebrated crusader in the Baltic region; that in *Vox clamantis* Gower was overtly in favour of action against the Saracens, as he appears to be even in the Dedication directed to Henry IV; and that his criticism of the Crusades, in the answer to Amans, may therefore be ironic. Against the first point, it should be noted that the structure of *Confessio amantis*, and especially the explicit identification, at the end of the poem, of Gower with the penitent, Amans, left the poet free to voice at a distance, as it were, and with immunity through Genius, opinions unwelcome at court. Erasmus made equally tactless observations similarly indirectly and tactfully in writings which he addressed to popes and princes: the dialogue – and, in Gower's case, the confessional form – was ideally suited to such candour. Of course, it leaves the reader unsure which of the two voices is authentic, but we can note that neither Gower nor Erasmus provided, let alone developed, the case for war or crusade as we might have expected them to do if their true opinions inclined that way: the case for war is allowed to go by default. The passages in *Vox clamantis* and in the dedication of the *Confessio* which lament the reluctance of knights to go and fight the Saracens and of popes to summon crusades instead of wars for their own worldly and territorial gain, might be interpreted less as an exhortation to go and fight Muslims than as an expression of dismay that western knights and popes gave priority to wars of acquisition: Gower's words, like Erasmus's, seem calculated to shame warriors engaged in inter-Christian struggles into diverting their energies to defend Christendom from paganism. Both Gower and Erasmus certainly believed that, if wars had to be fought by Christians, then there was more justification for them being fought against pagans rather than against other Christians; it was the lesser evil. Yet both express serious reservations about the virtue and wisdom of such campaigns, either as a defence against, or as a way of proselytizing, the pagans.

Gower's views on crusades are ambivalent – to the same degree that Erasmus's comments on wars against the Turks are. Both writers were caught on the horns of a dilemma, all too aware that while the threat posed by the Muslims was serious it demanded, in all likelihood, a military solution that was incompatible with Christ's own words and example. Not saddled with responsibility for taking action, both writers vacillated in their attitudes to crusades.

Like Erasmus, Gower was equally appalled by the contrast between the example of the Apostles and the actions of his own contemporaries, especially the clergy and the pope:

> How now that holy cherche is went,
> Of that here lawe positif
> Hath set to make werre and strif
> For worldes good.[128]

Gower put the matter more forcefully in *Vox clamantis*:

> Peter preached, of course, but today's pope fights. The one seeks souls, the other greedily seeks riches. The first was skilled for God's law, the second kills, and yet God maintains no such law as that. The one arouses faith through his innocence, not by force; the other rouses armies on parade'.[129]

No doubt he had in mind the Avignon pope, Clement VII, but his words would have served as a text for *Julius exclusus*.

In his search for an explanation of wars, Gower is even less satisfactory than Erasmus. In the Prologue to the *Confessio*, Gower remarks how widespread and common wars have become in Christendom, every man now seeking revenge; he predictably explains this by Adam's sin, but he also notes – apparently in defiance of his statement elsewhere about war being against nature – the proclivity of man to conflict, compounded as he is of warring humours:

> ... for his complexioun
> Is mad upon divisioun.
> Of cold, of hot, of moist, of drye:

> For the contraire of his astat
> Stant evermore in such debat,
> Til that o part be overcome,
> Ther may no final pes be nome.[130]

Nevertheless, peace

> ... is the chief of mannes welthe,
> Of mannes lif, of mannes helthe.[131]

Peace is 'as it were a sacrament',[132] and 'of alle charite the keie';[133] 'withoute pes ther may no lif be glad'.[134] In short, 'Pes is the beste above alle erthely thinges.'[135]

Gower is as convinced as Erasmus of the profits of peace and, like Erasmus, he commends it to kings generally, 'these othre princes cristene alle'.[136] The ruler who has ambitions to be considered worthiest will eschew wars, which bring remorse: 'blod is schad, which no man mai restore'.[137] The king should consult the welfare of his people first,

> And suffre noght this poeple be devoured,
> So schal thi name evere after stonde honoured.[138]

To this end he should beware of councillors commending war and listen to God: 'Let god ben of thi counseil in this cas.'[139] A good councillor is beyond price to a king, but the king must weigh up himself what is reasonable and then resolve on peace 'for love of him which is the kyng of hevene'.[140]

Altogether, it is difficult to find an aspect of war covered by both Gower and Erasmus where their sentiments are not closely similar. Both acknowledge that, despite all the arguments against it, war is especially and perversely prevalent in their own times, and that church and Christianity have so far failed to balk man's irrational and (as they see it) unnatural lust for battle. Both deplore the sufferings which war inflicts on undeserving people who have no control over its conduct nor profit from its outcome. Both are equivocal about a just war, conceding that it is conceivable and permissible, but only as a very last resort and within the constraints of mercy and charity. Both Gower and Erasmus are ambivalent about war with the Saracens or Turks, preferring mission but conceding – by implication rather than direct statement – some possibility of justification for armed combat. Both urgently recommend peace to kings as being a more honourable and prestigious policy than war and as better serving the welfare of their subjects as well as the spiritual health of themselves.

While there is little that Gower advances that is not discussed or advocated by Erasmus, there are matters which are treated only by him. He is far more expansive, though not much more illuminating, on the causes of war; he alone recommends a long-neglected – but not quite forgotten – medieval theme, the necessity to conduct war humanely (or as he would have put it, in as Christian a way as possible) in respect of weapons used and the protection of non-combatants; and Gower says nothing about ways to prevent wars or cure man's weakness for them, although by his address to Henry IV he was actively and consciously contributing to that prevention in the same way that Erasmus did in his time. On the subject of prevention Erasmus is far more imaginative, urging compromise and concession, denouncing obstinacy over rights (which were often rationalizations of greed), and advocating resort to an arbitrator, particularly the pope. One should not forget, however, that the medieval papacy, while it had rarely been approached to arbitrate, had despatched innumerable missions to reconcile warring factions and powers (even though it had also played its shameful part in exploiting conflict or mobilizing armies).

The notion of compromise was also current in juridical circles and a not unusual resort in the ecclesiastical courts of the day; certainly some canon lawyers viewed their role in terms of promoting reconciliation rather than litigation over rights, for example. Charity, *caritas*, was their guiding light, as it was in much that Gower wrote about war, and we should beware of regarding Erasmus's pursuit of charity or Christian love as a sixteenth-century discovery. There is much about Erasmus's thoughts on war and peace which was familiar in the Middle Ages – not popular, any more than his views could be called 'popular' in his own time – and his originality seems to lie often not in his substance but in his expression, his sublime eloquence, artful and copious rhetoric, and rasping wit – a case of 'what oft before was said but ne'er so well expressed'. His influence, however, is not just to do with style.

That Erasmus rather than Gower is celebrated as offering a revolutionary view of war has much to do with the advent of printing, his genius and vigour as a polemicist and publicist, and his participation in two events which cast their shadows over Europe for the next five centuries – the Renaissance and Reformation. He was pre-eminently the schoolmaster of the classical education which dominated European culture and upbringing from his time almost to ours. He was also the voice of moderate, rational

Reformers. And he was the first international 'best-seller' of the printing press, his Latin providing a highway into multifarious vernacular translations and versions. Gower, despite being read and appreciated into the seventeenth century, and being translated into Spanish and Portuguese, remains – because of his dated vernacular – a much more parochial and neglected figure even in England. Erasmus throughout his life argued passionately, resourcefully and repeatedly against war. By sheer volume and eloquence, as well as by his unique standing as a European publicist, he has captured the attention and admiration of subsequent generations of readers who have found their own thoughts echoing, or perhaps set in train by, his words.

That so much coincidence of ideas should exist between Erasmus and Gower is not really surprising, for not only was Erasmus well versed in the relevant medieval texts but the two writers had in common many classical sources, directly in the case of Erasmus, at second hand in Gower's case via the works of St Augustine and later mediators of Antique thought. Nevertheless, since from the same sources many other men drew quite different conclusions, we should beware of dismissing the similarities between the views of Erasmus and Gower on war as simply a matter of textual determinism, instead of recognizing the harmony of spirit, insight and compassion which they so emphatically shared.

Notes

1 .   L.E. Halkin, *Erasme parmi nous* (Paris, 1987), p 41. For further discussions of Erasmus on war, see also R.P. Adams, *The Better Part of Valour* (Seattle, 1962), and A.G. Dickens and W.R.D. Jones, *Erasmus the Reformer* (London, 1994), *passim*.
2 .   'Charon', printed in C.R. Thompson, ed, *The Colloquies of Erasmus* (Chicago and London, 1965), pp 388–94.
3 .   Unless otherwise indicated, all quotations of Erasmus in this chapter are based on the translations in the University of Toronto's *Collected Works of Erasmus* (various eds, Toronto, 1974–), cited henceforward as *CWE* followed by volume and page numbers.
4 .   *CWE* X, p 205.
5 .   *CWE* LXXXV, pp 112–13, lines 87–8.
6 .   *CWE* X, p 205.
7 .   See note 2 above.
8 .   On this, see Dickens and Jones, *Erasmus the Reformer*, p 69.
9 .   *CWE* LXXXV, pp 338–9, 372; item nos. 119, 141. For notes on these poems, see *CWE* LXXXVI, pp 696–701, 729–30.
10 .   *CWE* XXVII, pp 156–97 (which includes a valuable introduction). Another text with revealing commentary is in P. Pascal and J. Kelley Sowards, *The 'Julius Exclusus' of Erasmus* (Bloomington and London, 1968).

11 . *CWE* LXVI, pp 1–127, where it is accompanied by an illuminating commentary in the general editor's Introduction to the volume.
12 . For a recent discussion of the 'philosophy of Christ', see Dickens and Jones, *Erasmus the Reformer*, particularly chapter 3.
13 . *CWE* XXVII, p 129.
14 . *Ibid*, pp 283, 310.
15 . M. Mann Phillips, *The 'Adages' of Erasmus: a Study with Translations* (Cambridge, 1964), p 327. The Adages cited here which have not yet been published in *CWE* are from this edition.
16 . Mann Phillips, *Adages*, pp 330–2.
17 . *Ibid*, pp 335–9 for what follows in this paragraph.
18 . *CWE* XXVII, pp 300–1.
19 . *Ibid*, p 314.
20 . *Ibid*, p 287.
21 . Mann Phillips, *Adages*, pp 344–5.
22 . *CWE* LXVI, p 11.
23 . Mann Phillips, *Adages*, p 344.
24 . *CWE* XXVII, p 286.
25 . *CWE* XLIX, pp 2–3.
26 . *CWE* XXVII, p 54; compare *CWE* XLIV, p 14.
27 . *CWE* XXVII, p 139.
28 . Mann Phillips, *Adages*, p 297 (summarizing the Adage 'Pot hits Pot').
29 . *CWE* XXVII, p 55.
30 . *CWE* LXVI, p 184.
31 . *CWE* XXVII, p 285.
32 . Thompson, *Colloquies*, p 13.
33 . *Ibid*, pp 131–3.
34 . *CWE* XXVII, p 52.
35 . *Ibid*, p 317.
36 . *Ibid*, p 316.
37 . *Ibid*.
38 . *CWE* XXXIV, p 188.
39 . *CWE* XXVII, p 283.
40 . Mann Phillips, *Adages*, p 320.
41 . *CWE* XLIV, p 14.
42 . Mann Phillips, *Adages*, p 323.
43 . *CWE* XXVII, p 286.
44 . Mann Phillips, *Adages*, p 304.
45 . *CWE* XXIII, p 224; XXVII, p 285.
46 . *CWE* XXVII, p 285.
47 . *Ibid*, p 55.
48 . *Ibid*, p 54.
49 . *Ibid*, p 139.
50 . *Ibid*, p 282.
51 . Mann Phillips, *Adages*, pp 310–11.
52 . *CWE* XXXIV, p 188.
53 . *CWE* XLIX, p 3.
54 . *CWE* XXVII, p 286.

55 . Mann Phillips, *Adages*, p 298.
56 . Thompson, *Colloquies*, p 13.
57 . *CWE* XXVII, pp 139, 296, 306; Mann Phillips, *Adages*, pp 310, 327.
58 . *CWE* XXVII, p 53.
59 . *CWE* XLIX, pp 3–4.
60 . Thompson, *Colloquies*, pp 324–6.
61 . *CWE* XLIX, p 10.
62 . Thompson, *Colloquies*, p 325.
63 . *Ibid*, p 14.
64 . *Ibid*, p 131.
65 . *CWE* XXVII, p 314.
66 . *CWE* XLIX, p 4.
67 . *CWE* XXVII, p 284.
68 . *CWE* LXVI, p 3.
69 . *CWE* XXVII, p 283.
70 . E.g. Thompson, *Colloquies*, pp 11–15, 388–94.
71 . *CWE* XXVII, p 286.
72 . Thompson, *Colloquies*, p 391.
73 . *CWE* XXVII, p 55.
74 . *CWE* XXIII, p 234.
75 . CWE XXVII, p 284.
76 . *CWE* II, p 281.
77 . *CWE* XXVII, p 311.
78 . *Ibid*.
79 . Thompson, *Colloquies*, p 293.
80 . *CWE* LXXI, p 119.
81 . *CWE* XXXIII, p 303.
82 . *CWE* XXVII, pp 306–7.
83 . *CWE* LXVI, p 192.
84 . On these developments see I.S. Robinson, *The Papacy 1073–1198* (Cambridge, 1990), pp 325–7; C. Morris, *The Papal Monarchy: the Western Church from 1050 to 1250* (Oxford, 1991), pp 20–1; and A.H. Bredero, *Christendom and Christianity in the Middle Ages* (Grand Rapids, 1994), pp 105–29.
85 . For the texts of Lateran decrees cited here see *Decrees of the Ecumenical Councils*, ed N.P. Tanner, 2 vols (London and Georgetown, 1990), I, pp 199, 222.
86 . *Ibid*, p 203.
87 . *Ibid*, p 224–5.
88 . Except where otherwise indicated, what follows on just wars is drawn from F.H. Russell, *The Just War in the Middle Ages* (Cambridge, 1975).
89 . Robinson, *The Papacy*, p 327.
90 . P. Heath, *Church and Realm, 1272–1461* (London, 1988), pp 195–6.
91 . See J.H. Barnie, *War in Medieval English Society: Social Values and the Hundred Years War, 1337–99* (London, 1974), particularly chapter 5. For scepticism about the degree of disillusion with the Crusades, see the works by Siberry cited below in note 127.

92 . This theme threads its way through Bredero's thought-provoking book, *Christendom and Christianity*.

93 . Quoted by Bredero, *Christendom and Christianity*, p 106.

94 . Excellent studies of particular episodes of papal diplomacy can be found, but they are almost wholly incidental to works which are focused on quite different issues – constitutional, legal, national and so forth.

95 . See Russell, *The Just War, passim* on this subject.

96 . Heath, *Church and Realm*, pp 111, 195–6.

97 . *Ibid*, p 111.

98 . *Ibid*, pp 107–10, 231, 279–80, 284.

99 . *Ibid*, pp 11–12, 284.

100 . J. Coleman, *English Literature in History, 1350–1400* (London, 1981), pp 72–3.

101 . Nicholas Upton, *De studio militari*, ed E. Bysshe (London, 1654).

102 . *The Essential Portions of Nicholas Upton's 'De Studio Militari' before 1446, Translated by John Blount, Fellow of All Souls (c. 1500)*, ed F.P. Barnard (Oxford, 1931), pp 28–9.

103 . Quoted by Morris, *Papal Monarchy*, p 333.

104 . M. Keen, *Chivalry* (London, 1984), pp 73–7.

105 . Heath, *Church and Realm*, p 327.

106 . *Mirk's Festial*, ed T. Erbe, Early English Text Soc., Extra Ser., 96 (1905), p 241.

107 . Barnie, *War in Medieval English Society*, pp 117–38.

108 . Still the best edition is *The Complete Works of John Gower*, ed G.C. Macaulay, Early English Text Soc., Extra Ser., 81 & 82 (1900–1).

109 . *Confessio amantis*, Book III, lines 2201 ff.

110 . *Ibid*, lines 2258, 2288.

111 . *Ibid*, 'In Praise of Peace', lines 175, 179–80.

112 . *Ibid*, lines 323–6.

113 . *Ibid*, Bk. III, lines 2261–2.

114 . *Ibid*, Bk. III, line 2263.

115 . *Ibid*, Bk. III, lines 2226–34.

116 . *Ibid*, Bk. III, lines 2235–40.

117 . *Ibid*, Bk. III, lines 2267–9.

118 . *Ibid*, 'In Praise of Peace', line 113.

119 . *Ibid*, Bk. III, lines 2294–5.

120 . *Ibid*, 'Prologus', lines 892–4.

121 . *Ibid*, Bk. III, lines 2273–7.

122 . *Ibid*, Bk. III, lines 2361–480, in particular lines 2394–7.

123 . *Ibid*, Bk. III, lines 2283–4.

124 . *Ibid*, 'In Praise of Peace', lines 281–6.

125 . *Ibid*, Bk. III, lines 2485–546.

126 . *Ibid*, Bk. III, lines 2485–546.

127 . E. Siberry, 'Criticism of crusading in fourteenth-century England', in P.W. Edbury, ed, *Crusade and Settlement* (Cardiff, 1985), pp 127–34, especially p 130. This essay complements her book *Criticism of Crusading 1095–1274* (Oxford, 1985), the conclusions of both being that the crusading ideal was

largely unscathed by criticism which was directed rather against failures in, and abuse of, practice.

128 . *Confessio amantis*, Prologus, lines 246–9.

129 . E.W. Stockton, ed, *The Major Latin Works of John Gower* (Seattle, 1962), p 125 [Bk. III, cap. vi of *Vox clamantis*].

130 . *Confessio amantis*, Prologus, lines 975–82.

131 . *Ibid*, Bk. III, lines 2265–6.

132 . *Ibid*, 'In Praise of Peace', line 309.

133 . *Ibid*, 'In Praise of Peace', line 90.

134 . *Ibid*, 'In Praise of Peace', line 86.

135 . *Ibid*, 'In Praise of Peace', line 63.

136 . *Ibid*, 'In Praise of Peace', line 380.

137 . *Ibid*, 'In Praise of Peace', lines 103–5.

138 . *Ibid*, 'In Praise of Peace', lines 125–6.

139 . *Ibid*, 'In Praise of Peace', lines 127–30.

140 . *Ibid*, 'In Praise of Peace', lines 141–7.

7. Josse Clichtove and the Just War

Howell A. Lloyd

In 1519 Josse Clichtove, doctor of theology and distinguished teacher in the University of Paris, published a treatise *De regis officio (On the Duty of a King)*, addressing it to King Louis II of Hungary. Four years later he produced another 'little work', *De bello et pace (On War and Peace)*, this time addressed to 'Christian princes' in general. Such books of advice to princes were much in vogue among members of the humanist circles in which Clichtove moved. Most notably of all, only three years before the appearance of the Parisian doctor's *De regis officio*, Erasmus had dedi-cated to the future Emperor Charles V his *Institutio principis christiani (The Education of a Christian Prince)* with its vigorous denunciation of 'this long-lasting and detestable frenzy among Christians for making war'.[1] As for Clichtove's *De bello et pace*, this too had its immediate Erasmian precursors. The *Querela pacis (Complaint of Peace)* had fol-lowed hard on the heels of the *Institutio principis*; and both had been preceded in 1515 by the edition of the *Adages* which contained Erasmus's much-enlarged version of his 'Dulce bellum inexpertis' ('War is pleasant to those without experience of it'), a version further refined in the edition of 1523. Thus Clichtove's two specific excursions into the field of political writing coincided very closely with the period when Erasmus's propa-ganda in the cause of peace reached its crescendo.

In the content of their respective contributions, too, there was much correspondence. Both drew upon a similar range of classical and biblical sources, with Clichtove displaying as great a liking as Erasmus's for Latin poets, though references to the Old Testament figured much more con-spicuously in Clichtove's work. Of course, no more than his other contemporaries could Clichtove match Erasmus's literary flair. Whereas the latter wore his learning lightly, weaving allusions seamlessly into his

145

aphoristic prose, the former relied upon direct quotations and explicit citations to substantiate his elaborately phrased contentions. Even so, those contentions tallied by and large with Erasmus's positions. Their accounts of rulership revolved around the proposition that a prince's best means of leading his subjects to virtue lay in the example which he provided through the probity of his own life.

The emphasis might differ: thus Clichtove gave greater prominence than Erasmus to the need for the prince to submit to the laws,[2] and insisted upon his duty to protect the liberty of the church – a matter upon which Erasmus barely touched.[3] Yet both subscribed to an essentially Stoic conception of the prince's mental and moral orientation as the prime condition of beneficent rule. This meant, to Clichtove, that he must 'subdue concupiscence of the mind';[4] to Erasmus, 'that perverse and vulgar fancies should be removed from his mind'.[5] The prince must cultivate wisdom. Much therefore depended upon the company he kept and the instruction he received. He must avoid 'flatterers', as both agreed,[6] and take the advice of 'learned men', who should be, by Clichtove's recommendation, 'of proven diligence in the conduct of affairs' – 'men learned', as Erasmus put it, 'through long experience of affairs and not after the manner of petty maxims'.[7] Instructed accordingly, and fore-warned meanwhile of the dangers of tyranny, the prince should aim to rule with mildness and mercy, loving truth and cultivating good faith, not only in his dealings with his own people but also in his relations with other rulers.[8]

But on a critical aspect of those relations, an aspect central to Erasmus's preoccupations, his views and those of Clichtove sharply diverged. In the *Institutio*, as in the 'Dulce bellum' and the *Querela pacis*, Erasmus denounced wholesale the evils of war and the motives of those who engaged in it, animadverting sardonically on the very notion that a war might be 'just'.[9] For his part, Clichtove devoted to the question of war and peace the sixteenth chapter of his *De regis officio* as well as the whole of his other treatise. In the chapter's first section he dilated on the benefits of peace, drawing, like Erasmus, on the evidence of the natural order and, again like Erasmus, citing Juvenal on man as the only creature disposed to use his weapons on his own kind.[10] But, Clichtove continued, it did not follow 'that there is no reason for undertaking war'. True, 'it is necessary above all that when war is undertaken it should be just and commenced for a legitimate cause'. Nevertheless, there were such causes. They included the eviction of foreign invaders, the protection of provinces and of possessions – above all, 'the defence of holy religion against the enemies

of the faith'. 'A prince,' concluded Clichtove, 'eager to emulate remarkable deeds in such glorious military fashion will wage wars with the
greatest commendation.'[11] And in his *De bello et pace* the sequence of the
argument recurred. The treatise opened by differentiating, conventionally
enough, between *pax domini* and *pax mundi* on the one hand and between
bellum domini and *bellum mundi* on the other, defining the last of these as
'that which is waged against justice and equity among those who ought to
be bound together by love'. In *De bello* Clichtove proposed to deal with
'the peace of the Lord' and 'the war of the world'.[12] A denunciation of war
might therefore be expected; and so, for a dozen chapters, it proved.
Demonstrably deriving his material in numerous passages from Erasmus's
'Dulce bellum' and *Querela*,[13] Clichtove commented afresh on the peaceful order of nature, on the blessings of peace, on the destructiveness of war,
on the duty of Christian princes and of Christians in general to live
peaceably together in accordance with Christ's teachings. Clergymen in
particular ought not to incite princes to war[14] – an adjuration which
Erasmus repeatedly pronounced in the strongest terms.[15] And yet, having
reiterated such pronouncements, Clichtove proceeded to embark upon a
series of chapters which reaffirmed all the principal grounds of the
medieval doctrine of the just war.[16]

Wars were sometimes punishments inflicted by God's command upon
perpetrators of 'abominable deeds'. They were justifiable in general 'for
the defence of one's country and one's kinsfolk',[17] though the 'law of
nature' underwrote the quite specific right to 'peaceful transit across
another's land', and so licensed resort to arms to vindicate that right.[18]
Wars of all these kinds were 'wars of the Lord'[19] and therefore, by
definition, just. This did not mean that anyone could legitimize them
simply by invoking divine sanction. It was true that 'all animate and
inanimate beings' enjoyed the right to self-defence 'by divine and natural
and human law, for it is given to whomseoever to resist force with force
(when no other means of flight and safety are left)'.[20] Yet for war as such
to be just, it must be warranted on earth by legitimate authority. Such
authority was in the hands of 'the prince' who 'is constituted governor and
administrator of the whole commonwealth so that he may defend it against
its enemies'.[21] Furthermore, a war could not be just unless it were properly
conducted, and so 'military discipline is necessary' for the avoidance of
robbery and rapine. As soldiers all too often perpetrated these evils owing
to lack of pay, princes must take care to deny them that pretext.[22] Even so,
justice required that the people be not oppressed 'by immoderate and
burdensome taxes'.[23] All these conditions being met, a prince might still

engage in war only for a 'just cause': redress of injury, punishment of crime, defence of the innocent against oppression, defence of the church – and always with the ultimate aim of securing peace and justice.[24] There remained one time-honoured cause which appeared to place Clichtove in some difficulty. In a statement regularly incorporated into subsequent discussions of the topic, Cicero had identified as the fundamental justification of war the recovery of misappropriated rights and possessions.[25] On this Clichtove resorted to dialectic.[26] On the one hand, it did not seem legitimate for Christian princes to make war in order 'to bring back to their authority towns seized at the limits of their kingdom' or 'to recover some entire region annexed by titles of their ancestors and appropriated by foreign princes'.[27] On the other hand, to tolerate such losses was plainly to leave 'a wide open door for injustice to go rioting about the world'.[28] So princes should first explore by diplomatic means all possible avenues of settling the dispute by peaceful means; and, 'when they have investigated everything and there remains no other way', then they should 'fight it out with arms'.[29]

Apart from his usual array of Scriptural and classical references, Clichtove rested his case in these chapters principally upon the authority of Augustine, the *fons et origo* of medieval just war doctrine. A great deal of the relevant Augustinian material was available in Gratian's *Decretum*,[30] a source which Clichtove readily acknowledged. In places Clichtove went beyond Augustine, as in accepting the opinion of Bishop Isidore of Seville on the validity under 'natural law' of 'resisting violence with force',[31] a view traceable to Roman law which the bishop of Hippo had nonetheless opposed.[32] To all this Erasmus had made his antagonism abundantly plain by the time Clichtove wrote. In the *Institutio* he had rounded explicitly on Augustine who 'in one or two places does not condemn war: but the entire philosophy of Christ teaches against war'.[33] In the 'Dulce bellum' he had likewise dismissed the relevant tenets of Roman law, despite the efforts of 'dialecticians, sophists' and the rest to 'distort the gospel' into agreement with them, and had singled out for special stricture wars to recover 'some petty township or other'.[34] Why, then, did the Parisian theologian, whose views on rulership and armed conflict tallied with Erasmus's in so many respects, adhere nevertheless to justifications of war which his fellow-humanist had urgently rejected?

There is a twofold answer. The first consists in the intellectual context, in differences between the theological positions at which Erasmus and Clichtove respectively arrived despite the 'humanist' predilections they had in common. The second lies in the political context, in the immediate circumstances amid which Clichtove penned his political writings.

Born about 1472 at Nieuport in Flanders, Josse Clichtove came to Paris in 1488 and entered the Collège de Boncour. Graduating in arts in 1491, he continued to study philosophy for a year or more before turning to theology, whilst still residing at the same college. In 1498 he obtained his bachelor's degree in theology, and then proceeded to the Collège de Navarre and the Sorbonne. He took the *licence* and finally his doctorate in 1506, having meanwhile been ordained into the priesthood.[35] As a student he necessarily followed the statutory curricula grounded upon the works of Aristotle in philosophy and the Bible in theology, though with heavy reliance in practice upon such textbooks as the *Summule logicales* of Peter of Spain and the *Sententiae* of Peter Lombard.

The practice was scarcely sufficient for a man of Clichtove's ambitious intellect: an ambitiousness encouraged by contact with leading figures in the ferment of Paris's academic world. His compatriot Charles Fernand of Bruges, soon to join the Benedictine order, taught him Latin at Boncour and introduced him into the circle of Robert Gaguin, general of the Trinitarian order and enthusiast for Petrarch, poetry and rhetoric. Gaguin's enthusiasms also embraced the ideas of the Italian humanist Giovanni Pico della Mirandola, would-be synthesizer of ancient philosophy, who had twice visited Paris shortly before Clichtove's own arrival there. Chief among the latter's preceptors was Jacques Lefèvre d'Étaples who, in the year when Clichtove took his arts degree, visited Florence in his turn and was powerfully influenced both by the Platonist Marsilio Ficino and by Giovanni Pico himself. For two decades from 1494 Clichtove collaborated with Lefèvre in producing improved manuals of Aristotelian philosophy for student use, and assisted as well in his master's revisionist editorial work on a range of other texts, including the neoplatonist treatises attributed to Dionysius the Areopagite. Meanwhile he produced pedagogical works of his own on grammar and rhetoric, in the shape of commentaries on treatises by two of the leading teachers of the Italian *quattrocento*: the *De eloquentia* of Gasparino Barzizza, and the *Elegantiolae* of Agostino Dati.

These interests, in the purification of language, the establishing of authentic texts, the recovery and reinstatement of the Platonic tradition in conjunction with a revivified Aristotle, were the hallmark of mainstream humanist concerns. But other influences contributed to inform Clichtove's mental and spiritual world. No student of philosophy in the Paris of the

1490s could escape exposure to nominalism with its logical rigour and ,aversion to speculative theology – and least of all Clichtove, who at the Collège de Navarre shared lodgings with the brilliant Jacques Almain, pupil of the outstanding nominalist teacher John Mair.[36] No more could a theologian at that college escape the legacy of Jean Gerson, its most celebrated luminary and chancellor of the university a century before.

Gerson's theology had embraced a form of mysticism whereby the highest levels of the human soul might experience truth and virtue to the full. That experience sprang from divine 'illumination', a concept pregnant with significance for the status and function of the clergy who were the agents of its realization on earth through preaching and administering the sacraments.[37] The concept recurred explicitly in Clichtove's own writings, notably in sermons to members of monastic orders whose ranks some of his closest friends had joined.[38] It was central to the teachings of the thirteenth-century Franciscan St Bonaventure, to Gerson the greatest teacher whom the university had ever known – and was traceable from him in turn to St Augustine.[39] And to Augustine, that major influence upon Renaissance thought,[40] Clichtove himself owed central features of his philosophical and theological positions. Time and again, in his writings and sermons, he cited Augustine: on 'wisdom' (*sapientia*), the knowledge of divine things, accessible through contemplation on a basis of prior mastery of other sciences;[41] on 'charity' (*caritas*), whereby the soul was drawn towards the universal and towards God, as distinct from the worldly preoccupations of succumbers to 'avarice' (*cupiditas*), which, in Clichtove's view, was best eradicated by the strict observance of religious vows;[42] on the mystical significance of numbers, a key to wisdom by Augustine's account, and the subject of a treatise of Clichtove's in which he described the bishop of Hippo as 'the weightiest authority in the whole church'.[43] True to that assessment, he drew more frequently upon Augustine than upon any others of the Fathers of the Church, apart from St Jerome, for the notably patristical approach he adopted for his work as a professional theologian.

Now, much of this was acceptable enough to Erasmus. Himself an editor of patristic texts and an indefatigable advocate of the relevance of classical literature to the Christian message, he repeatedly prayed in aid Augustine's famous endorsement of 'converting the works of the Egyptians to grace the temple of the Lord'.[44] Impatient of numerology, he nonetheless seized upon Platonic and neoplatonic ideas for some of the most vibrant passages in his writings, not hesitating to couple the name of Dionysius with that of Augustine as guides in the quest to understand

God's word.[45] The famous peroration in his *Moriae encomium* (*Praise of Folly*) was a hymn to mysticism, replete with allusions to Augustine's vision of ineffable bliss;[46] while images of the faithful in Christ exposed to 'illumination of knowledge of the brightness of God' (*ad illuminationem scientiae claritatis Dei*) radiated in his *Enchiridion*.[47]

But Erasmus arrived at such positions as these by a different route from Clichtove's, and a different theological perception. However conspicuous education and teaching may have been among his concerns, his experience as a university student was relatively brief. It left him contemptuous of the curricula which Clichtove sedulously followed for 18 years, and hostile towards the academic theologians whose ranks the latter joined. Nothing could be sharper, in his view, than the contrast between bickering theologians immersed in their esoteric private arguments, on the one hand, and Christ's apostles, on the other, imbued with His 'charity' in terms of long-suffering and lack of self-preoccupation, and making it manifest 'by the example of their way of life'.[48] That example and the spirit that informed it were accessible to all Christian believers. Ancient learning, when considered from the unique vantage point of the Cross, might be invaluable for interpreting the allegories and nuances of the biblical record. Yet the 'philosophy of Christ' was not the preserve of academics, and still less of priests and monks. For that philosophy was 'as common and open to everyone' as the light of the sun: it 'prevents no one from approaching', for all that there might be 'some grudging person who may keep himself apart'.[49]

Plainly set forth in the preface to the version of the New Testament that Erasmus published in 1516, such contentions could almost have been calculated to antagonize scholars of Clichtove's stamp. The Sorbonne doctor subscribed to no view of the common availability of vital theological truths. In his commentary on the first chapter of Pseudo-Dionysius's *Celestial hierarchy*, he himself had shown how the members of the priesthood ought rightly to keep themselves apart: 'for not all men have the sanctity to assume that dignity, nor do all men have the knowledge of divine things which is neccessary for understanding religious matters'. Thus, the 'spiritual mysteries' were matters not for the 'profane multitude', but for the 'most sacred priesthood'.[50] Those 'mysteries' were the sacraments of which priests were the custodians. Above all, they re-enacted Christ's redeeming sacrifice in the miracle of the mass, the vehicle of grace, for the ministry of which they alone were sanctified and consecrated. Accordingly, they must observe purity of life, uncontaminated by worldly dealings.[51] Hence Clichtove's insistence upon chastity and fasting, crucial marks of the separateness at issue, and requirements no less stern of the secular than of the regular clergy. To argue otherwise – as Erasmus indeed had argued – was to be advocate 'of a diabolical doctrine'.[52] It was true that far too many of the clergy had deviated, and continued lamentably to deviate, from the requirements of asceticism and all that it signified. They must therefore be reformed: restored, in the case of the regulars, to conformity with the original rule of their order, and, in the case of the seculars, to a condition compatible with the discharge of their sacerdotal functions.

This meant enforcing the law and traditions of the Church in all their rigour. As Clichtove declared, 'whoever does not obey the Church ought to be taken for a heathen (*ethnicus*) and a publican', and to disobey its commandments was to be 'a despiser of God (*Dei contemptor*)'.[53] For, *pace* its mystical components, the religion he professed was ultimately a religion not only of clerical elitism but also of external constraints: of divine law as the Church interpreted it, of canon law, of ecclesiastical authority. These constraints, coupled with the sacraments, afforded an indispensable counterweight to the degradation which was the condition of fallen man.[54] It was a view far removed from Erasmus's vision of human society at large as a 'great monastery', such that 'every man according to his power should strive to attain the target of Christ who was crucified for all'.[55]

'According to his power': the differences between Clichtove and Erasmus were evidently fundamental. They emerged, moreover, in the course of writings published at a time of crisis in the Church's affairs. Precipitated by Luther, the crisis compelled Erasmus to dissociate himself from the German revolutionary and eventually to engage the latter in open debate. He did so, however, in terms of 'the power of the human will' entirely consistent with the optimistic conviction of human potential which he had long since expressed. Man was 'that noble creature for whose sake alone God fashioned this marvellous fabric of the world'; and by 'the power of the human will' man 'can devote himself to or turn himself away from those things which lead to eternal salvation'.[56] This, then, was the conviction that sustained him in his persistent propaganda against war. If men in general and princes in particular would only will it, the prospect of peace on earth was not an impossible dream. Indeed, 'it should not be very difficult to achieve, if everyone would desist from deluding himself with his own concerns', and 'if Christ should be with us in our planning'.[57] Given that conviction, no compromise was admissible with arguments to the effect that war might in certain circumstances be justified, for such arguments could serve only to seduce men away from the objective which otherwise lay within their reach.

But Clichtove did not share Erasmus's conviction. Notwithstanding his humanist leanings, he adhered in his theology to a conception of fallen man rooted in the position of the later Augustine. For him, 'the inclination of our will [is] towards evil and the performance of evil' owing to the 'defect and perversity' of human nature, itself the legacy of the sin of Adam and irremediable by human effort or desert.[58] Against that inclination stood the bulwark of the Church – its law, its traditions and, above all, its sacraments, with the ministry of which the clergy were charged. Erasmus seemed to decry that bulwark, and Luther assailed it. Clichtove denounced them both, and in doing so was driven to renounce as well his allegiance to his mentor Lefèvre d'Étaples, his friendship with whom foundered on the question of clerical celibacy,[59] an essential ingredient of his view of the clergy's distinctive status. Meanwhile he devoted himself to renovating the clergy's sense of that status and their sacerdotal function, in efforts which contributed directly to the position which the Church itself would adopt at the Council of Trent.[60]

It was the same perception of the human condition that underpinned Clichtove's views on the question of war. Man through his sinfulness continually waged war upon God. Yet war as such was a reversal of the process, a punishment which God inflicted upon man for his sins.[61] War was thus a manifestation at once of human wickedness and of divine justice. Accordingly, those who engaged in it acted as God's instruments, as long as their aims in doing so were compatible with His ultimately benevolent purposes towards mankind. Hence an oxymoron, a device so seductive to humanist lovers of rhetoric: 'Among the true worshippers of God, wars themselves are peaceable in so far as they are waged not for cupidity or cruelty, but for peace.'[62] The case for the just war followed inexorably from these premises. While conflicts and the horrors that went with them were profoundly to be deplored, they were also inevitable, owing to the condition of fallen man; and wars motivated and conducted in accordance with divine and natural law were necessary correctives to the effects of that condition. To deny altogether the legitimacy of war on the part of the well-intentioned was to release wickedness to go rioting at will about the world. Indeed, by Clichtove's account, the use of war in 'the last resort' was comparable with the Church's use of 'excommunication for reproof of the stubborn'. And the comparison, as he saw it, was specifically relevant to princes who aimed with just cause 'to recover their possessions'.[63] Even so, his observations on that feature of the just war theory were further conditioned by considerations of a very different order.

Although Clichtove came from a tolerably prosperous family,[64] his education at Paris and, especially, his doctorate in theology were costly investments on which his official earnings as a university teacher could have brought him only a modest return.[65] His attempts after taking his first degree to avail himself of the *droit des gradués* by securing an ecclesiastical benefice seem to have been unsuccessful.[66] Insofar as he hoped thereafter for material and professional advancement, his prospects in an age of patronage depended upon the support of the influential. That support was forthcoming. Clichtove obtained it partly through his connection with the highly reputed Lefèvre d'Étaples and partly through his own pedagogical abilities, reinforcing the links which he forged by these means through addressing his written works to appropriate dedicatees. Even before gaining his *licence* in theology, he was acting as tutor to offspring first of the Briçonnet, financiers, prelates and counsellors to the kings of France from Louis XI onwards, and then of the d'Amboise whose leading member, Georges, was cardinal archbishop of Rouen and, in effect, first minister to Louis XII.[67] By the opening of the reign of Francis I, however, Clichtove's principal pupil was Louis Guillard, descendant of royal secretaries and son of Charles Guillard who had held office as second *président* in the Paris *parlement* since 1508 and served repeatedly on royal diplomatic missions, including Francis's campaign of 1519 to win election to the imperial crown.[68] It was his involvement with the Guillard that brought Clichtove face to face with political affairs and their impact upon ecclesiastical matters.

In 1513 Pope Leo X had designated Louis Guillard bishop elect of the see of Tournai in Hainault. The appointment was sensitive both in ecclesiastical and in political respects. At 22 years of age Guillard was too young by five years for full episcopal status, and in any case was still in minor orders. Tournai itself lay in the march between Valois France and the Habsburg Netherlands, a region of endemic political and military dispute. By the treaty of Senlis (1493), Tournai had been confirmed as parcel of the French royal domain. But the position was inherently unstable. Its instability was exacerbated in the very year of Guillard's appointment, when Henry VIII of England seized Tournai on the strength of his alliance with Maximilian of Habsburg and Ferdinand of Spain and his recent recognition by the late Pope Julius II as rightful king of France.[69] Supplementing the town's fortifications with a new citadel, Henry proceeded to earmark its bishopric for his own minister, Thomas Wolsey. Papal confirmation was obtained, subject to Guillard's remaining absent from the diocese and refusing to swear allegiance to the English crown. While Guillard did indeed decline so to swear, he nonetheless maintained his claim; and a prolonged 'battle of the bishops'[70] ensued. Meanwhile Wolsey embarked upon the diplomatic manoeuvres which culminated in the famous treaty of 'universal peace' proclaimed at London in 1518. Those manoeuvres were facilitated by the ascendancy in the Netherlands of councillors urging the benefits of peace with France upon the young Archduke Charles of Habsburg, a policy which encouraged Erasmus in his pacific addresses to the future emperor and to which he alluded directly in the dedicatory epistle of his *Querela pacis*.

In subsidiary agreements to the Treaty of London, King Henry conceded the restoration of Tournai to France. Louis Guillard at last took possession of the bishopric. For assistance with his episcopal duties in a difficult diocese he called upon the services of his mentor, Clichtove, whom he appointed to a benefice in the town. Clichtove tackled his role with characteristic devotion. Properly discharged, episcopal duties included the regular holding of diocesan synods for the discipline and instruction of the clergy.[71] At the synod Guillard convened in April 1520 Clichtove preached two sermons, the substance of which informed the statutes the bishop subsequently published. The preacher reproved the local priests for scandalous misbehaviour, stressed the requirement of obedience to the hierarchy, and waxed eloquent upon the errors of Luther whose 'diabolical doctrine' – a favourite phrase – threatened to 'demolish the ecclesiastical order'.[72] But the opportunity which Guillard and Clichtove both clearly recognized to make Tournai a laboratory of clerical reform was as short-lived as the international peace that had facilitated it. In 1521 hostilities broke out afresh between French and imperial forces, in Italy, in Navarre and on France's north-eastern borderlands where Robert de La Marck, lord of Sedan, took up arms on King Francis's behalf. Once more Wolsey donned his mantle as arbiter of peace, convening conferences to the purpose at Calais and at Bruges. Whatever the English minister's underlying intentions, his overt efforts were frustrated, not least by the attitude the emperor struck at Bruges, where he was reported to have affirmed every man's obligation under divine law to claim his right.[73] Evidently, in Charles's view the relevant right in his own case included the ancient Burgundian claim to Tournai, to which his troops were laying siege even as the talks continued. At the end of November the town surrendered.[74] By then Bishop Guillard, and Clichtove with him, had retired to Paris.

The loyalty the frustrated bishop had displayed towards France warranted some compensation for his eviction. It came in a form made available through disloyalty on the part of one of his episcopal colleagues. In 1518 Érard de La Marck, brother of Robert of Sedan and pluralist bishop both of Liège and of Chartres, renounced his allegiance to Francis I, apparently through pique over the king's failure to support him for a cardinal's hat, and threw in his lot with Charles of Habsburg. The king promptly seized the temporalities of his diocese of Chartres, and three years later granted them, with the 'fruits' of the spiritualities as well, to Louis Guillard. But the grant excited the opposition of the cathedral chapter, the canons claiming that through the *de facto* vacancy of the see the administration of its perquisites appertained by right to them. Litigation followed before the *parlement* of Paris. The dispute was compounded by Érard de La Marck's continued assertion of his entitlement to the perquisites at issue, or at least to an indemnity assessed upon Guillard's presumed resources as *de jure* bishop of Tournai.[75] In due course Guillard agreed to indemnify his rival. He endeavoured to honour the agreement through the sale in the Netherlands of cloth purchased in France from funds delivered by him to compliant merchants. The merchants proved unreliable, with embarrassing consequences for the bishop.[76] So the wrangle persisted, attaining the proportions of a significant diplomatic incident. At length Pope Clement VII ratified a formula, approved by the monarchs concerned, for a financial settlement satisfactory to the episcopal parties, coupled with a redistribution of bishoprics which left Guillard in possession of Chartres. The principal losers were the canons of Chartres, whose sufficiently tenable objections were simply brushed aside. Yet the entire episode, driven by motives of financial gain and prolonged by commercial manoeuvres, seemed designed to ridicule Clichtove's thesis on the 'separate' status and way of life of the clerical elite, and the sacerdotal responsibilities which ought to be their exclusive preoccupation.

It was in the midst of this episode that Clichtove produced his *De bello et pace*. As he did so, in 1523, war was again in the offing. While the French king prepared to lead his armies afresh in Italy, English troops were poised again to land in France with Imperial support from the Netherlands and elsewhere, including now the forces of Francis I's renegade constable, the duke of Bourbon.[77] Past experience showed that in such a conflict possession of Tournai and its environs would once more become a live issue.[78] So Clichtove reached for his pen, to suggest in the course of a general argument on behalf of peace that, while war for acquisitive purposes was unjustifiable, a prince might justly fight to recover what was rightfully his. Of course, the French claim to the territories of which Tournai formed a part was historic, traceable to the ancient treaty of Verdun of 843. But historical precedent did not figure in Clichtove's statement of the case for a just war. He grounded it upon higher authority: the law of nature and of nations, coupled with Scripture and with the teachings of the Fathers of the Church. If Francis would regulate his policies by such considerations as these, he could with justice prosecute his claim to the marcher lands on the north of his realm – especially now that all possible avenues towards a peaceful settlement had been explored, in the years leading up to the treaty of 'universal peace' and in subsequent negotiations. And the effect of King Francis's successfully resorting to arms would be to release Louis Guillard from his spiritually dangerous predicament, to extricate him from the morass in which the Chartres affair was immersing him ever more deeply, and to reinstate him in his bishopric of Tournai where he and Clichtove could resume the work of reform which they had begun.

'Nowadays', observed Erasmus, 'men have become so accustomed to war that they can scarcely imagine anyone whom it does not please'.[79] His own campaign against war certainly jarred with the military conditioning of the leaders of Renaissance Europe. Humanist precepts served even to reinforce that conditioning, as scholars drew the battle-loaded histories of Greece and Rome to the attention of princes already eager to emulate the deeds of their ancestors.[80] They shared that eagerness with noble elites instructed from boyhood in warlike pursuits and so poised to approach war itself as the most glorious of field sports. Of course, their expectations were often disappointed, in an era of change in the conduct of war, of development in military technology and professionalization of military personnel. But such changes tended to underpin extensions of princely power, as the mounting costs of war stimulated enlargement of the apparatus of government to enhance royal revenue-raising capability. Although there were moments when the case for peace tallied with the manoeuvres of politicians such as Wolsey, in general high-minded intellectuals who urged that case argued against both the ethos and the perceived interests of those to whom they looked for patronage. Even humanists rarely urged it with complete conviction. In England Thomas More, Erasmus's friend and an ornament of Henry VIII's court, described in his *Utopia* (1516) how the citizens of that commonwealth 'detest and abhor' war and yet accepted the need to engage in it for the defence of their country or the support of oppressed neighbours.[81] In his *Diálogo de las cosas ocurridas en Roma* (1527) the Castilian Alfonso de Valdés, admirer of Erasmus and secretary to the Emperor Charles V, conceded the legitimacy of war for reasons of self-defence and motives of 'just vengeance'.[82] Meanwhile in France Claude de Seyssel, translator of Greek histories and royal diplomat, maintained in his *Grant monarchie de France* (1519) that, while princes 'ought to love and seek peace', they were authorized 'by divine and human law' to make war in order 'to help and defend' their allies or 'to recover one's own which has been unlawfully taken'.[83]

It would have needed a bolder man than Josse Clichtove to defy the prevailing political, social and intellectual trend. His character has been interpreted as that of a timid man, deferential to his superiors, unwilling for reasons of 'prudent foresight', as he himself explained, to accept in 1517 an offer of appointment as confessor to the future Charles V[84] – though Erasmus thought him unacceptable 'to the courtiers' owing simply to his being 'too thin and having scarcely ten hairs on his head'.[85] Considerations of prudence may also have contributed to his abandonment of his long-standing friendship with his mentor Lefèvre d'Étaples as the latter became suspected of radical sympathies, and his subsequent alignment with the Sorbonne in condemning the teachings of Luther. Yet that condemnation was entirely in line with Clichtove's own theological and ecclesiastical convictions. Throughout the 1520s he expressed his convictions vigorously and fruitfully, in sermons, in anti-Lutheran tracts, above all in his activities at diocesan and provincial synods. At Tournai, at Chartres, most notably at Paris in 1528 where the synod of Sens convened under the aegis of the Chancellor and Archbishop Antoine Duprat, Clichtove figured not merely as a participant but as the framer of statutes for the discipline of the clergy. The terms of those statutes were to reverberate in the decrees of the Council of Trent;[86] and Tridentine pronouncements on the mysteries of the sacraments, together with the distinctive status and functions of the clergy, would inform the position and the fortunes of the Church for generations to come. Thus the Parisian doctor caught the tide of history. He caught it as well through his endorsement, however qualified and from whatever motives, of the legitimacy of war undertaken 'with the advice of prudent men'.[87] It is a fortunate intellectual who can discover so close a concurrence of his convictions with the dictates of prudence and of interest. But proponents of war have not lacked intellectual support, throughout the ages.

Notes

1. *Institutio*, LB IV, 610F. Citations from Erasmus's writings refer to the ten-volume edition of his *Opera omnia* published at Leiden in 1703–6, and conventionally identified by the initials 'LB' followed by volume and column numbers.
2. *De regis officio* (Paris, 1519), fos 18v–21r. Cf. *Institutio*, LB IV, 592D, 595D, 602A; *Panegyricus*, LB IV, 530C.
3. Cf. Erasmus's remarks on the prince's duty to support 'the piety of priests' with his dismissal of the monastic life as 'a kind of idleness': *Institutio*, LB IV, 607B, 598A.
4. *De regis officio*, fo. 13v.
5. *Institutio*, LB IV, 584E.
6. *De regis officio*, fos 44v sqq; *Institutio*, LB IV, 583F sqq.
7. *De regis officio*, fo. 23v; *Institutio*, LB IV, 562D.
8. *De regis officio*, fos 53r–55v, 36v–47v; *Institutio*, LB IV, 571F–573D, 566E, 600B, 603C.
9. *Institutio*, LB IV, 609A; 'Dulce bellum', LB II, 961B; *Querela*, LB IV, 639F.
10. Juvenal, *Saturae*, XV, 159–71.
11. *De regis officio*, fos 57v–58v.
12. *De bello et pace* (Paris, 1523), fo. 4v.
13. J. Hutton, 'Erasmus and France: the propaganda for peace', *Studies in the Renaissance* 8 (1961), pp 108–9.
14. *De bello et pace*, fos 24v–27r.
15. 'Dulce bellum', LB II, 967C; *Querela*, LB, IV 634C–635B.
16. The standard work is F.H. Russell, *The Just War in the Middle Ages* (Cambridge, 1975). The doctrine is summarized by J. Barnes, 'The just war', in N. Kretzmann, A. Kenny and J. Pinborg, eds, *The Cambridge History of Later Medieval Philosophy* (Cambridge, 1982), pp 771–84.
17. *De bello et pace*, fo. 30r.
18. *De bello et pace*, fo. 30v.
19. *De bello et pace*, fo. 31r.
20. *De bello et pace*, fo. 34v.
21. *De bello et pace*, fo. 32r.
22. *De bello et pace*, fos 32v–33v.
23. *De bello et pace*, fo. 33v.
24. *De bello et pace*, fos 32, 35.
25. *De bello et pace*, fo. 32r; Cicero, *De officiis*, I.xi.36.
26. *De bello et pace*, fos 35v–38r.
27. *De bello et pace*, fo. 35v.
28. *De bello et pace*, fo. 37r.
29. *De bello et pace*, fo. 38r.
30. Notably, Causa 23, quaestiones 1–8: a total of 165 canons.
31. *Decretum* D.1 c.7.
32. *Digest* 1.1.3. See Russell, *Just War*, pp 56 and 96, note 23.
33. *Institutio*, LB IV, 608E.
34. 'Dulce bellum', LB II, 961B, 965A.

35 . Jean-Pierre Massaut, *Josse Clichtove, l'humanisme et la réforme du clergé*, 2 vols (Paris, 1968), I, p 205. Massaut's study, rich in material and in insights on many aspects of Clichtove's career, provides the fullest study of its subject's work and milieu. Some corrections and amendments on points of detail are proposed in the account by J.K. Farge, *Biographical Register of Paris Doctors of Theology, 1500–1536* (Toronto, 1980), pp 90–104. The older work by J.A. Clerval, *De Judoci Clichtovei Neoportuensis, doctoris theologi parisiensis et carnotensis canonici vita et operibus (1472–1543)* (Paris, 1894), is seriously defective.

36 . On the survival of medieval logic see the remarks by E.J. Ashworth, 'The eclipse of medieval logic', in Kretzmann, Kenny and Pinborg, eds, *Cambridge History of Later Medieval Philosophy*, pp 791–2. On Almain and Mair respectively, see Farge, *Biographical Register*, pp 15–18, 304–11.

37 . For Gerson's views on the *status perfectionis* of the clergy and their functions, directly appointed by Christ, of 'illuminare per doctrinam et praedectionem, perficere per sacramentorum ministrationem', see J.L. Connolly, *John Gerson, Reformer and Mystic* (Louvain, 1928), p 105; L.B. Pascoe, *John Gerson: Principles of Church Reform* (Leiden, 1973), p 153.

38 . See, for instance, quotations from Clichtove's manuscript commonplace book, in Massaut, *Josse Clichtove*, I, pp 370, 390.

39 . É. Gilson, *La philosophie au moyen âge*, 2nd edn (Paris, 1952), pp 714, 446.

40 . Cf. P.O. Kristeller, *Studies in Renaissance Thought and Letters* (Rome, 1956), pp 355–72.

41 . On Augustine's conception of wisdom, see É. Gilson, *The Christian Philosophy of Saint Augustine*, ed L.E.M. Lynch (London, 1961), pp 115–26, 305. Cf. Massaut, *Josse Clichtove*, I, pp 240–1, 245, 271–3; also E.F. Rice Jr, *The Renaissance Idea of Wisdom* (Cambridge, MA, 1958), pp 4–13.

42 . Clichtove, *De laude monasticae religionis* (Paris, 1513), fo. 13r: 'At vero cupiditas ipsa est terrenorum affectio: potissimum per tria praedicta religionis vota imminuitur, debilitatur et frangitur'. Cf. Gilson, *Christian Philosophy*, pp 118–20, 136–42.

43 . *De mystica numerorum significatione* (Paris, 1513), fo. 2r.

44 . *Antibarbari*, LB X, 1731C; *Enchiridion*, LB V, 25F. Cf. Augustine, *De doctrina Christiana*, 2.40.60: *Patralogia Latina*, XXXIV, ed. J.-P. Migne (Paris, 1887), col. 63.

45 . *Enchiridion*, LB V, 29F.

46 . M.A. Screech, *Erasmus: Ecstasy and the Praise of Folly* (London, 1980), pp 172–3.

47 . LB V, 28A.

48 . *Moriae*, LB IV, 465A–471A, citing St Paul's definition of 'charity' (I Corinthians xiii).

49 . *Paraclesis*, LB V, 140B.

50 . Clichtove, *Theologia vivificans* (Paris, 1515), fos 53v–54r.

51 . Clichtove, *De vita et moribus sacerdotum* (Paris, 1519), fo. 16r.

52 . *De vita*, fo. 61v ('diabolici dogmatis').

53 . *De vita*, fo. 51r.

54 . Massaut, *Josse Clichtove*, II, p 391.

55 . Erasmus, Epistola CCCXXIX (Letter to Volz), LB III (i), 346B, D.

56 . *Enchiridion*, LB V, 55C; *De libero arbitrio*, LB IX, 1220F–1221A.

57 . *Institutio*, LB IV, 610F.

58 . Clichtove, *Sermones* (Cologne, 1535), fos 7F, 151F–152A; cf. Clichtove, *De necessitate peccati Adae* (Paris, 1519), fo. 28r ('ex corruptione naturae per Adae peccatum inducta'), also fo. 35v ('opera iustitiae humanae non meruerunt talem ac tantum redemptorem'). For Augustine's position, see G.R. Evans, *Augustine on Evil* (Cambridge, 1982), pp 121–2.

59 . Massaut, *Josse Clichtove*, II, pp 182, 374.

60 . Massaut, *Josse Clichtove*, II, p 348.

61 . *De bello et pace*, fo. 40r: 'Bella in deum gerimus ... Quid mirum ergo videri debet: si & deus in nos bellum retorqueat?'

62 . *De bello et pace*, fo. 32v, crèditing the formulation to Augustine, *De diversis ecclesiae observationibus* [sic]: 'Apud veros dei cultores, etiam ipsa bella pacata sunt: quae non cupiditate aut crudelitate, sed pacis studio geruntur.'

63 . *De bello et pace*, fo. 38r.

64 . Massaut, *Josse Clichtove*, I, pp 99–100.

65 . Cf. L.W.B. Brockliss, 'Patterns of attendance at the University of Paris, 1400–1800', *The Historical Journal* 21 (1978), pp 526–30.

66 . M.J. Kraus, 'Patronage and reform in the France of the Préréforme: the case of Clichtove', *Canadian Journal of History* 6 (1971), p 47.

67 . The Briçonnet network is conveniently described by R.-H. Bautier, 'Guillaume Briçonnet, évêque de Meaux, et la haute administration du royaume', *Journal des Savants* (1987), pp 79–87. On the d'Amboise see M. Harsgor, *Recherches sur le personnel du Conseil du Roi sous Charles VIII et Louis XII*, 4 vols (Paris, 1980), II, pp 918–69.

68 . On Louis Guillard's ancestry, see A. Pommier, *Chroniques de Souligné-sous-Vallon et Flacé*, 2 vols (Angers, 1889), I, pp 125–34. For Charles Guillard's role in the Imperial election campaign, P. de Vaissière, ed, *Journal de Jean Barrillon, secrétaire du Chancelier Duprat (1515–1521)*, 2 vols (Paris, 1897–9), II, p 120.

69 . On these events see C.G. Cruickshank, *The English Occupation of Tournai, 1513–1519* (Oxford, 1971), pp 1–12, 143–4. On the immediate diplomatic background, J.J. Scarisbrick, *Henry VIII* (London, 1968), pp 31–7. On the long-term question of possession of Tournai, D. Potter, *War and Government in the French Provinces: Picardy, 1470–1560* (Cambridge, 1993), especially pp 39, 44–5.

70 . The term is Cruickshank's, who provides a detailed narrative: *English Occupation*, pp 143–87.

71 . R. Doucet, *Les institutions de la France au XVIe siècle*, 2 vols (Paris, 1948), II, p 724.

72 . Cf. above, n 52. Clichtove's efforts at Tournai are described by Massaut, *Josse Clichtove*, II, pp 34–41: quotations from the synodal sermons at pp 36–8. The synod of 1520 was the only one held at Tournai between 1509 and 1568.

73 . J.G. Russell, *Peacemaking in the Renaissance* (London, 1986), p 109.

74 . R.J. Knecht, *Renaissance Warrior and Patron: the Reign of Francis I* (Cambridge, 1994), pp 176–80.

75 . L.E. Halkin, *Les conflits de juridiction entre Érard de La Marck et le chapitre cathédrale de Chartres* (Paris, 1933), pp 56–7, 63–8.

76 . H. Dubief, 'Les opérations commerciales de Louis Guillart, évêque de Tournai, puis de Chartres, en 1524', *Revue du Nord* 43 (1961), pp 149–54.

77 . S.J. Gunn, 'The duke of Suffolk's march on Paris in 1523', *EHR* 101 (1986), p 596.

78 . Cf. Potter, *War and Government*, p 267.

79 . 'Dulce bellum', LB II, 951E.

80 . Perhaps the outstanding instance is the distinguished Hellenist Guillaume Budé's *L'Institution du Prince* (1518/19), addressed to Francis I and replete with such examples despite its author's protestations that princes 'can increase their renown more surely through peaceful than through warlike acts' (cf. C. Bontems, L.-P. Raybaud and J.-P. Brancourt, eds, *Le prince dans la France des XVIe et XVIIe siècles* (Paris, 1965), pp 6, 71–5, 112 and 75–139 *passim* for the text of the tract).

81 . Thomas More, *Utopia* (London, 1968), p 118.

82 . J.A. Fernandez-Santamaria, *The State, War and Peace. Spanish Political Thought in the Renaissance, 1516–1559* (Cambridge, 1977), pp 38, 47, 153–5.

83 . C. de Seyssel, *La monarchie de France*, ed J. Poujol (Paris, 1961), pp 190–1.

84 . Kraus, 'Patronage and Reform', pp 66–8.

85 . Letters to More and to Beatus Rhenanus, in P.S. Allen, ed, *Opus Epistolarum Des. Erasmi Roterodami*, 11 vols (Oxford, 1906–47), III (1517–19), nos. 597 (p 4), 628 (p 51).

86 . Massaut, *Josse Clichtove*, II, pp 207, 226, 283–4, 340–1.

87 . *De bello et pace*, fo. 38r.

8. 'Wise and Experimented': Sir William Pelham, Elizabethan Soldier and Landlord, *c.* 1560–87

R.W. Ambler

Towards the end of January 1575, Edward Woodshawe wrote to Lord Burghley from Antwerp, asking him to send over in secret either Sir William Drury or Mr William Pelham, 'both wise and experimented in martial affairs'.[1] Pelham's reputation was based on his work as a military engineer with experience of active service in Scotland and France, together with a period of soldiering in Ireland in 1569 and 1570. He had also been lieutenant of the ordnance since 1567 and his military career had another 13 years to run, ending with his death at Flushing in December 1587 while serving with the earl of Leicester in the Low Countries.

Despite the apparent and, for the period, characteristically episodic nature of his career, the post of lieutenant of the ordnance provided a degree of continuity: Pelham was one of a relatively small number of professional soldiers with a permanant position in government service. It also provided the basis for the establishment of a landed estate since, as one of three younger sons of another Sir William, from Laughton in Sussex, Pelham's only inheritance was a third share of a £20 annuity from his father's lands left to him in 1538 when he was still a minor. By the time of his death he had accumulated an estate in north Lincolnshire with a clear annual value of some £980, although his debt to the crown was said to be £8807 14s 5½d.[2]

His first recorded experience in the field, when 4000 Frenchmen were evicted from the port of Leith in 1560, was also the first act of siege warfare of the reign of Elizabeth. Pelham's role as commander of the pioneers – the 'trench maister' – marked his involvement in a developing branch of military science, although it never achieved the degree of either theoretical or practical coherence and continuity that it did on the mainland of Europe because of the intermittent English experience of foreign warfare. The

limited opportunities for English engineers were reflected in criticisms of
Pelham's conduct at Leith. According to the military writer Humphrey
Barwick, his lack of practical experience – having 'neither served in
Fraunce, nor with the Emperour' – meant that he left his trench open to
attack by the French at a cost of 200 lives.[3] Other accounts, however,
commended the diligence of Pelham and his men and said that the 'opinion
of their slackness' was 'offered wrongfully, since there is no day and
scarcely any night on which they lose not some of their blood and decrease
the enemy's force'. He was said, together with other officers, to deserve
'commendation to the Queen'.[4]

Insofar as it is possible to discern any theory underpinning the conduct
of the siege of Leith and Pelham's part in it, older-style tactics were
combined with more modern elements of siegecraft. The fortifications the
besiegers faced had been begun in 1549 under the direction of an Italian
engineer. With work carried out in 1559, they were the most advanced of
their type in Britain. The English pioneers constructed fortified 'mounts',
one of which on the south side of the town was named after Pelham and
contained 1200 soldiers. It 'was cast square with four bulwarkes at euery
corner, and 12 battering pieces placed in places conuenient' in an attempt
to dominate the fortifications of Leith through artillery fire. While this use
of mounts looked back to the practice of the previous century, entrench-
ment was a response to newer developments in the science of fortifications. In these, well-placed artillery played a central part, although,
whatever the place of military science and theory in the conduct of the
siege of Leith, hunger was an important factor in bringing the French to
reach terms with their besiegers.[5]

Within two years Pelham was on the European mainland in command
of the pioneers at Le Havre in November 1562, as well as serving at the
siege of Caen the next year. Le Havre brought him experience among
fortifications built to guard the Seine estuary which were part of the earlier
military legacy of French fortress warfare. This had reached a peak under
Henry II in the middle of the sixteenth century. Yet lack of artillery and
money among their Huguenot allies meant that the English forces were not
involved in prolonged siege warfare. According to Sir John Smythe, a
vigorous protagonist of the continued use and usefulness of English
archers, it was the main concern of Chatillon, the French commander, to
have the assistance of English archers at Caen. The thousand Englishmen
Pelham is reported as having taken there in February 1563 included
pioneers, but although the castle was said to have been 'trenched about' the
works were not deep and the siege was over by 2 March.[6]

Despite its fortifications Le Havre was said to be weak, needing reinforcements to sustain it against the French Catholic army. Pelham's work in its defence brought increasing demands for manpower as the works were elaborated: in November 1562 he requested a thousand more men than the 200 he had so that 'the least molehill about the town shall not be lost without many bloody blows'. Although wounded in the leg Pelham remained active and became a counsellor of the English commander, Ambrose Dudley, earl of Warwick. He was involved in negotiations on the terms of surrender in July 1563 and served as hostage during the English withdrawal.[7]

Warwick's patronage was to be important in Pelham's later advancement, but Pelham had also begun to be recognized as an expert in fortifications and in 1564 he became involved in schemes which were in progress to remodel the defences of Berwick. The whole system there had become obsolete by the early sixteenth century and improvements were begun during the reign of Henry VIII. Despite these the fortifications remained weak and particularly vulnerable to artillery attack. Sir Richard Lee, who, with Sir Thomas Palmer, had reported on the Border defences in 1550, was ordered to begin the replacement of the medieval works at Berwick in 1558. Both Lee and Palmer were experienced in new methods of fortification: Lee had seen service on the continent and training under the Bohemian Stefan von Haschenperg in the short-lived Office of Works established by Henry VIII; Palmer had worked at Boulogne in the 1540s. Lee was often away on other business and so unable to exercise constant supervision over his plans. The Italian engineer Giovanni Portinari had been consulted about the Berwick works in the spring of 1560. When in April 1564 Lee breached the medieval wall, the anxiety aroused in London about both the nature and the cost of his work led to Portinari being consulted again with another Italian, Jacopo Contio. Pelham was ordered to go with them to Berwick but although there were differences over the way the works were to be continued, in which Pelham and Lee tended to agree against the two Italians, they were resolved in a way which typified the English approach to military science in the period. Lee was left with considerable discretion in carrying out the proposals but, despite the interest in them in the 1560s, changing political and financial priorities meant that the new defences were only partially completed. Berwick still had only its medieval wall to the south and south-west, although the work that Lee did carry out remains largely intact, refaced in more recent times. The inclusion of Pelham in the commendation the earl of Bedford conveyed to Cecil for the way in which differences among the Berwick engineers had been overcome reflected his role as a pragmatist in a situation where financial exigencies were a powerful solvent of theory.[8]

Pelham's expertise in fortifications continued to be recognized in work he was asked to undertake in the 1570s, although the constant necessity to adapt and refurbish meant that he had little scope to demonstrate any capacity for innovation. In July 1574 he was associated with Lord Cobham and Sir William Winter in putting the forts of the Medway and the Isle of Sheppey on an operational basis to meet the threat of an attack by Spanish warships from the Flemish ports. The existing forts, together with the Gravesend 'Bulwerkes', were to be furnished with artillery, while a new fort was to be erected at Sheerness. Pelham and Winter also recommended that Queenborough, which was considered as a possible anchorage for the English fleet, should be refortified. Here Pelham was again working on modifications to works in which Richard Lee had been involved nearly 30 years before when he had been brought back from France to strengthen Queenborough and the blockhouses on the mouth of the Medway before moving on to work at Tynemouth and Berwick. Pelham's and Winter's plans for Queenborough were curtailed by the need for 'good husbandry' and only partly accepted. They were ordered to 'forbear all other fortifi-cations', limiting their work to the construction of a sea-wall and the plans drawn for them by Robert Lieth at a cost of 40 nobles were abandoned.[9]

In December 1576 Pelham visited Hull in response to the corporation's requests to the Privy Council for relief from the burden of maintaining its fortifications which he was ordered to 'view and survey' with others 'of skill and judgment'. They had been built on the orders of Henry VIII from 1541 and were another example of the partial and piecemeal application of continental models in England. Again, Pelham's work was that of repair rather than fundamental refurbishment. His largest piece of new work, the addition of a jetty to protect the fort's south blockhouse, epitomized the limitations which fluctuating military pressures and financial commitment imposed on his development as a military architect.[10] It was, however, a role in which his expertise continued to be recognized. In November 1585 he was involved with Sir Walter Raleigh, Lord Burghley and others in a discussion in the presence of the queen of the fortifications at Portsmouth where disagreements had arisen over the work of William Pearce, an able theoretician who lacked experience in directing works. As a result of their mediation Pearce was requested to submit new plans and estimates.[11]

It was Pelham's experience of defensive works that drew him into the Irish campaign against the rebels Gerald, earl of Desmond and James Fitzmaurice Fitzgerald. He had been asked to go to assist in improving the defences of the Pale in August 1579; he found the forts and castles, including Dublin, needing attention and requested artificers from England for this work. It was in Ireland that he was knighted by the Lord Justice, Sir William Drury, and on Drury's death in October 1579 Pelham succeeded to his office, assuming leadership there until a new viceroy could be despatched.[12]

The military problems which the Fitzmaurices' and Desmonds' rebellion created for Sir William were substantially different from those of his earlier campaigns. Instead of relatively static siege warfare, the operations in Ireland were more mobile and concerned with establishing territorial supremacy in the areas of rebellion, while allies such as the Butlers were also alive to the possibility of making personal territorial gains. At first the rebels did attempt to adopt a defensive stance, but the outmoded defences of their castles were quickly battered down, while the fort they constructed at Smerwick was dismissed as 'a vain toy'. Although Sir William wrote to Walsingham requesting that ten gunners, two carpenters and two saltpetre men be sent to him, he experienced considerable difficulties in moving 'the great ordnance' around so that sea-borne material was crucial to his plans. The ultimate effect of his attacks was to force the rebels into the open countryside.[13]

Whatever the nature of the campaign, the financial constraints imposed by a wary central government were as constant in Ireland as on military engineering and were no less significant because of the different conditions in which they operated. In December 1579 Sir William's request for supplies brought a response referring to the 'evil ordering' of earlier provisions. He was reminded that the rebels in Kerry and Munster had gathered 'great quantities of victuals for their relief' which he should 'cause ... to be intercepted for the maintenance and relief of Her Majesty's garrisons'. While he received money in the course of 1580 – £10,000 in May together with victuals and other material – the Privy Council continued to pursue potential 'defalcacions of munition and victual'.[14]

With Munster and Leinster in arms, Sir William was unable to make much headway in 1579. His ally the earl of Ormond was left in Waterford to prepare for a western campaign while Sir William returned to Dublin. Government support was yielded only reluctantly, with sufficient money, munitions and victuals for 2000 men for three months. 'I would to God,' Ormond said, 'I could feed soldiers with the air, and throw down castles with my breath, and furnish naked men with a wish', although Burghley commented that there were more in the queen's pay in Ireland than there had been for hundreds of years. Returning to Waterford Sir William began his campaign in February 1580. He had reported the dangers of the rebellion in November 1579, including the rumours fostered by Dr Nicholas Sanders, an exiled English recusant who had landed with James Fitzmaurice, that a navy had been prepared in Italy 'to come to the relief of the Papists ... at the equal charges of the King of Spain and the Bishop of Rome'.[15]

The fear that Sanders and Fitzmaurice would be able to secure a base drew Sir William into winter movement, although his preparations were hampered by shortage of supplies. Desmond had allowed Spanish and Italian troops, who had garrisoned castles, into his country. Sir William marched out of Waterford to Limerick with some 1400 men: half his Irish army. Lacking pack animals and carriages, he was 'compelled to levy 300 churles' to carry provisions and could take no tents. He then moved on from Limerick to Glin and into Kerry, laying the country bare from Listowel to Tralee while Ormond, who had reached Cork, also went westward. They met at Rathkeale on 10 March and moved in parallel to the west and on to Dingle to meet supply ships, 'wasting and spoiling the country' as they went. The difficulties of overland transport meant that supply by sea, especially of ordnance, was crucial, although the ships Sir William's forces hoped to meet had in fact moved on to the Shannon. Desmond, who had gone that way, believing them to be Spanish, also razed the countryside. The progress of Sir William's army on the Dingle peninsula was halted by heavy snow and as they struggled back to Tralee, where the abbey was garrisoned, they were unable to retrace their route over the Corkaguiny mountains and lost men and horses fording the swollen River Feale.[16]

After meeting his supply ships at Carrigafoyle Sir William was able to attack the castle there, which was held by 16 Spaniards and about 50 Irishmen. When it was taken he moved on to attack Desmond's other castles on the Shannon. After they saw the fate of Carrigafoyle, Askeaton's defenders abandoned it as Sir William unloaded his ordnance, while the garrison at Ballyloghan set fire to the castle and fled after it was approached by bands of foragers. Desmond and the 600 men he still had in the field were pursued into Kerry, and from May 1580 Sir William began operations to scour the Dingle peninsula. The great fires which marked Ormond's progress could also be observed 15 miles away across Dingle Bay. Despite Desmond's stiff resistance to a sortie by 300 soldiers in mid-April, the campaign became a hunt for him. Sir William returned to Limerick and laid plans to hold down the rebels' country with garrisons which would eat up supplies of food while they starved. The struggle was now largely confined to Kerry. The English fleet blockaded the coast while the rebels were contained within an area too poor and mountainous to sustain them. By late July Sir William had, however, received a 'most comfortable letter' from Burghley informing him that Lord Grey de Wilton had been appointed to replace him as Lord Deputy in Ireland. He left the country in early November, after handing over his sword of office in September.[17]

The devastation of the countryside during Sir William's Irish campaign was characteristic of warfare in the country during this period, both the internecine feuds of its Gaelic lords and the hostilities under Grey and later Essex and Mountjoy. This, together with the absence of well-developed defensive systems in the towns and castles of Ireland, gave little scope for the application of any of the more technical military skills Sir William had acquired, apart from the application of artillery fire to defensive works, which offered little or no challenge to an experienced gunner. Powers of decisive personal leadership were an asset during the difficult and, as in February 1580, remarkable marches of the campaign and in the summer of 1580 when Sir William remained at the head of his army during the marches into Kerry, emerging, according to contemporary annalists, 'nobly triumphant'.[18]

Not only did the policy of laying waste the countryside damage the enemy, but the seizure of food and especially livestock made up for deficiencies in the army's supplies, although 'the spoil made in the country of corn, as well by the rebels as by the army' brought such dearth that in the west of Ireland supplies by sea became crucial. Lack of adequate provisions and munitions was a constant problem which contributed to the unpopularity of service there. The queen's reluctance to provide adequate resources was compounded by the poor quality of what was available. Sir William found that the stock of provisions contained only sour beer, biscuit which was almost mouldy and unusable beef, while bread sent from Dublin to Cork in the time of Sir William Drury was musty. The effect as well as the use of the tactic of seizing cattle was demonstrated vividly when Sir William with Admiral Winter, the commander of the fleet, returned to Castlemaine at the head of the Dingle peninsula and came upon a herd reported to contain 4000 or 5000 cows. It was driven into the camp and slaughtered, although when the starving people of the country asked Winter to leave some he spared 12 or 13 cows, a few goats and 400 sheep. Sir William reported to the queen in August 1580 that the rebels were 'continually hunted' and kept from their harvest while he had taken 'great preys of cattle from them'. The poor people who lived by their labour and milk cows were so distressed that they offered 'themselves with their wives and children rather to be slain by the army than to suffer the famine that now in extremity beginneth to pinch them'.[19]

As well as demonstrating the ferocity of warfare in sixteenth-century Ireland, the capture of the castle at Carrigafoyle in March 1580 showed that the country's relatively undeveloped fortifications were unable to withstand sustained and planned attack by artillery. The overland marches with inadequate transport which Sir William had undertaken meant that he was also dependent on supply by sea for ordnance. The commander of the troops in the castle 'reported himself to be an excellent engineer', but Sir William was able, after unloading the artillery, to set up a battery. The bombardment with three cannon, a culver and a culverin, which lasted for nearly two days, was, according to his account, arranged to 'make the fall of the house to fill the ditch of the barbican' and choke the flankers so that the castle became 'assaultable'. Some Irish and an English rebel who attempted to escape by swimming away from the castle were killed, while the rest retreated deeper into it. After further fighting the commander, six other Spaniards and 'certain women' surrendered and were all 'presently hanged saving the captain' who was kept 'for a day or two to learn what is intended, and how they have been succoured and relieved'.[20]

The particular hardships of his Irish campaign elicited Sir William's admiration for the soldiers of the country, to whom 'all the soldiers of Christendom must give place'. They lived 'under unhappy stars ... for the climate will yield no better'; the difference between their lot and that of the soldiers who served in places like Berwick was 'as is between an alderman of London and a Berwick soldier'. He had had only limited opportunities to apply his knowledge of military engineering, but the recommendations Sir William made towards the end of his service in Ireland reflected his expertise and interests. The 'aptest way to establish this province in due obedience,' he wrote, 'is to fortify the haven towns' under the supervision of an engineer with 'skilful men ... sent for that purpose' who were capable of working with the large amounts of turf that needed to be used. His plans for Munster entailed a garrison of 1200 men living off the country, a fleet of five galleys and a series of coastal fortifications and fortified bridges protected from within by the prohibition of trade in weapons and munitions.[21]

The last campaign in which Sir William was involved was in the Netherlands, where he served from 1586 until his death in 1587. While conditions there called for the application of his experience of fortification and siegecraft, it was a period of his career which was significant less in this respect than for the light it throws on the influence of politics and faction on military life in the period. Pelham had probably visited the Low Countries in 1575 as a result of the request for his assistance which Edward Woodshawe made to Lord Burghley, although the advice he gave was not highly regarded by the contemporary military historian Sir Roger Williams. According to him, Pelham's report that Flushing was incapable of withstanding a prolonged attack showed how 'we were not very great Captains at that time; for then being without fellowe, he was accounted our chiefest souldier'. That comment was probably coloured by the jealous disputes which developed between Williams and other soldiers in Leicester's entourage. They were part of the confusion of largely irrational concerns which became particularly evident in Sir William's case during his last period of active service.[22]

The waterways and lowlands of the Netherlands meant that crossing places and passages through marshland were of considerable strategic significance, halting the advance of armies and protecting communications. The 17 provinces also had more than 200 walled cities, 150 chartered towns and more than 6000 villages. Where they were not already fortified they could be strengthened with earthworks which could be relatively easily constructed, giving scope for the application of the techniques which had spread from Italy in the 1540s. An estimated 43 kilometres of modern defences were built in the Netherlands between 1529 and 1572. Warfare in these conditions needed a high degree of organization in which sustained supplies were deployed in support of commanders who employed military science in either siegework or defence. Whatever his failures as a soldier or statesman during his period as commander-in-chief in the Netherlands, Leicester at least recognized the need to respond to these conditions and appointed a master general of artillery, a general of fortifications and a colonel of pioneers.[23]

Sir William Pelham's appointment as marshal of the army was a reflection not so much of his particular skills as a military engineer as of his more general expertise in military organization. Leicester had 'no such man to govern the armye' and the repeated requests for Sir William's services were part of Leicester's plans to transform his following in the Netherlands into an organization which was more like a military headquarters than a court. The fact that this was not easily achieved is indicative of what has been described as 'the tangled confusion of private and public interests that characterised the Elizabethan scene', in which it was impossible to separate civil and military affairs and which spread into military life. Leicester asked for Sir William's assistance in the middle of December 1585 but he did not arrive in the Netherlands for another seven months, held back by the queen: 'ynough to break the hart of any gentleman in the world of his sort and derserving, that were not armyd with his vertue and constancy'.[24]

Sir William's position on Leicester's staff did not prevent some employment of his more specialist military skills when they were needed in the field. He was actively involved in reinforcing the Dutch pioneers at Doesburg in August 1586. His comment that they were 'beastlie ... having begon their trench everie shott makes them run awaye' reflected the divisions which bedevilled Leicester's military operations. It was at Doesburg that Leicester and Sir William lost their way in the trenches and Sir William was shot in the stomach. Although he was to carry 'a bullett in his bellie' as long as he lived, he had recovered sufficiently later in the month to take part in the attack on the Spanish train at Warnsfeld, where Sir Philip Sidney was fatally wounded after lending part of his equipment to Sir William, who had come lightly armed. The campaign of the autumn of 1586 ended in October, when Deventer was secured by Sir William after English and Irish soldiers were infiltrated into the town and its magistracy replaced.[25]

The delays in Sir William's posting illustrate the complex interrelationship between the politics of the court of Elizabeth and military affairs which was particularly evident in the case of Leicester's involvement in the Netherlands. 'The fruit of faction,' he wrote, 'will fall out as it hath done in England.' Divisive rivalries based on the emotive areas of honour and precedence added their particular element of irrationality to these complexities. Their effect on military operations was, according to Leicester, 'like to bringe our quarrell from the enemie to a priuate revenge among ourselues'. This was manifested dramatically in Sir William's quarrel with Sir Edward Norris during a drinking bout at the quarters of Count Hohenlohe in Geertruidenberg in early August 1586. Hohenlohe, who had a considerable affection for Sir William, 'hurld a cover of a cupp' at Norris's face, cutting his forehead, after Norris had 'caried himself not all the best' towards Sir William in a dispute centred on the giving and drinking of pledges. 'What man living,' Leicester wrote, 'would goe to the feild and haue his officers devyded almost into a mortal quarrell?'[26]

As Leicester prepared to return to England in November 1586 the queen expressed her fear of the 'emulacion and faction' likely to grow between her servants if either Sir William Pelham or Sir John Norris were left in command over the other. In the event Sir William also left the Netherlands and in April 1587 he was with Leicester and the earl of

Warwick at Bath, where he 'received benefit from the waters'. Leicester asked in May of the same year that Sir John Norris be replaced by Sir William, who probably returned to the Netherlands with him in July 1587. Sir William's attempt to raise the siege of Sluis by a landward attack was abandoned and the town surrendered on 5 August. When Leicester prepared to leave the Netherlands for the last time in 1587, he reported on 17 November that Sir William was 'wonderfully decayd'. He wished to return to England if he was able – 'I pray God,' Leicester wrote, 'he may com alyve' – but he died the next month at Flushing.[27]

Apart from his periods of active service, the stability provided by the office of lieutenant of the ordnance, one of the few full-time military appointments of the period and which he held from 1567 until his death, gave Sir William Pelham's career a continuity which was not available to most of his fellow soldiers. It was one of the increasing number of appointments made for life by letters patent which provided a degree of security of tenure for their holders. Yet, despite its place at the heart of the nation's military life at a period when the relationship between the state and its sources of military supply were beginning to change in response to new demands, his appointment reflected the Tudor network of office and patronage rather than any significant development in the professionalism of the military. There is little doubt that he owed his post to the patronage of Ambrose Dudley, earl of Warwick, under whom he had served at Le Havre in 1562 and who was master of the ordnance for 30 years from 1560.[28]

The Office of Ordnance was responsible for the supply to the armed forces of heavy guns, small arms, metal and shot, and such ancillary supplies as rope and wood, together with spades, axes and similar tools. The growth in military expenditure by the state from the mid-sixteenth century meant that it became one of the central departments of government, with a developing bureacracy. By the sixteenth century the office of master had become one of dignity, although even Warwick carried out a certain amount of routine administration and his membership of the Privy Council meant that the procedures developed at the Office were always subject to the changing priorities as well as control of the Council. The post of lieutenant had been created in 1544 and carried a salary of 100 marks with accommodation at the Minories, one of the storehouses and properties in and near the Tower of London in which the Ordnance was based. It was a salary which placed Sir William, as one of a group of 71 royal servants who had between £50 and £100 a year, just inside the top half of the approximately 400 royal servants who had annual fees of £20 or more.[29]

In his work on fortifications and in his Irish campaign Sir William had felt the effects of the exercise of economy in government expenditure on both defence and the prosecution of war. Finance was also central to his work at the Office of Ordnance. The lieutenant of the ordnance had been responsible for its expenditure since 1546; although £6000 was provided on a yearly warrant for routine commitments, a great deal of the money with which he dealt was in excess of this, with drafts from central government varying according to perceived military needs. While Sir William's lack of any other permanent office meant that he did not augment his annual stipend through the accumulation of office, the opportunities afforded by his position at the Ordnance brought sufficient rewards for him to build up his north Lincolnshire landed estate.[30]

The nature and extent of these rewards were, like his appointment to the Office, indicative of the extent to which this important part of government activity remained trapped within the prevalent mores of office-holding rather than developing a functional response to the more complex and sustained demands of new types of warfare. Some of the opportunities afforded to Sir William by his office are less well-defined than others, but all of them illustrate the same tension between the possibility of new professional responses and the constraints imposed by the particular situation in which he operated. This tension characterized the whole of Sir William's military career and was accentuated by the administrative routine of the Office of the Ordnance, which had developed the capacity to deal with the whole process of equipping the armed forces by the late 1550s.[31]

The purchase of stores and equipment by the Ordnance Office was an area where connection remained significant. Since gunpowder was perishable it was bought on a regular basis, giving Pelham a degree of control over suppliers. In 1574 he was empowered by the Privy Council to issue licences to those members of the Company of Grocers who wished to buy saltpetre from the government's suppliers. While guns and cannon needed renewing less frequently, their purchase was an important part of Sir William's work. His accounts for 1584 included the charges of Harman Harrison of the Ordnance for travel to Sussex in connection with artillery being made there for fortifications on the south coast, and there was similar expenditure at other times. Since the Pelhams were one of a number of substantial landowners who had operated forges and furnaces in the Weald from the 1540s, using skilled iron workers brought in from northern

France, Sir William had family connections in the armaments-manufacturing industry.[32]

In 1586, the year before Sir William's death, William Painter, clerk of the ordnance from 1560 until 1594, was charged with embezzlement. Like Sir William, Painter had as his patron the master of the ordnance, Ambrose Dudley, earl of Warwick, who for a time was also caught up in the affair. The allegations made against him were never substantiated but the fact that George Hogge, clerk of deliveries and one of Painter's not entirely disinterested protaganists, was from a family of Sussex ironmasters illustrates the tangle of connections which lay behind the Office's work of supply. While Sir William was not involved in these proceedings, the way in which his estate was built up from the fruits of his office illustrates, within the context of military affairs, the extent to which a major department of government could also provide an accepted base from which to advance family and personal interest.[33]

As lieutenant of the ordnance, Sir William had the use of the large surplus which could accumulate on his account. His advantage was increased by the fact that the presentation of this account was often delayed. The surplus was not inevitable and for the first six years in which he held the Office there were deficits, but from 1574 he held an accumulated sum which grew, with some fluctuations, from £5348 4^{1}/2d to its highest point of just over £8840 in the year of his death, when it became repayable. This debt to the crown was one of the factors that delayed his departure to join Leicester in the Low Countries. It continued to be an encumbrance on his estate until after his death.[34]

There is no neat correlation between Sir William's purchases of property in Lincolnshire, which totalled some £7000, and the clear availability of the resources which would enable him to do this. He began to acquire land in the county in 1564, before his appointment to the Ordnance, but after his service at Leith and Le Havre, at a period when his expertise in fortifications was being recognized. He had spent £1520 before his appointment to the Ordnance and just over half the £5624 laid out after this was used in 21 transactions up to 1574, when he began to enjoy the advantages of an accumulated surplus in his account. From then until purchases ceased in 1583 he spent £2596 on 11 pieces of property. While the value of the 21 purchases made between 1567 to 1574 varied, the smallest being £10 for two cottages and land bought from William Tenny of Great Limber, Sir William also laid out large sums in individual transactions. These began with his first purchase – property in the villages of Great Limber, Killingholme and Stallingborough for £1000 in 1564 –

but were spread throughout the period he was active in the land market. His two largest – £1500 each for lands which had belonged to the monastery of Newsham and former monastic property at Newstead on Ancholme – were made during the period he was at the Ordnance Office, although one was before a surplus was available, the other after.[35]

A further area reflecting the changing nature of military life in the period was conflict over the method of paying troops in which Pelham became involved. This was particularly evident during the Le Havre campaign which was, significantly, before he had secured the rewards of permanent office and arose out of changes to established practices. These in their turn stemmed from the need to develop new responses to the problem of pay in the increasingly large armies of the sixteenth century. The changes were particularly contentious because of the way they challenged the position and, more significantly, the perquisites of professional army officers. The system of payment by poll, under which captains were issued only with enough money to pay the men who were counted as being under their command, rather than paid a lump sum based on muster returns, was intended to cut down wastage. Wages were handed direct to the men rather than passing through the captains' hands. When payment by poll was used for the pioneers at Le Havre, Pelham refused to allow it and stood 'so much upon his reputation that he will pay them as every captain here pays his soldiers', although the Privy Council had ordered that the 800 labourers under his command should be viewed daily and paid individually. Pelham was suspicious of the amounts allowed to the ordinary soldiers when they undertook pioneering work, while there were said to be discrepancies in the number of men he had on his pay books: 724 in one and 920 in another. Warwick as commander of the expedition had to explain these to the Privy Council. In May 1563 the clerk of check of the labourers reported that Pelham had forbidden him to make a further count of the labourers under his command and had said he would have no man meddle any further with his doings.[36]

The method of paying troops remained as much an issue 25 years later in the Netherlands, where captains still wished to maintain procedures more appropriate to mercenary companies than to a large field army. Pay was some £40,000 in arrears by the second half of 1587, although from 1586 the queen had insisted against strong opposition on payment by the poll. This method meant that captains were no longer able to gain through the death or absence of men said to be under their command, while they also stood to lose when they advanced money to soldiers who later died or deserted. Sir William's role as a member of Leicester's rudimentary command meant that he was still, if less immediately than in his earlier career, caught up in this, as he was in the whole issue of the supply of the army. When a muster was proposed in October 1586, Sir William wrote to Leicester that he could 'not perceive how the same may be orderlie done'. The soldiers 'not hearinge of moneye' were justly discontented and flocked around him by the hundred whenever he went out. He did not know how to alleviate their misery. Some had no money, others no clothes, and large numbers of them were barefoot while every day many fell sick.[37]

Any attempt to encapsulate the process of historical change, particularly one which has such wide ramifications as that of military development, through prosopography and especially through the life of a single individual inevitably raises questions about their particular relevance or representativeness. In 1567 Pelham had prepared a treatise, 'Mr Pellham's devise for harquebusyers', which its recipient, Cecil, endorsed. It was one of a growing number of papers on military topics which appeared in the second half of the sixteenth century. Although it remained unpublished, its interest lies in the way it shows the same mixture of innovation and conservatism set in the particular context of the English situation that characterized the whole of Pelham's military career. His advocacy of the arquebus rather than the longbow was part of a vigorous debate on their relative merits. This continued into the seventeenth century and coloured the attitudes of writers such as Humphrey Barwick, Sir John Smythe and Sir Roger Williams, all of whom had described actions in which Sir William was involved: Leith, Caen and in the Netherlands respectively. Pelham's position was indicative of progressive attitudes but the novelty of his ideas was tempered by the fact that this type of handgun had been used on the continent since the early sixteenth century and in the English army, albeit to a limited extent, from the reign of Henry VIII. His attitude illustrates the way in which even a professional English soldier of relatively high standing and in touch with developments in military affairs which were changing both the logistics and conduct of war could still be hesitant in his approach to military innovation, conscious of precedent and mindful of the lessons to be drawn from past glories and traditions. Even when the companies of arquebusers advocated by Sir William were set up, he still wished to see the 'use of the bow' continued in the villages 'according to the statutes' and 'by some more pleasant means to draw youth thereunto'. Training in the use of the arquebus was to be set firmly within the context of what were perceived as traditional English pursuits and carried out 'at the times heretofore used for the sports of Robin Hood, Midsummer, Lords and Ladies'.[38]

The essential symmetry of Sir William Pelham's career with the wider context of English military life in which he secured advancement does, however, point to the way in which it was representative of the process of military change in England in the sixteenth century. Here the wisdom which was attributed to him by Edward Woodshawe in 1575 was the ability to adopt the best means to accomplish an end, while the qualities attributed to him as an 'experimented' soldier were, in the contemporary sense, those which related to his practical experience. This hardly constituted the basis for a revolution in military affairs but rather a situation where adaptation rather than innovation was the engine of change.[39]

Notes

Part of the research on which this essay is based was carried out with the support of the Economic and Social Research Council (Project R00 23 1368 on the development of the Yarborough landed estate, Lincolnshire, 1565 to 1948) whose assistance is gratefully acknowledged. I am also indebted to Dr Anne Mitson who worked with me on this project.

1 .   HMC, *Calendar of the Manuscripts of the Marquis of Salisbury,* Part II (London, 1888), pp 84–6.

2 .   PRO, PROB11/27; Lincolnshire Archives (hereafter, LA), YARB 5/1/1, fo. 20v.

3 .   C. Duffy, *Siege Warfare: the Fortress in the Early-Modern World, 1494–1660* (London 1979), pp 140–41; C.G. Cruickshank, *Elizabeth's Army,* 2nd edn (Oxford, 1966), p 152; Humphrey Barwick, *A Breefe Discourse Concerning the Force and Effect of All Manuall Weapons of Fire, and the Disability of the Longe Bowe of Archery, in Respect of Others of Greater Force now in Use* (London [1594]), pp 4r–4v.

4 .   *CSPF, 1559–1560,* pp 600–1.

5 .   S. Mowat, *The Port of Leith: its History and People* (Edinburgh [1994]), p 114; John Stow, *The Annales or General Chronicle of England ...* (London, 1615), pp 641, 643; C. Oman, *A History of the Art of War in the Sixteenth Century* (London, 1937), p 223; B.H. Nickle, 'The military reforms of Prince Maurice of Orange', unpublished PhD thesis, University of Delaware, 1975, pp 163–4; G. Chalmers, ed, *Churchyard's Chips Concerning Scotland: Being a Collection of his Pieces Relative to the Country; with Historical Notices and a Life of the Author* (London, 1817), pp 97, 102–3, 104, 105, 109; J. Bruce, ed, *Annals of the First Four Years of the Reign of Queen Elizabeth by Sir John Hayward,* Camden Soc., 7 (London, 1840), pp 66–7; J.B. Black, *The Reign of Elizabeth, 1558–1603* (Oxford, 1936), pp 40–1.

6 .   Oman, *Art of War,* p 408; Duffy, *Siege Warfare,* pp 50, 106; J.R. Hale, ed, *Certain Discourses Military by Sir John Smythe* (New York, 1964), p 97; Stow, *Annales,* pp 652–3.

7 . *CSPF, 1562*, pp 425, 439, 499, 500; *CSPF, 1563*, pp 271–2, 394, 466, 483; V. Toussant, ed, *Pièces historiques relatives au siège du Havre par Charles IX en 1563* (Havre, 1862), p 17.

8 . J.R. Hale, *Renaissance War Studies* (London, 1983), pp 88, 96; M. Merriman and J. Summerson, 'Berwick upon Tweed', in H.M. Colvin, ed, *The History of the King's Works*, 6 vols (London, 1963-82), IV (ii), pp 648, 651, 656, 657; I. MacIvor, 'The Elizabethan fortifications of Berwick-upon-Tweed', *The Antiquaries Journal* 45 (1965), pp 64–7, 76–81, 84–8, 92–3; *CSPF, 1564– 1565*, p 156; A. Saunders, *Fortress Britain: Artillery Fortification in the British Isles* (Liphook, 1989), pp 59–61; Duffy, *Siege Warfare*, pp 41, 140; *CSPF, 1563*, pp 404, 425.

9 . *APC, 1571–1575,* new ser., 8, pp 271–5, 281, 285, 289–90; *CSPD, 1547– 1580*, p 486; H.M. Colvin and J. Summerson 'The River Medway', in Colvin, ed, *History of the King's Works,* IV (ii), pp 479, 481; Hale, *Renaissance War Studies*, p 85.

10 . *APC, 1575–1577*, new ser., 9, pp 246–7; K.J. Allison, 'Fortifications', in *VCH: Yorkshire. East Riding*, i: Kingston Upon Hull, ed K.J. Allison (Oxford, 1969), pp 414–15; Duffy, *Siege Warfare,* p 140.

11 . *CSPD, 1581–1590*, p 288; M. Biddle and J. Summerson, 'Portsmouth and the Isle of Wight', in Colvin, ed, *History of the King's Works*, IV (ii), pp 520– 21.

12 . *APC, 1578–1580*, new ser., 11, pp 224–5; C. Falls, *Elizabeth's Irish Wars* (London, 1950), p 128; *Calendar of the Carew Manuscripts preserved in the Archiepiscopal Library at Lambeth, 1575–1588* (London, 1868), pp 211– 12, 312; R. Bagwell, *Ireland under the Tudors with a Succinct Account of the Earlier History*, 3 vols (London, 1885–1890; repr. 1963), III, pp 27, 29–31.

13 . Duffy, *Siege Warfare*, p 144; *CSPI, 1574–1585*, p 184; *Calendar Carew MSS*, pp 169, 268.

14 . *APC, 1578–1580,* new ser., 11, pp 337–8; *APC, 1580–1581,* new ser., 12, p 58.

15 . Falls, *Irish Wars*, p 132; Bagwell, *Ireland*, III, pp 29–31, 37–8; *Calendar Carew MSS*, p 172.

16 . G. Morton, *Elizabethan Ireland* (London, 1971), p 56; S.G. Ellis, *Tudor Ireland: Crown, Community and the Conflict of Cultures, 1470–1603* (London, 1985), p 280; Falls, *Irish Wars*, p 132; Bagwell, *Ireland,* III, pp 40, 41–2; *Calendar Carew MSS*, pp 216, 236–7.

17 . *Calendar Carew MSS,* pp 237–8, 241, 243, 313–14; Bagwell, *Ireland*, III, p 43; Morton, *Elizabethan Ireland*, p 57; Falls, *Irish Wars*, pp 132–3; *CSPI, 1574–1585*, p 237; *APC, 1578–1580*, new ser., XI, pp 291–2

18 . Morton, *Elizabethan Ireland*, p 134; Falls, *Irish Wars,* p 135; Bagwell, *Ireland,* III, p 47.

19 . Falls, *Irish Wars*, p 133; *Calendar Carew MSS*, pp 165–6, 220, 293; Morton, *Elizabethan Ireland*, p 131; Bagwell, *Ireland,* III, pp 47, 48, 54.

20 . Morton, *Elizabethan Ireland,* pp 129–30; *Calendar Carew MSS*, pp 237–8; Bagwell, *Ireland,* III, p 42.

21 . *Calendar Carew MSS*, pp 219, 274–5, 284–7.

22 . HMC, *Calendar Salisbury MSS*, Part II (London, 1888), pp 84–5, 88–90; *The Works of Sir Roger Williams,* ed J.X. Evans (Oxford, 1972), pp xxx–xxxi,

180

121.

23 . Nickle, 'Military reforms', pp 70, 158, 162; C. Wilson, *Queen Elizabeth and the Revolt of the Netherlands* (London, 1970), pp 10–11; G. Parker, *The Military Revolution: Military Innovation and the Rise of the West* (Cambridge, 1988), pp 12–13; G. Parker, *The Army of Flanders and the Spanish Road, 1567–1659* (Cambridge, 1972), p 11.

24 . Wilson, *Queen Elizabeth*, p 89; W.T. MacCaffrey, *Queen Elizabeth and the Making of Policy, 1572–1588* (Princeton, 1981), pp 359–60; J. Bruce, ed, *Correspondence of Robert Dudley, Earl of Leicester, During his Government of the Low Countries in the Years 1585 and 1586*, Camden Soc., 27 (London, 1844), pp 28, 37, 126, 136, 345–6, 394.

25 . J.L. Motley, *History of the United Netherlands: from the Death of William the Silent to the Twelve Years Truce, 1609*, 4 vols (London, 1875), II, pp 39, 145–6; *Leicester Correspondence*, pp 401, 407, 478–80; F.G. Oosterhoff, *Leicester and the Netherlands, 1586–1587* (Utrecht, 1988), pp 98–9.

26 . *Works of Sir Roger Williams*, pp xxx–xxxi; *Leicester Correspondence*, pp 391–3

27 . *Leicester Correspondence*, p 452; Oosterhoff, *Leicester and the Netherlands*, pp 135–6, 176; · *CSPD, 1581–1590*, p 402; H. Brugmans, ed, *Correspondentie van Robert Dudley graaf van Leycester en andere documenten betreffende zijn gouvernement-generaal in de Nederlanden*, 3 vols (Utrecht, 1931), II, p 275; III, p 310.

28 . W.T. Macaffrey, 'Place and patronage in Elizabethan politics', in S.T. Bindoff, J. Hurstfield and C.H. Williams, eds, *Elizabethan Government and Society: essays presented to Sir John Neale* (London, 1961), pp 101, 105, 107; R. Ashley, 'The organisation and administration of the Tudor Office of Ordnance', unpublished BLitt thesis, University of Oxford, 1973, pp 42, 80.

29 . Cruickshank, *Elizabeth's Army*, p 121; Parker, *Military Revolution*, p 147; Ashley, 'Office of Ordnance', pp 39, 80–81, 92–3; *CPR, 1566–1569* (London, 1964), p 108; Macaffrey, 'Place and patronage', p 111.

30 . F.C. Dietz, *English Public Finance, 1558–1641* (New York and London, 1932), pp 36, 112; PRO, E351/2618–28; R.C. Braddock, 'The rewards of office-holding in Tudor England', *Journal of British Studies* 14/2 (May 1975), pp 35–6; Ashley, 'Office of Ordnance', p 53; LA, YARB 3/3/2/1: 'A Digest or Particular of the Real Estate of the Earl of Yarborough within the County of Lincoln'.

31 . Parker, *Military Revolution*, p 147; Ashley, 'Office of Ordnance', p 80.

32 . Dietz, *Public Finance, 1558–1641*, p 36; *APC, 1571–1575*, new ser., VIII, p 210; PRO, E351/2626; H. Cleere and D. Crossley, *The Iron Industry of the Weald* (Leicester, 1985), pp 117, 119, 126–7, 149, 315, 318, 363.

33 . R. Ashley, 'Getting and spending: corruption in the Elizabethan Ordnance', *History Today* 40 (November 1990), pp 48–52.

34 . PRO, E351/2618–28; Ashley, 'Getting and spending', p 52; *CSPD, 1581–1590*, p 703.

35 . LA, YARB 3/3/2/1. fos 2, 4–11, 14–15, 18–31, 34–9, 40–48.

36 . Parker, *Military Revolution*, p 147; Cruickshank, *Elizabeth's Army*, p 152; *CSPF, 1563*, pp 271, 282, 303, 349.

37 .   J.E. Neale, 'Elizabeth and the Netherlands, 1586–7', *EHR* 45 (1930), pp 376, 380–1; Cruickshank, *Elizabeth's Army*, pp 152–3; BL, Cotton MS, Galba C.X, fo. 65r.

38 .   HMC, *Calendar Salisbury MSS,* Part XIII (Addenda) (London, 1915), pp 84–5; J.R. Hale, 'Armies, navies and the art of war', in R.B. Wernham, ed, *The Counter-Reformation and Price Revolution, 1559-1610.* The New Cambridge Modern History, Part III (Cambridge, 1968), pp 177–9; C.L. Gaier, 'L'invincibilité anglaise et le grand arc après la guerre de cent ans: un mythe tenace', *Tijdschrift voor Geschiedenis* 91/3 (1978), pp 382–4; Oman, *Art of War*, pp 324, 333; J.R. Hale, *The Art of War and Renaissance England* (Washington, 1961), p 22.

39 .   *Oxford English Dictionary,* 2nd edn, 1989, V, p 565; XX, pp 423–4.

9. A State Dedicated to War? The Dutch Republic in the Seventeenth Century

J.L. Price

The argument of this chapter is that not only did the Dutch state have its origins in war, but the common central institutions of the Dutch provinces were created as a direct response to the requirements of war and were primarily, indeed almost exclusively, concerned with preparations for and the prosecution of war throughout the century of Dutch greatness. The Dutch Republic which emerged with surprising rapidity as a major European power in the last decade of the sixteenth and the first decade of the seventeenth century was born in an armed rising against Spain, and took definitive shape in and through the consequent long war for independence. The external boundaries of the new state and its internal political and administrative structure, as well as the very survival of the Dutch state, were determined by the opportunities and demands of warfare. The Republic continued to live on intimate terms with war throughout the seventeenth century, and only after the end of the War of Spanish Succession was it able to enjoy a substantial period of peace in Europe. In brief, the Dutch state was the creation of war and war was its primary *raison d'être*: within this militant carapace the sense of a common identity was able to develop only slowly, and military and naval affairs remained the prime functions of the Dutch state until the fall of the Republic in 1795.

This aspect of Dutch history has been obscured by an historical myth, with its roots in the seventeenth century but perhaps reaching maturity only in the nineteenth, which depicts the Dutch people as essentially unwarlike, even in their period as a major power: their economic and cultural achievements are stressed and it is asserted that they fought their wars by proxy, through the use in their armies of foreign mercenaries, and that there were – and are – no military leaders among their popular heroes. The undoubted contemporary – and later – popularity of Tromp and De Ruyter as heroes of naval warfare casts some doubt on this latter argument. Yet there is perhaps a real question here: how could a society which was so heavily and continuously involved in war apparently remain relatively uninvolved in military affairs and unaffected by military values? The answer is unlikely to be found in a putative national character, but in rather more tangible factors.

One clue can be found in the peculiar nature of the Republic's territorial ambitions: it had none, in Europe at least.[1] As the hopes of gaining control of large parts, if not all, of the southern Netherlands from the Spanish faded, or were dropped, in the early years of the seventeenth century, the Republic was left with no desire to expand in Europe. Any extension of its territory was seen as likely to bring more problems than it was worth. In particular, new areas could not easily be absorbed into the Dutch political system; even the parts of Brabant brought under Dutch control by the war with Spain were unable to get admission, or rather readmission, to the States General because of the reluctance of the seven provinces to share power with another member. Reconquering more of Brabant or bringing other areas (such as, perhaps, East Friesland) under Dutch control would only have exacerbated this problem, which in the case of Brabant was made even more sensitive by the fact that the great majority of its population was Catholic, which made it even less easy to assimilate.

This lack of aggression stemmed not from the supposed pacific nature of the Dutch people, but from the economic priorities of Dutch society. Apart from achieving independence and then defending it, the prime aim of Dutch political leaders at every level was the maintenance and increase of general prosperity. They could be combative in their use of naval power in the defence of their shipping and trading interests, for example, but their priorities were always clearly economic, not the honour or reputation which motivated contemporary monarchies. Similarly, the Dutch were willing to use military as well as naval force in their colonial campaigns, but here again the primary aim was not the conquest of territory or the control of new subjects but the pursuit of trading advantage. Their failure to maintain their colonial position in Brazil must, in part at least, be explained by economic considerations – after Portugal's break with Spain, Dutch merchants realized that they did not need territorial control to profit from the Brazilian trade.

Again, the use of foreign personnel in its armies and navies did not mean that the Dutch were naturally more inclined to peaceful pursuits than others: rather, the Republic was prosperous and relatively few Dutch people found service in the army or navy an attractive alternative to civilian life. The Republic had a population of only around two million at its peak, and with a booming economy there were unavoidable labour shortages so the use of foreigners in the army and navy was only part of a broader movement of economic immigration. This was a consequence of demography and economics rather than national character, and in any case its extent has perhaps been exaggerated.[2]

The Dutch also seem to have avoided one of the most important results of the 'military revolution', the growth of the apparatus of the state. The association between the changes in warfare in the early modern period and an increase in the power of central government and the size of government bureaucracies has become almost a commonplace in recent studies,[3] but the Dutch Republic remained resolutely decentralized politically, and the bureaucracy attached to the States General remained remarkably slim. However, it should be noted that military and naval affairs were, formally at least, controlled from the centre: the army was a single army of the Republic, not an agglomeration of provincial armies; and the five admiralties were also, at least formally, Generality institutions.[4] What there was of a centralized state in the Republic was concerned with military matters, and that it existed at all was to a large extent the result of the constant need during the war with Spain for joint military action by the rebel provinces. It is no accident that the only document remotely resembling a constitution that the Republic ever knew, the Union of Utrecht of 1579, was essentially a military alliance. To this limited extent the Republic fits in with the theory of the military revolution – without the need for concerted action in war, there might never have been a Dutch state at all.

The Dutch case fits rather better another aspect of the military revolution, Michael Robert's stress on the changes in organization and tactics which culminated in the successes of the Swedish army under Gustavus Adolphus.[5] The reforms carried out in the Dutch army by Maurice and his cousin William Louis of Nassau in the 1590s foreshadowed and to a large extent anticipated the innovations of the Swedish king,[6] though perhaps the regular pay and effective logistic support provided by the Dutch political and administrative system from this point on were even more important. What seemed at the time a desperately hand-to-mouth effort financially, looks much more impressive in retrospect. All states had difficulty finding the money to pay their troops, and prolonged warfare usually led to what was in effect bankruptcy under one disguise or another, but the Dutch state, even in these early and most fragile years, managed to find the resources necessary for the regular and reliable support of its armed effort on both land and sea. This ability to pay for its wars more efficiently than other governments became a hallmark of the Dutch state in the seventeenth century and, both cause and consequence, it could borrow money considerably more cheaply than other countries – or, rather, the province of Holland could, which brings us to the peculiar nature of the Dutch political system.

For this success in achieving independence from Spain and establishing the position of a major power in Europe was the work of a political system which was not only republican but also decentralized. Both contemporaries and later commentators have agreed that a strong leader and a central government capable of overriding particularism in the interests of the state as a whole were necessary for survival in the harsh world of the seventeenth century: the Dutch state broke both these rules and yet survived and prospered. The provinces enjoyed a high degree of autonomy even if they were not sovereign – the issue was never completely clear – and this was particularly evident in fiscal matters. Not only could the provinces not be forced to pay for policies they had not agreed to, but they collected and to a large extent spent their own taxes themselves. Moreover, although later in the seventeenth century successive princes of Orange as *stadhouders* and captains-general could be portrayed as providing the strong leadership necessary for military success, the reorganization of the army, the first victories against Spain and the attainment of quasi-independence at the truce of 1609 all came in a period when the position of Maurice within the political system was much weaker than after the coup of 1618.[7] In other words, military effectiveness was attained by a system which largely lacked a quasi-monarchical element to balance the centrifugal forces of provincial particularism.

The Dutch state was and remained minimal: there was a heavy load of government in the Republic, but it came and was controlled at the local, town and provincial levels. The Republic was permanently marked by its origins as an alliance embodied in the Union of Utrecht for the prosecution of the war for independence from Spain. In the course of time it became more than this, and a sense of the indissolubility of the Union developed; in addition, the growth of the status and political power of the princes of Orange provided another significant unifying factor in Dutch life. Nevertheless, the Generality and its institutions remained very limited in size and primarily concerned with military affairs, to this extent supporting the idea of a link between the demands of warfare and the development of the state, yet at the same time casting doubt on the need for any considerable degree of centralization and bureaucracy.

As has been noted in the Introduction to this volume, one prominent argument to arise out of the idea of a military revolution in this period is that the increasing costs of this new type of warfare overstretched the resources of the early-modern state. If the state was to survive, however, these costs had to be met by squeezing extra revenue from reluctant taxpayers, and this could be achieved only by suppressing representative institutions and strengthening the coercive powers of the centralized state. In brief, absolutism was the political answer to the problem of keeping up with the military escalation of the time. Only in this way could the state gain control of sufficient resources from economies still hampered by endemic low productivity. Absolutist France survived; the aristocratic republic of Poland-Lithuania did not.

The Dutch Republic is the most telling counter-example to this argument: it was at the centre of European conflicts from its very inception until the second decade of the eighteenth century, yet it proved able to preserve its republican and particularist political system – and survive. The apparently inexorable logic connecting the demands of warfare with centralization and absolutism break down in this case. It is clearly not that the Dutch were able to avoid having to support large modern armies and navies: however much they may have wished to devote themselves to peaceful trade, they found themselves heavily involved in the European wars of the period, not to mention the quasi-warfare that was inseparable from colonial expansion. Indeed, war was more a normal than an abnormal state of affairs for the Dutch until the early eighteenth century. The war for independence from Spain lasted until 1648, with only the uneasy truce of 1609–21 as a respite. In addition, in the first half of the seventeenth century the Dutch were directly and indirectly involved in the Thirty Years War, which not coincidentally also ended at the Peace of Westphalia. After this point, the Dutch may have hoped for a lasting peace in which to pursue their economic priorities, but instead they found themselves forced into three damaging wars with England, the third of which coincided with the beginning of a series of even more threatening conflicts with Louis XIV's France which dominated the last decades of the century and lasted until the Treaty of Utrecht in 1713. Only then could the financially exhausted Dutch state enjoy a prolonged period free from serious international conflict.

Apart from these major wars, their strategic position and economic interests also drew the Dutch into other military and naval actions and expense. Even before the beginning of the Thirty Years War, they were drawn into military intervention in neighbouring territories of the Holy Roman Empire, most notably as a consequence of the Jülich-Kleve succession dispute after 1609, and protection of their vulnerable eastern border encouraged a continuing presence in this region. Also, the importance of Dutch trade with the Baltic meant that naval intervention in the conflicts of the area was not only frequent but had to be a constant element in Dutch strategic thinking – the 'mother trade' had to be protected. This is perhaps a useful reminder that, though the Dutch may in principle have preferred peaceful trade, where the use of force might be expected to further their economic interests they could be ruthless.

This characteristic is also shown by the history of the Dutch trading empire outside Europe. The chief weapons of the Dutch in this enterprise were, of course, the two chartered trading companies – the East India Company (VOC) and the West India Company (WIC) – which acted to some extent as privatized extensions of the Dutch state. In the East, open or covert warfare was a built-in part of the VOC's strategy to oust the Portuguese from their established positions and to ward off the challenge from the English and other would-be competitors. In Africa and, especially, the Americas military and naval force played an even greater role, and for much of its existence the WIC was as much a privateering and belligerent organization as it was a trading one. The most spectacular example of this orientation – made inevitable perhaps by the entrenched position of the Iberian powers in the Americas – was the attempt to conquer Brazil. Before this enterprise was finally given up, the conflict in and around Brazil had drawn in considerable help from the Dutch navy as well as large subsidies from the States General, and it was the reluctance of Holland in particular to continue to give significant financial help to the failing company which finally sealed its fate. These colonial hostilities involved a considerable expansion of the Dutch experience of war in the seventeenth century and, in so far as the VOC and WIC can be considered extensions of the state, a similar increase in its involvement in warfare as well.

War was thus a normal situation for the Dutch state in the seventeenth century, and this meant that it had to support large armed forces on a permanent basis. It is easier to give figures for the size of the Dutch army than for the navy, though as with all seventeenth-century statistics regarding military or fiscal affairs a certain amount of caution is required as to just what such figures mean. The 1590s saw both the consolidation of the Dutch political system and the creation of an effective Dutch army, and from this point until the Treaty of Utrecht the Dutch state maintained a military force big enough to make it a major power in Europe.

The available figures suggest that the army rose from around 30,000 men in the mid–1590s to over 50,000 on the eve of the Twelve Years Truce (1609–21); during the truce the numbers may have fallen to about 28,000 but no lower; and the resumption of hostilities with Spain brought the numbers back over 50,000 again and by 1632 to around 75,000 where they remained until the 1640s saw a reduction to just over 60,000.[8] After the peace in 1648 the army was run down to a low point of 24,000 men in 1661, but war with England and Münster brought the numbers back up to over 50,000 in 1667 and, although there was then a brief fall, by 1671 the threatening international situation had brought it up to nearly 65,000. The war with France from 1672 onwards caused a fresh escalation of army size to a peak of 93,000 men in 1674, and subsequently even in peacetime numbers never dropped much below 40,000 and wartime strengths were 64,000–87,000 after 1688. A new high was reached in the period 1695–7 with over 100,000 men, and though the brief peace then allowed numbers to halve, the return of war after 1702 brought new heights of military effort from the Dutch with the army reaching almost 120,000 by 1707.[9]

Even allowing for the partly fictional nature of all accounts of troop numbers in this period, these figures represent a major achievement as well an enormous burden for the Dutch state. It is rather less easy to present useful figures for the navy, as ships varied in size and function, and until after the middle of the century there could be no simple division into ships-of-the-line and the rest.[10] However, it is clear that from the very beginning the Republic had to maintain a more or less large fleet, though until the mid-century attempts were made to keep costs down by hiring privately owned vessels for specific purposes and campaigns rather than maintaining an all-purpose permanent navy.

The Dutch needed a navy for a wide range of purposes: apart from protecting strategic and commercial interests through a battle fleet and convoy protectors, ships had to be found to blockade the Flemish coast and deal with the Dunkirk privateers, as well as to provide a wide variety of services on the inland waterways. In 1631, for example, the admiralties were supporting 199 ships, of which 65 were employed on the rivers and canals, while 76 were involved in convoy protection (of these 13 were for the herring fleet and six for the other fisheries), and only 45 allocated to the Flemish blockade and the North Sea.[11] Defeats for the old-style Dutch navy in the first Anglo-Dutch War led to the development of new fleet of purpose-built warships, and from this point on the Republic had to maintain a navy which could prove a match for that of England or France – or even both combined, as was the case in the critical year of 1672. Only after the English revolution of 1688, with the potential double naval threat removed, could the Dutch afford to slacken their effort at sea and allow themselves to be overtaken in numbers of front-line ships not only by England but by France as well.[12]

The relative costs of war on land and sea varied throughout the century according to the particular circumstances facing the Republic. Despite spectacular incidents, and despite the damage done to Dutch economic interests by the Dunkirk privateers,[13] the war against Spain was fought primarily on land, and it was the army which absorbed the greater part of state resources during this period. Expenditure on the navy could and did vary much more erratically than that on the army, but the evidence suggests that the land campaign cost at least twice as much as the war at sea for the whole of the period up to the treaty of Münster.[14] For the next two decades the emphasis switched to the sea: the shortcomings in the Dutch navy revealed in the first Anglo-Dutch War led to a major rebuilding and reorganization of naval forces, while the international situation presented the Republic with no great immediate threat to its security on land. Consequently, while the period of political domination by Johan de Witt saw the peak of Dutch naval strength in this century, it was also a time when the army was run down in size and relatively neglected, with consequences that were all too apparent in the summer of 1672, when French troops nearly overran the Republic. From this point on, the defence of the Republic's independence against the perceived threat from France became the first priority again, although until 1688 the fear of a renewed naval attack by England meant that naval spending also had to be kept high. It seems to have been the combination of these two financial drains over a long period which finally crushed the resilience of the Dutch – or rather of Holland's – fiscal system by the end of the War of Spanish Succession.[15]

It is both revealing and appropriate that the chief financial instruments of the Republic's central government were primarily concerned with military (including naval) expenditure. In most countries, the cost of warfare can be – however inaccurately – expressed as a percentage of the government's annual expenditure; in the Dutch Republic such a procedure makes little sense: here the financial machinery of the central government was designed to deal primarily with the costs of warfare, and other expenditure was incidental. Even the salaries of diplomats were absorbed in the *staat van oorlog*[16] (and assigned to Holland). A reconstruction of the Republic's total expenditure has been made for 1641 by M. 't Hart, and the result is instructive: 89.5 per cent went directly to pay for the war and 4.4 per cent on servicing the debt, which can also be regarded as part of the costs of warfare as it had been incurred very largely for this purpose; 1 per cent went on the costs of diplomacy, leaving just over 5 per cent for administrative and other expenses.[17] There is no reason to believe that this year was other than typical, not only for the years of the war with Spain but throughout the whole history of the Republic; if we judge the function of a state by what it spent its money on, then the Dutch state was concerned with warfare and everything else was incidental.

Although in nearly all European states the greater part of expenditure went on war and related matters, the sheer concentration of the central institutions of the Republic on warfare does raise some questions about the nature of the Dutch state and, indeed, whether it constituted a true state at all. Although the Union of Utrecht was never intended to be a constitutional document, it does give some clues as to why the polity that indirectly arose out of this agreement should have been so singular. The Union brought together a number of provinces represented in the States General of the whole of the Netherlands in order to form a closer alliance for the better prosecution of the war against Spain.[18] In form the Union was a military and political alliance between – presumably – independent signatories, and the Dutch state that grew out of this agreement was profoundly affected by these origins. In one aspect this state was no more than an alliance between autonomous, if not sovereign, provinces and the States General and other Generality organs of government enjoyed only those powers which were specifically delegated to them by the unanimous consent of the provinces.

Throughout the history of the Republic the doctrine of provincial autonomy was central to the Dutch idea of the nature of their polity: the existence of a single sovereign, either individual or corporate, was not seen as a necessary part of the definition of the state. However, in the course of time – and more quickly than perhaps might have been expected – the assumption grew that the Republic was more than an *ad hoc* agglomeration of provinces. This process took some time, if only because the new state had to be defined in its geographical extension by the accidents and process of war, but the first major political crisis of the new state, during the 1609–21 truce, demonstrated that a sense of unity was able to triumph over provincial separatism. As the seventeenth century wore on it became progressively more clear that the new state would remain united despite, or perhaps because of, the extent of provincial autonomy.[19]

It is perhaps only from the perspective of the unitary modern state that the Dutch Republic looks odd or illegitimate as a workable polity. The two activities which it can be argued were the vital activities of the state – war and diplomacy – were indeed the province of the central government of the Republic. The States General was the forum where the delegates of the seven provinces came together to decide matters of common policy, and foreign relations were one of its main concerns. It formally received ambassadors, made treaties and decided on peace or war. The direction and administration of the army and navy were likewise ultimately the responsibility of the States General. However, in such a devolved system it was perhaps inevitable that the actual practice should have been somewhat different from the theory.

Although ambassadors were sent out by the States and formally reported back to this body, in practice foreign relations were normally managed by either the *raadpensionaris* of Holland (formally the legal adviser of the states of the province, in practice its prime minister) or the prince of Orange, depending on which of these was the dominant political force in the Republic at any particular time. Thus this area of state responsibility was to a great extent either devolved to the political leader of Holland or privatized under the direction of the prince, but policies and certainly decisions had still to be endorsed by the States General and, because important decisions had to be unanimous, in effect by all the provinces. The official address of the States General was High Mightinesses (*Hoog Mogende*) and as such they represented the Dutch state to the outside world.[20] In the end, whether the prince or Holland was the driving force behind the Republic's foreign policy, this remained the arena where formal expression was given to that policy. So the Republic's foreign relations were one area where the Dutch state, though it had little or no autonomy, acted as the coordinator to provide an indispensable common policy for the seven constituent provinces.[21]

The Dutch state was also responsible for the organization and administration of the army and the navy. That the military forces on both land and sea were Generality, and not provincial, institutions needs to be stressed, as this fact has often been obscured by concentrating on the practical devolution within the system. In retrospect, what is perhaps surprising is not that there was a great deal of influence at provincial level over both army and navy but that these were national forces at all. Given the degree of decentralization of political power in the Republic, it might have been expected that there would have been provincial armies and navies, coming together in a more or less coordinated way for common purposes. It has to be admitted that this is how the navy often seemed to operate in practice, but formally, despite the plethora of local admiralties, it remained a Generality institution, and the army, although also affected by the in-built centrifugal tendencies of the Republic, was much more clearly both led and organized effectively from the centre.

To take the army first, it was controlled and organised by the Council of State (*Raad van State*) drawing its authority ultimately from the States General.[22] This college was staffed by representatives of all the provinces, but the greatest influence was probably normally exercised by successive princes of Orange[23] and its permanent officials, the secretary and treasurer-general, as the members sitting for the provinces were limited to three-year terms of office. It drew up the yearly military budget, organized the logistic support of the army and directed its movements. Ultimate authority for decision-making lay with the States General, and the Council of State acted on its authority: the Dutch army was the army of the state in both theory and practice.

However, it was hardly likely that the army would be totally unaffected by the provincial autonomy which was so characteristic of the Dutch system. Provincial influence on the army was exercised in a number of ways but the most important was probably the system by which the troops were paid. The repartition system meant that the provinces paid directly those regiments and companies assigned to them in the *staat van oorlog*, with the treasurer-general checking that such payments had been properly made. This could have meant an effective devolution of the army into provincial forces, especially in the case of Holland, which had nearly 60 per cent of the army in its pay, but this does not seem to have happened. One reason why this provincialization did not take place was that army units were not necessarily posted to the provinces that paid them. This was particularly important in the case of Holland: most of the troops paid by this province were in fact garrisoned or employed elsewhere in the Republic. For example, in 1653 the province was responsible for the payment of 28 companies of horse and 231 companies of foot, but of these only four companies of horse and 51 of foot were actually garrisoned within Holland.[24] The repartition system could lead to serious difficulties, as in 1650 when Holland refused to agree to the proposed military budget and ended up by effectively – and irregularly – dismissing some of the troops assigned to its repartition, but did not in practice lead to the disintegration or the weakening of central command.

Although the navy was also formally a federal force, central direction was much less effective in this case than in that of the army. The admiralties were in theory Generality institutions, but they were effectively under the control of the provinces in which they were situated. There were five of them: in Zeeland, Friesland, and no fewer than three in

Holland, where internal rivalries produced separate admiralties for the Maas at Rotterdam, at Amsterdam and for the Northern Quarter (with its headquarters regularly alternating between Hoorn and Enkhuizen). The local admiralties were run by boards of directors appointed by the States General and including members from outside the home province, but it is clear that the interests of the provinces in which the admiralties were based were pre-eminent. In Holland devolution went even further in practice, as smooth cooperation between Rotterdam, Amsterdam and Hoorn/Enkhuizen was not always easy to achieve, to say the least. Two main problems arose out of this effective decentralization of the navy: with five separate sources of squadrons, it was difficult to coordinate the overall activities of the fleet; and the proliferation of administration and, especially, dockyard and ship-building facilities proved inefficient.

Similarly, the financing of the navy was significantly less centralized in practice than that of the army. Although they never produced enough money to support all naval activities, the basic sources of revenue for the admiralties were the convoys and licences,[25] effectively import and export duties, levied on trade. These were collected by the admiralties separately in areas of the Republic assigned to them,[26] and thus opened up possibilities both for individual corruption and for provinces to pursue their own interests at the expense of the country as a whole. There was a standing temptation for provinces to enforce the convoys and licences less strictly within their own borders in order to attract trade, and the amounts of money and lucrative contracts passing through the hands of local admiralty officials offered opportunities they could not always resist. In the long term the weakness of central direction and logistical control was a serious flaw in the Dutch naval system, and tended to undermine the effectiveness of the fleet, but all attempts to introduce more effective centralized control and facilities were shipwrecked on the reef of provincial particularism.[27]

In sum, the Dutch Republic – even in its years of greatness in the seventeenth and early eighteenth century – was a peculiar polity when judged by both contemporary and later conceptions of the proper nature of the state. It was first and foremost an alliance between quasi-autonomous provinces for the successful prosecution of war, or for defence if a rather more modern terminology is used, but had otherwise few of the characteristics that have been seen as typical of the state in early-modern Europe and, in particular, it was a far cry from the centralized and bureaucratic state supposedly encouraged, if not required, by the demands of warfare in this period. The apparatus of government at the centre was minimal, even by contemporary shoestring standards, and the range of responsibility of central government was notably narrow. There was not even a super-provincial court for the Union at The Hague: the provincial judicial systems were self-contained and did not recognize any right of appeal to a Generality court.[28] There was some Generality jurisdiction but this was largely limited to its own officials and the Generality lands, and the use of *ad hoc* central courts for particular and usually politically contaminated cases – such as the trial and politically inevitable condemnation of Oldenbarnevelt in 1619 – failed to lead to the establishment of any more lasting central jurisdiction.[29]

In sharp contrast to what was at least supposed to be the case in the more conventional states of contemporary Europe, political power in the Dutch Republic was rooted formally as well as practically at provincial or even sub-provincial level. It was not that the provinces enjoyed a considerable amount of autonomy from the central government, but rather that the provincial states were prepared to delegate certain powers and tasks to the Union. The ultimate power of decision-making remained with the provinces. Moreover, political power was devolved in practice even further: in some provinces there was an intermediate level of government in the states of the quarters,[30] but more fundamentally, political authority was vested in the members of the provincial states rather than in the states themselves. Thus in Holland, for example, unanimity was required for decisions on important matters, and none of the 18 voting towns (i.e., those represented in the States of Holland) could be forced to go along with any policy its delegation had not voted for. So the root of political power in this province lay with the oligarchies of the voting towns and, *mutatis mutandis*, this local basis of authority can be seen in the other provinces as well – though in most of them the grass-roots power of the nobility and other rural notables was at least as important as that of the town regents.[31]

The Generality did not display that bureaucratic expansion that was to be expected of the early-modern state; just as the range of activity of the central government in the Republic remained sharply restricted, so did the size of its personnel. This is not to say that there was no growth of administration, especially in response to the need to finance and control the army and the navy, but such growth occurred at the level of provincial government or even lower. The inhabitants of the Dutch Republic were heavily taxed and much governed, but taxes were collected and regulations administered at the level of town or rural district; even where the officials concerned were formally part of the provincial apparatus they were in effect controlled by the local oligarchies.

One of the reasons why the powers of central government could remain so restricted was the absence – after the abjuration of Philip II in 1581 – of a monarch. The princes of Orange did act to some extent as a unifying force, and at times were able to increase the effective influence of central direction in the state, especially Frederick Henry[32] and William III[33] at the peak of their powers, but even they had to work through the provinces rather than circumvent their powers. Their authority was based on their position as head of the army, member of the Council of State, and *stadhouder* of a majority of the provinces, which brought them considerable formal powers and even greater informal influence through patronage. In any case it seems that they were at best able to increase their control over the existing functions of the Generality, in foreign policy and warfare particularly, but not to extend its scope or challenge provincial autonomy.

In any case, the crucial impediment to any significant increase in the powers of the central government, whether exercised by the princes of Orange or not, was the power of the regents of Holland. Throughout the seventeenth century the province of Holland contained about 40 per cent of the Republic's population and a much greater proportion of its wealth. The principle of provincial autonomy prevented Holland from being outvoted by the six smaller provinces, and enabled it to make its financial superiority pay in terms of control of policy – its quota of Generality expenses was very nearly 60 per cent. Up to 1618 and subsequently during the two stadhouderless periods (1650–72; 1702–47) the Republic was effectively governed from and through Holland, and at other times the princes of Orange had to work in cooperation with the States of Holland. By a judicious use of their powers and patronage the princes could influence the regent elite of the province, but they could never subordinate them either to their will or to the authority of the Generality. The state gained a degree of coherence from the power and influence of Holland, and to this extent provincial autonomy worked to strengthen the Union.

The structure of the Dutch political system meant that only a limited number of functions needed to be carried out by the state, but warfare was clearly one of the most important of these centrally controlled matters. Apart from directing and administering the army and the navy, the scope of central government was minimal. Foreign relations and diplomacy were formally controlled by the States General, but in practice were to a great extent delegated to the princes of Orange or the *raadpensionaris* of Holland and their advisory councils. To a limited, but nevertheless important, extent economic policy could be determined at the centre: the tariffs of the convoys and licences had to be fixed by the Generality, though uniform enforcement was unattainable, and the charters for the great trading companies – the East and West India Companies – were granted and enforced by the state. In addition the state administered the Generality lands and its own – minimal – bureaucracy, and had a legal jurisdiction over its own personnel, together with a theoretically unfounded but occasionally effective power to set up courts to try what were effectively seen as crimes against the state, as in the case Oldenbarnevelt and his co-accused. All of this adds up to a state which is a far cry not only from the modern state, but also from the burgeoning bureaucracies of the early-modern state.

In terms of the conventional wisdom of the period, as well as of many later historians, this should have been a dangerously inefficient system, making it difficult for the Dutch state to defend itself in a threatening international environment. As B.M. Downing has pointed out, 'cumbersome, particularist estates were serious obstacles to military modernization and the proper conduct of early modern warfare'.[34] The Dutch Republic should, perhaps, have gone the way of Poland-Lithuania. It did not, and instead proved to be one of the most successful states of the seventeenth century in terms of military effectiveness. The Republic was able to maintain a large, well-organized and regularly paid army and navy throughout the century and well on into the eighteenth century as well. In size, these forces were large enough to keep it in the front rank of European powers, and in terms of its ability to pay its troops on time it remained far ahead. Downing suggests that the weakness of the central government was counteracted by the rule of the oligarchy of Holland,[35] and there is a measure of truth in this observation, but it ignores the degree to which – in contrast to most other matters – military affairs were indeed controlled by and through the Generality.

Certainly, Holland's role was crucial: its wealth and the relatively cohesive and stable nature of its regent elite provided both the necessary finance and the coherent policies that the Republic needed. The financial contribution was vital and can be illustrated by a comparison of the state debt with that accumulated by Holland alone. By the end of the seventeenth century, Holland's provincial debt had risen to just under 200 million guilders, and to over 300 million after the War of Spanish Succession. In contrast, the state debt at the end of the century was only just over 19 million and, though it had risen to 61 million by 1715, it remains clear that the Dutch Republic fought its wars on the basis of the credit of the province of Holland.[36] This single province was ultimately responsible for the payment of nearly 60 per cent of Generality expenditure, including the support of the state debt. However, there are other factors which need to be taken into account to explain the effectiveness of the Dutch state in its sharply delimited but important role. Apart from the specific contribution of the regents of Holland, there is the degree of cohesion that existed, or at least developed in the course of the early seventeenth century, within the oligarchy of the Republic as a whole. Whatever the differences between the provinces, urban elites, nobles and rural notables could unite behind the task of defending the Union. The princes of Orange too were important in helping to provide a sense of common purpose, though their role may have been more significant in focusing attention on, and preventing neglect of, the army, than in strengthening central government in any significant way.

The Dutch state began as a military alliance between effectively autonomous provinces and this remained its primary functions throughout the history of the Republic. Over time, the Union became something more than this, but the evolution of a sense of Dutch identity was slow and uncertain[37] and it does not seem an exaggeration to end with the assertion that the Dutch state, even more than was the case in other contemporary countries, was first and foremost dedicated to war.

Notes

1.   E.H. Kossmann, *In Praise of the Dutch Republic: Some Seventeenth-Century Attitudes* (London 1963), pp 3–4.
2.   See H.L. Zwitser, *'De militie van den staat'. Het leger van de Republiek der Verenigde Nederlanden* (Amsterdam 1991), chapter 3, which suggests that the proportion of foreigners in the Dutch army varied from 40 to 60 per cent.
3.   See Introduction to this volume .
4.   'Generality' is used here as a short-hand term for the institutions of central government, i.e., those associated with the States General etc.
5.   M. Roberts, *The Military Revolution, 1560–1660* (Belfast 1956).
6.   B.H. Nickle, *The Military Reforms of Prince Maurice of Orange* (Delaware 1975).
7.   A son of William of Orange, Maurice was the effective leader of the army and *stadhouder* of most of the provinces during the establishment of the Dutch state.
8.   M. 't Hart, *The Making of a Bourgeois State. War, Politics and Finance during the Dutch revolt* (Manchester 1993), pp 43–5.
9.   Zwitser, *'De militie van den staat'*, pp 175–6; and 't Hart, *The Making of a Bourgeois State*, pp 43–5.
10.   The best study in English is J.R. Bruijn, *The Dutch Navy in the Seventeenth and Eighteenth Centuries* (Columbia, SC, 1993), and it is significant that he provides no overall figures for naval strength before the late seventeenth century, when comparative numbers of ships-of-the-line can be given.
11.   't Hart, *The Making of a Bourgeois State*, pp 51–2.
12.   Bruijn, *The Dutch Navy*, p 148.

13 . For a general account of the activities of both the naval and privateering activities of Dunkirk in this period, see R.A. Stradling, *The Armada of Flanders. Spanish Maritime Policy and European War, 1568–1668* (Cambridge 1992); and R. Baetens, 'The organization and effects of Flemish privateering in the seventeenth century', *Acta Historiae Neerlandicae* 9 (1976), pp 48–75.

14 . 't Hart, *The Making of a Bourgeois State*, pp 50–63.

15 . R. Liesker, 'Tot zinkens toe bezwaard. De schuldenlast van het Zuiderkwartier van Holland 1672–1794', in S. Groenveld, M.E.H.N. Mout and I. Schöffer, eds, *Bestuurders en geleerden* (Amsterdam, 1985), pp 151–60.

16 . The 'state of war': this was the annual allocation of military costs to the charge of the provinces.

17 . 't Hart, *The Making of a Bourgeois State*, pp 61–2.

18 . For a recent treatment of the subject, see S. Groenveld and H.L.Ph. van Leeuwenberg, eds, *De Unie van Utrecht* (The Hague, 1979).

19 . The classic account of the constitution of the Dutch Republic is R. Fruin, *Geschiedenis der staatsinstellingen in Nederland*, ed H.T. Colenbrander (The Hague, 1901); a more modern, brief treatment can be found in S.J. Fockema Andreae, *De Nederlandse staat onder de Republiek* (Amsterdam, 1961). See also J.L. Price, *Holland and the Dutch Republic in the Seventeenth Century* (Oxford 1994), Part III.

20 . See J. Heringa, *De eer en hoogheid van den staat. Over de plaats der Verenigde Nederlanden in het diplomatieke leven van de zeventiende eeuw* (Groningen, 1961).

21 . There were eight provinces in the Republic but Drenthe, although formally an autonomous province of the union, was not represented in the States General. The Generality lands – those areas, largely of Flanders and Brabant, outside the core provinces but part of the territory of the Republic – were governed by the Generality, and were an unsung area of autonomous operation by the Dutch state.

22 . The Council of State had originally been intended as the central governing body of the state, but one of the chief changes made during the definitive establishment of a workable system of government in the 1590s was the sidelining of the Council to make way for the States General to take its place at the centre. From this point on the Council was largely restricted to military affairs, where it acted somewhat as a committee of the States General with only delegated authority. Cf. A.Th. van Deursen, 'De Raad van State en de Generaliteit, 1590–1606', *Bijdragen voor de Geschiedenis der Nederlanden* 19 (1964), pp 1–48.

23 . This is technically untrue: Maurice was count of Nassau-Dillenberg, not prince of Orange, until the last years of his life when he finally inherited the title from his eldest brother, Philip William. Also, although he headed the army, he was never awarded the title of captain-general.

24 . Zwitzer, *'De militie van den staat'*, pp 36–7.

25 . The *convooien en licenten* were originally charges on shipping to pay for naval convoys and special payments to allow trade with the enemy.

26 . As there were admiralties in only three of the seven provinces, this system meant, for example, that both Rotterdam and Amsterdam collected revenues

from areas outside Holland.

27 . See Bruijn, *The Dutch Navy*, p 39, for Frederick Henry's attempts in the 1630s to reform the system through bringing fleet and blockade operations under the control of a single body of councillors and also by setting up a main operational base at Hellevoetsluis.

28 . Holland and Zeeland had two appeal courts in common – the *Hof van Holland* and the *Hoge Raad* – staffed by judges from both provinces, but their essentially provincial character remained.

29 . See Price, *Holland and the Dutch Republic*, pp 284–6.

30 . Overijssel and Gelderland, plus a somewhat analogous division between the town of Groningen and the Ommelanden in Groningen (*Stad en Lande*).

31 . Cf. J.L. Price, 'The Dutch nobility in the seventeenth and eighteenth century', in H.M. Scott, ed, *The Nobility of Western Europe in the Seventeenth and Eighteenth Century* (forthcoming).

32 . *Stadhouder* of most of the provinces and captain-general 1625–47.

33 . *Stadhouder* of most of the provinces and captain-general 1672–1702.

34 . B.M. Downing, *The Military Revolution and Political Change. Origins of Democracy and Autocracy in Early Modern Europe* (Princeton, 1992), p 233.

35 . *Ibid*, pp 234, 237–8.

36 . These figures were taken from E.H.M. Dormans, *Het tekort: staatsschuld in de tijd van de Republiek* (Amsterdam, 1991), pp 80–1, 142–7.

37 . Cf. P.J.A.N. van Rietbergen, 'Beeld en zelfbeeld. "Nederlandse indentiteit" in politieke structuur en politieke cultuur tijdens de Republiek', *Bijdragen en Mededelingen betreffende de Geschiedenis der Nederlanden* 107 (1992), pp 635–56.

Index